DOING THE OPPOSITE

A life, its lessons
and building success

By Jeff Dewing

Contents

Acknowledgements

In the course of a lifetime, we all receive more blessings from the people who shape, influence and help us than can ever be acknowledged in a few brief paragraphs in a book. As a child, my parents, grandparents and extended family gave me a start in life full of love, guidance and kindness. As time passes, and now I find myself as a grandfather, my own family and wife Michelle bring me more happiness than I thought possible.

There have been so many others I am grateful to, from my primary school teacher Sandra Terry who inspired me during my childhood, to the countless people who have selflessly helped and educated me ever since. From dusty engineering sites to boardrooms and the life-changing Vistage group, countless people have supported me on my life journey. Any triumphs I have had are down to their support, and any failings are my own.

Business can be a harsh environment and sometimes friendships are sorely tested by circumstance. One of my remaining ambitions is to sit alongside such people and laugh at the past we shared and the things we endured together. You know who you are.

I would also like to thank my editorial team, headed up by my writer James Wills (now close friend), for their incredible support and guidance throughout this project.

Prologue

Not so long ago, I had £7.60 in my bank account and was struggling to feed my children.

Aged 39, I was bankrupt. The taxman had taken my house, my car and my self-respect. In a matter of months, I had seen my life collapse. I went from owning a successful business and a football club, to claiming benefits to try and put food on the table.

In 2012, I started a new business in my garden shed. Just eight years later it was about to be sold for tens of millions of pounds.

My journey is the tale of a working class, East End lad done good, who lost it all and hit rock bottom hard, but who managed to battle back.

This book highlights the lessons in life which helped me to recover, and some of the principles I believe you need to follow to find happiness and fulfilment, not just in your bank balance, but in life itself.

As for that multi-million pound deal? There was a slight hiccup. People in China started coughing.

Chapter 1:

Eastenders

We were the traditional East End London family. All those Cockney clichés? I lived them. The doorstep was kept scrubbed, you were respectful to your elders or you got a clout, the front door was always unlocked, people were always popping in and out of each other's houses. It was a real community, people looked out for each other. The only thing missing from the cliché was the Kray twins.

Even though the early 70s were not so long ago, it was a totally different society in terms of lifestyle and culture. The welfare society did not exist to the same extent and, for most people in our part of London, you worked or went hungry and every penny counted. My parents just did their best every day to put food on the table. Everyone lived hand to mouth. For years, my Mum made all our clothes and a real treat for us wasn't a foreign holiday, it was half a pint of shrimps from the fish van outside the pub.

We were old East End stock. On my mother's side my Grandfather Bill (William) was from Leytonstone, near the Orient football ground, and was a carpet fitter all his life. He was so terrified of electricity he would never allow the immersion heater to be switched on and they lived with cold water for years. I am surprised he even turned the lights on.

His brother Herbert Butler was an extraordinary man. He had become involved in Labour Party politics from an early age and was one of the main opponents of fascist Oswald Moseley's Blackshirt movement in Hackney in the 1930s. He went onto become an MP in 1945 and remained in Parliament until he retired in 1970, which wasn't bad going for a kid from the East End. There is now a statue of him in Hackney for his services to the community.

On my Dad's side, his family was from Walthamstow. My Grandad Frank was an incredibly talented carpenter and a 'jack of all trades'. He also loved playing around with car engines. When we went to visit him, he would be tinkering with a V8 engine on the living room floor while my Nan Lillian, who constantly had a cigarette in her mouth, was trying to cook dinner.

Frank's main occupation was a television engineer – in those days you had big heavy televisions with valves in the back - and he would repair those, but carpentry was always his passion. He was a lovely man. For all the times he called my Nan 'a silly old cow' they were obviously devoted to each other and had a generally happy life. Frank worked his entire life to provide for his family, to slowly pay off the mortgage, pottered about in his workshop and saved every penny for a rainy day.

My Dad had left school at 15 which everyone did in that part of society back then. Go to school, leave at 15, get a job. He started working for a guy called Charlie Climan who had a haberdashery and who would fix irons, washing machines and different bits and pieces. Because my Dad had grown up tinkering with machinery, dissembling radios and rebuilding them, fiddling with electronics, he was also a real 'jack of all trades'. Eventually he started concentrating more on refrigeration because it was a good trade. Everyone had a fridge, but no-one knew how they worked, so you would always be kept busy repairing them.

Like a lot of couples back then my Mum and Dad met at the local social. A couple of times a year most communities had a big community party with a band when everyone dressed up in their finest. Even though he was painfully shy with strangers, my Dad asked my Mum to dance and their relationship grew from there.

My Mum and Dad courting in 1962.

My Mum was unusual in that she was an accountant's clerk and worked in an office environment, whereas on my Dad' side everyone had always worked with their hands. They were soon married, moved into my Mum's parents' house, and saved hard for a mortgage to buy a £3,000 three-bedroomed mid terrace house in Grove Park Avenue in Chingford (right next to the old Walthamstow Dog stadium). In those days, living in Chingford was seen as a real step up from Walthamstow, but as they lived right on the border it was anything but affluent. It sounded posher on envelopes though.

My Dad had a ridiculous work ethic. His view was you worked until the job was done. Later, when he was running his own business, he never got home before 1am in the morning and went to work at 10am every day, seven days a week, apart from the odd Sunday when my Mum put her foot down and said "we need to go out and do something with the kids". Because he believed in working late until a job was finished, he was terrible at getting up in the morning, which meant he struggled to hold down a conventional job. That was one of the reasons he started his own business, so no-one could tell him off for being late.

He set up as a fridge engineer, but in truth his heart was never truly in it. My Dad loved tinkering with electronics, designing things and didn't want to spend his life repairing fridges. Thankfully, a friend of his, Jim Laidler, owned a large electronic store in Hoe Street in Walthamstow, which sold radios, turntables, disco equipment and electronic components. Jim wanted to open up another shop in West Green Road in Tottenham called Radio Unlimited and asked my Dad if he wanted to run it. That invitation changed our family's entire future. Despite my Dad working every hour God sent, after the first year or so, the shop simply wasn't making enough money and Jim announced he would have to close it. My Dad then asked if he could buy it. Nowadays that wouldn't be seen as too unusual but back then, for a married man with kids to buy a failing business was a brave decision. Mum and Dad got another mortgage, changed the shop's name to Radio Corner, and tried to make a go of it. They struggled for a couple of years and then Dad decided he wanted to change it into a car accessories shop. He was forced to go to his Dad and ask for financial help.

Dad's shop in West Green Road, Tottenham.

Having saved every spare penny for years, for once his Dad put his hand in his pocket and invested in the business. This was a major leap of faith for him, spending money went against all his principles, but I like to think it was a matter of trust. He knew my Dad would do everything he could to succeed and I guess he just wanted his son to be happy. His risk paid off. They both loved playing around with electronics and cars, my Nan would go in every day and open the shop up, and it was a real family business. It brought them together. It also brought in more money, and while we were hardly flush, my Mum could buy clothes instead of making them, and cash wasn't a constant concern.

My Dad then bought a building behind the shop in West Green Road which had a garage area with an office above it. Selling car accessories, it made sense to then offer servicing and MOT's etc. He was inventing gadgets for cars the boy racers liked and the rooms upstairs gave Dad a proper space to invent and build even more things. Nowadays management consultants use tools like the Ikigai circles to help people identify what their passions and strengths are and how to make money from them (I will explore Ikigai later in this book). My Dad followed these principles, naturally. He had a passion for tinkering with electronics and cars and so created an environment where he could profitably do it. The first floor of the building became his electronics factory and a new business was born called Swift Electronics. One of his first inventions was a snazzy brake light. He bought some square plastic trunking, cut it to the right length, installed a load of inline car bulbs, bought shiny red reflective Perspex for one side, wired it all up and fitted it under the rear bumper of cars. When the driver put the brake lights on, this whole thing shone bright red like the sun. All the boy racers thought this was the dog's bollocks, they were flying off the shelves. He couldn't make them fast enough.

In the early 80s, one of the biggest crimefighting TV shows was Knight Rider with David Hasselhoff, who had a talking car called K.I.T.T. On the front of K.I.T.T.'s bonnet was a light strip where the light moved backwards and forwards in a horizontal pulse. I had just got my first van in 1983 and I wanted one, but the electronics to make the light move in this fashion was actually very complicated. I asked my Dad for one and he warned me it wouldn't be easy to replicate the smooth flow of the lights. One day I got home and there it was, laying on my bed, a K.I.T.T. light. I was so excited, I ran downstairs, got all my tools out, cut a hole in the front grille of the van and installed it. A Knight Rider light in Walthamstow! People would stand and point at it as I drove down the street.

He was truly ingenious. In those days rolls of carpets came wrapped round very strong cardboard cylinders, which the carpet companies would just throw out. My Dad noticed a company had a warehouse full of them and asked if he could have them. He would cut them down to about 1.2m long, cover them in fake leather vinyl fabric in whatever colour people wanted, put speaker electronics inside, a fabric mesh over the top and hey presto, you had an upright speaker which looked like a piece of furniture. The sound quality was also great as the sound waves came out of the top, would hit the ceiling and reverberate around the room. They cost peanuts to make but could command a high price and were flying out of the shop.

My Dad's speakers made from circular Carpet rolls.

As another example of his ingenuity, I had a Chopper bicycle at the time, and they were so popular they were always being nicked. One day I came home, and Dad had put an alarm on the back and a key console on the front. You would put the bike on its stand and take the key out.

If someone put the stand up without the key being in an alarm would go off, and this thing was loud. He even had a button on it I could press to make the alarm go off. What a bonus for a kid, my bike was now secure, and I could also scare the crap out of people by sounding the alarm as I rode past.

My Dad had the foresight to know the future of electronics was making things smaller and it appealed to his creative side. He then moved into making spy equipment. At one stage I believe he was making the smallest transmitters in the world. He would put listening devices in pens or plugs and they could transmit to an FM radio up to a mile away. He put together a cheap catalogue, put a weekly £6 advert in Exchange and Mart, and the orders came flooding in. Suspicious husbands, private detectives and James Bond wannabees couldn't get enough of them. He was making them for pennies and selling them from £45 up to a few hundred pounds.

He also developed a car tracker, which even the police started using. You could place it with a magnet under a vehicle and then electronically follow it. The BBC was making a documentary about spying and espionage and asked him to create a briefcase full of kit for them. He was actually selling these briefcases for around £100 but the BBC would hire it off him for £1,000 for a couple of weeks and return it when it was finished. If you want an indication of financial common sense at the BBC back then, that sums it up. I am not so sure it is any different now.

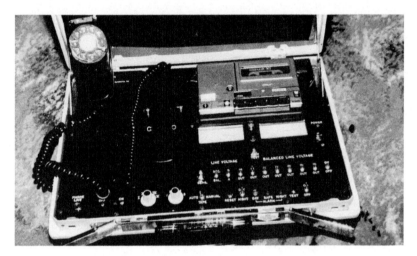

My Dad's super spy briefcase.

In those days, luxury 52-seater coaches were supplied to buyers with no PA or music system. Grey Green Coaches was a huge firm in Tottenham with hundreds of coaches. He designed a solution to put speakers above every seat, designed a PA amplifier and Radio Cassette system and had the contract to fit out all their coaches.

He was always creating something. One morning I woke up and was going downstairs when suddenly there was a screeching, ear piercing alarm sound. I didn't know what on earth was going on and ran screaming into their bedroom. He had designed and built his first burglar alarm and had fitted a pressure sensitive plate under one of the stair carpets and not told us. Every night he used to set the alarm before going upstairs to bed and always had to remember to avoid the booby-trapped step.

He even invented one of the first ever early police sirens. Back then, all emergency service vehicles had bells on them. He invented a little white box with five switches on, attached to a speaker, each giving a different siren noise, and a separate switch which played the sounds one after another. West Green Road was a typical shopping street with butchers and bakers, but it had yellow lines, nowhere to park, and people were always getting parking tickets. Dad put a siren on the front of the shop, had the box under a counter, and every time a traffic warden came up the street someone would warn him, and he would sound the siren. People were dashing out of shops, jumping in their cars and escaping tickets. The traffic wardens got so pissed off they eventually called the police but rather than arrest my Dad, he ended up having discussions with them about installing the sirens on their vehicles.

It never came about because he didn't have the knowledge or confidence to enter into such a large and financially challenging project. Instead, he walked away stating his company simply wasn't big enough to meet that level of demand.

One day he walked in our house with a plastic box with two circular dials on it. He plugged it into the TV and hey presto… a table tennis game for two people. You moved the bats on the screen with the circular dials, a ball bounced between the two, eventually going faster and faster. Atari later released an almost identical product (Atari Tennis) and made millions. The truth is my Dad could probably have made millions as well, but he didn't have the confidence or business nous. Entrepreneurs like Alan Sugar, another East London lad, were having the same sort of ideas, and making the same sort of new products as my Dad, but they went on to make millions. But there was a difference. My Dad never had the education, confidence or foresight to see how getting patents or intellectual property rights for these ideas, employing people to make them, and marketing them properly, could have potentially made him millions. He was also acutely shy in the company of strangers and was hesitant about being in situations he could not control. He was fine talking to customers and with people he knew, but to be placed in a room full of strangers having to make conversation or sell them an idea was painful beyond measure for him.

He never had the infrastructure, foresight or real desire to take such massive risks and expand his business beyond its comfortable boundaries. He loved the thrill of having an idea and seeing it come to fruition at his own hands. As long as he made enough money to pay the mortgage, pay the bills and have a good quality of life, that was fulfilling enough for him. It's easy to see his working life as a series of missed chances, but the fact is he created business ideas and made them profitable, created opportunities where none existed and made enough money from them for us to eventually live more than comfortably, that's an achievement most people never manage. He was happy doing what he loved and made money from it.

As for me, I had a blessed childhood. It was a warm and loving home. Dad was at work most of the time but Mum was always there to care and look after us. I grew up in the same house in Chingford they had bought all those years ago but Dad kept on improving it and, of course, with his work ethic, he did everything to the highest of standards. As my two sisters and then brother came along he did a loft conversion with three new bedrooms for us, so there was plenty of room. We had a garden to play in, a huge grass field opposite (which is now Arsenal's training ground), lots of friends, and were surrounded with love. That is enough for most children to flourish.

At school, from primary right up to secondary school, I was an average pupil. I used to try and compete with my cousin Carol who was the same age as me. However, she was naturally academically gifted and could read a page and absorb the content, whereas I had to read the page several times to absorb and really concentrate at every subject. Education didn't come naturally to me, but I worked hard in spurts, was always respectful and managed to be at the centre of school life. I loved most sports – diving was my strongest, which I competed across London in – and so I fitted in well with the sporting clique, but I also had natural empathy with the "nerdy crowd" as people now call them. I bridged the gap between the two groups and couldn't stand bullying, so even managed to stop some of the usual school conflicts between the two groups.

Back then you didn't have computer games - we made our own entertainment. We were always on our bikes, messing about in the woods. We used to get the bus to explore new parts of London, go to the local swimming baths, roller skating or ice skating, kicking footballs in the park. If it sounds idealistically simple, that's because it was. I had a loving family, friends, I was doing OK in school. Life was good. But I had one major problem.

From about seven years old I had a raging temper, far beyond that of a normal child. If things did not go my way, or I was asked to do something I didn't want to, I would fly into a blinding rage far deeper than a normal childhood tantrum. People talk about a red mist descending… I would get lost in mine and scream and rage. I put my Mum through hell. Dad never witnessed it much. Firstly, because he was always at work, and secondly, because I wouldn't have dared to kick off if he was there. One day, when I was about ten, she sat my Dad down and said, "You have to do something about this."

One Monday evening I was shocked when my Dad walked into the house at about 6pm, he was never home that early. He said, "Come on son, we are going to karate." I had never thought of doing karate before, the idea had never ever been mentioned. But off we went to the local karate club, took off our shoes, rolled up our trousers and started doing the basic stretches and movements the sensei showed us.

It was boring. I was stood there, sock-less, like a lemon doing Yoga-type stretches. We weren't doing any fighting, just movements, but when I started moaning, my Dad said we were going every week, so that was that. Of course, in time I got into it. I soon wanted the karate uniform (called a Gui), I made some friends, and eventually we began sparring with other pupils and the Sensei. One day while sparring with one of the other pupils, I got banged on the ear and the red mist descended. I totally lost it. I was raging, out of control, going for him with all the disciplines of karate totally forgotten and, bang, the next thing I knew I was flying through the air about fifteen feet backwards having been kicked in the chest by the Sensei. In that moment I learned a life lesson which has stayed with me ever since. **Losing my temper meant I**

lost control of the situation and the outcome. I learned when the red mist descended, the person most blinded by it was me. It is hard to be rational when you are angry, and if you are not in control of yourself, how can you control any situation to get the end result you want? Anger might be a natural reaction to certain situations, but you don't always have to follow its impulses.

I never properly lost my temper again for years. Karate taught me discipline and I went on to become a black belt. As well as controlling my temper, I also learnt another life lesson. My Dad had no interest at all in learning karate, but he didn't know enough about psychology to help me solve my anger problems. In those days no-one ever thought of sending an occasionally badly-behaved kid to a child psychologist, there were no TV shows about naughty steps, so he took me to a place he knew I would learn discipline. Most importantly, he sacrificed hours of his time for months to put me on the right path. He even got a brown belt himself. He showed me that **when there is a problem, sometimes long-term dedication and patience is the key to solving it.** Most people would have simply punished their children for losing their temper and hope that would solve the problem. But my Dad always seemed to think things through and look for long-term solutions. As a society we are addicted to the idea of a quick fix, entire industries and advertising campaigns are based upon promises of instant solutions and gratification, but the truth is, sometimes solving issues takes time, perseverance and a totally different approach.

If you ever need an illustration of proper parenting, my Dad taking me to Karate was one. But Karate was also central to the first big problem I had in life. I had taken to it very seriously and had been training three or four times per week and after a couple of years got my Brown belt.

I also played football for the school team and had a bit of a mouth on me. I was giving the other team a load of lip. Eventually they vowed to get me after the match but that was no problem for Mr Big Mouth, I had my mates with me, we could sort them out. After they threatened me, I didn't shup up, I started winding them up even more. Life lessons? Here's a minor one. When a gang of kids is waiting to get you, don't be slow in the changing rooms because all your mates might have buggered off by the time you come out. I came out, they were waiting, and I was on my own. I didn't feel so bloody clever or mouthy then. Running away seemed the better part of valour but our house was about ten minutes away and they were soon after me. I just kept running and escaped them until we were about 200 yards from home when they caught me at a bus stop and said they were going to do me. I got smacked around a bit, but my Karate skills kicked in and I put two of them in hospital. One had a broken jaw and one a fractured eye socket. The rest were a bit battered as well. In karate we were doing endless katas where you are taught to fight numerous people simultaneously. Repetition can lead to automatic responses which is why the armed forces, for example, train over and over again about how to respond to certain circumstances. Most of my reactions during that fight were simply because of what had been drilled into me, over and over again.

I didn't fight them and use my karate because I wanted to, I did so because I had to. I went into survival mode. If all of them had rushed me and got me on the ground I would have had no chance, they could have half killed me. But when I hurt the first two the rest had lost a little of their appetite for the fight. I hate to think what might have happened if today's knife culture existed back then. I might not be writing this now. I ran home in a blind panic and explained to my Mum what had happened. I was terrified because I knew I had hurt two of them quite badly and I knew an ambulance had been called by someone who had seen the fight. My Dad was at home for a change and he ran down there, saw the two lads being helped into the ambulance, and then ran back to the house and called the police. An officer soon came around and I explained what had happened. He first questioned how I had survived a fight with seven kids, leaving two of them in hospital. My Dad explained I had been doing karate for years, showed them my karate licence (which you needed to practice the sport back then). The police understood the circumstances behind the incident (even though I had been a dickhead and caused it) and the officer could see I was from a responsible family with no history of trouble or violence. The kids decided not to press charges, and nothing further was done.

I was in massive shock over what had happened. In a matter of minutes, I had badly hurt two people. I was terrified they were going to get revenge at some stage in the future, so I sat down and reflected on everything that had occurred and the realization hit me. I was a massive idiot. I had put myself in that situation. My mouth had led me into trouble, and I vowed to change my ways. As part of this process, I never told a single soul at school about it, not even my closest mates. I could have been the class hero, hard as nails Jeff who beat up seven kids, but my Mum and Dad sat me down and talked through it. There was no "Well done, son." They were not proud I had won the fight, but hugely disappointed I had been in one. They were mortified, devastated, and told me I had been lucky and must try to make sure nothing like that ever happened again.

We are all products of our environment. If you are brought up in a hostile environment, you will probably become hostile. If you are surrounded with love and generosity those traits become yours. A plant grows according to the soil it is planted in. You have to travel a long way to find a genuinely bad person, but you do not have to travel far to find a good person in a bad environment.

They treated it gravely, so I did too. Their reaction became my reaction. It was unacceptable to them, so it became unacceptable to me. If Dad had somehow given me approval for standing up for myself and using violence to defend myself, I might have been proud of winning the fight and got a "big man" attitude. But thankfully my parents were devastated by it. I can still see the look on their faces now, and I learnt no-one wins in a fight. Violence leads to more problems, not solutions. I never really had another fight. Even if you have the fighting skills to get out of trouble, a wise man doesn't put himself in situations where he has to use them.

So, with my temper issues solved, I muddled along at school. You learn life lessons in the silliest of ways. One day I was walking home with a mate, and I was walking on top of a wall which was only a couple of feet high. Eventually the wall had a gap for a driveway and my mate started daring and betting me I couldn't make the jump. I knew I couldn't, it was too far. Spiderman would have struggled. But still, I was umming and erring and he was trying to wind me up even more when it struck me. He was setting me a challenge he knew I would fail, and he would use that to tease me for ages afterwards. By failing, through my own actions, I would be giving him power over me. It was stupid. "I bet you can't. I bet you can't," he was saying. I replied, "You're right, I can't," and stepped off the wall. I had taken back control. This was the first time I experienced something which often happens in business, people set you up to fail.

Being challenged is a healthy process, it allows us to grow. But sometimes people set us tasks where the only result can be failure. Even by attempting such a task, you are handing power to others. Recognise this and step away. The American World War Two General, George Patton, said only by accepting challenges can people feel the exhilaration of victory. That might be true. But accepting impossible challenges is a different matter entirely - you simply use your energies to create inevitable failure.

Wall-walking aside, I also discovered a love for music. One day I came home and my Dad was building something in the living room. It was an electric organ. By then he could have afforded to buy one but, in true Dad fashion, he wanted to build one instead. He completed the project over about three to four months, doing a bit every night when he got home from work.

When it was finished, I sat down, determined to learn to play to impress him and to thank him for the hours of work he had put into building it. I listened to music, pressed the keys and tried to copy it. I couldn't read music at the time, but after five minutes of practice I could work out how to play a tune. I had a natural ear. My Mum and Dad liked 'Moonlight Serenade' so I listened to it a few times, and then played it for them. They were delighted and, as ever, I responded to positive reaction and wanted to learn more. I had music lessons at school, and in no time at all I was playing the violin, the trombone, the trumpet, the drums and the clarinet. I even got a part-time role in a commercial orchestra.

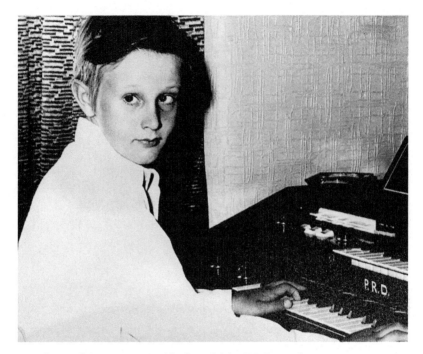

Me playing the Organ my Dad had just built. (P.R.D was his signature, Peter Ronald Dewing).

After playing the piano – pictured – I then went onto play the drums as well.

And the trombone.

The next life lesson I learnt was the joy of giving. When I was about ten, I took part in a school sponsored walk. It was twenty-four miles long and hundreds of kids took part. With the help of my parents, I spent weeks before it getting friends, family and relatives to add money to my sponsorship form. I had about three pages of people's names and was chuffed. I then completed the walk (it took eight hours) and my parents and siblings were at various check points to cheer me on. That night, I was knackered with blisters all over my feet, but I felt so proud. I remember when I was flagging a few times, all I could see was the names on those sponsorship forms and that gave me the strength to carry on.

In those days, my parents smoked John Player Special and you could buy a quality black oval tin with JPS printed in gold. The tins held fifty cigarettes. My Mum gave me an empty tin to begin collecting the money. Within about a week, the tin was brimming with 10p and 50p pieces, as well as a number of £1 notes and the odd fiver. The tin seemed to weigh a ton.

Then came the day when I had to proudly go to school to hand over all the money I had raised. However, the school had arranged for all the money to be handed in to a particular teacher at 3pm at the end of the school day. In those days, we all enjoyed free milk at school in the mornings, and I had a 'Humphrey' straw to drink it ("Watch out, watch out, there's a Humphrey about!" was the advertising slogan). At school there were also very under-privileged children who would receive free school meals and, being young, I could never really work out why that was.

Anyway, carrying this tin around created a lot of genuine interest from my school friends, and I was proud to tell them what it was for. In those days, if you got 50p a week pocket money you were rich. For 10p you could buy enough penny and half penny sweets to last you all day. I had also realised some kids never had any sweets, simply because their parents couldn't afford to give them pocket money.

After a few enquiries from my friends, one of them said, "God, I wish I had that much money. I have never got pocket money." In the spur of the moment, I reached into my tin and gave him a 50p piece. His face was a picture, he kept saying, "Are you sure? I can't take this!" I simply said, "It's yours, that's enough to buy sweets for a week." I felt wonderful seeing his reaction. During the rest of the day, I did the same thing for a dozen other kids I knew were on free school meals and couldn't afford sweets.

Then, just before I handed in my pot of money to the school, I had mixed emotions. I had enjoyed the elation of making people incredibly happy but was now fearful of what would happen when the school realised the money pot was short. I knew I would be criticised and would have to take it on the chin.

About a week later, my Mum was contacted by the school who naturally wanted to know where the money had gone. I explained that I had given some of the disadvantaged kids 50p each. After talking to me about responsibilities, she simply paid the £6 shortfall herself and made me do extra chores at home to pay it off.

I later labelled this type of behaviour as 'care without caring', which I will explain later in the book. But the important lesson life lesson was **look after the people around you before yourself and your reward will be incredible satisfaction.** Even though it is not the motivation, this behaviour means people you looked after will naturally look after you when the time comes.

But it wasn't long before I was in trouble again. When I was fifteen, I had some older friends who had left school, got jobs and liked to go for a pint in the pub. My Mum and Dad never went to the pub, so it was a novel experience for me. I looked old enough to get served. I would have three or four pints, stagger home and watch the room spinning. The trouble was pints aren't free and I was fifteen with no money, so I started sneaking downstairs and stealing a few quid out of my Dad's briefcase, which had the shop takings in it. After a few weeks, my Mum caught me red-handed. I tried to bullshit my way out of it, but I was bang to rights. She gave me a look of deep disappointment and told me to go school. I was mortified. I knew I was in big trouble for stealing and my Dad was probably going to kill me, but the guilt weighed more heavily on me than any fear. I was ashamed. Stealing was against every principle my parents had taught me and I had sunk to taking from my Dad simply so I could go and get drunk with my mates. I spent the next couple of days with a sick feeling of anticipation over when my Dad was going to confront me. I was in bed by the time he got home from work for the next couple of days, so I allowed myself a deluded glimmer of hope nothing was going to be said. The next day, walking home, I saw his car was parked outside the house. *Uh-oh.* I knew I was for it. I walked into the kitchen with dread. He asked if I was ok, how school went, did I want a glass of orange? It was all very normal. Then my Mum stood up and walked out of the kitchen and I knew this was it. The axe was about to fall. I was for it.

I half expected him to start shouting, but Dad simply asked if I had any plans for that night because he wanted to take me somewhere. I thought he was going to take me to the woods and kill me! Instead, he took me to a massive Airfix shop, pointed to a huge remote control model plane and said, "What do you think of that?" I said it was great. He said, "OK, we'll buy it, build it and go fly it."

He spent a load of money on the plane, the servos to fly it, the radio control, the works. He said, "Tomorrow night, and each weekend from now on, we are going to build it together and then fly it."

And that's what we did. He would leave work at a reasonable hour for a change, we would spend each evening poring over the plans, putting it together, constructing it bit by bit. When my mates called and asked if I was going to the pub I said "no, I was busy with my Dad". I loved spending quality time with him. We finished it, flew it and then built another. And another. I never went to the pub with my mates again until years later. Of course, being Dad, he went a stage further and designed a transportable tool kit for the planes. One of the problems with starting them was you needed to use a finger to get the propellers rotating, and sometimes the engine would kick in and you would whack your finger which used to sting... a lot. His tool kit even had an automatic starter. All the other flyers wanted a tool kit like his, he could have made good money from that too.

After being caught stealing, most kids would get a massive bollocking. Instead, like with the karate, my Dad had identified the problem and rather than using words, invested time in solving it. Time was precious to my Dad. He worked incredibly long hours but he realised the best thing he could do to stop me going to the pub and getting pissed was to spend time with me instead.

Looking back, the tendency of my Dad to do things the complete opposite to the usual way was a real foundation of my success.

My Dad.

The best solution is often not the obvious one. Doing the opposite to the expected can bring astounding results. There are countless examples of this in business. In the '80s, Apple started on its way to being the first trillion-dollar company by abandoning what the rest of the market was doing. While its competition was building PCs with separate towers and monitors and ever-increasing amounts of computing power, Apple decided not to compete in the race. Instead, it created the self-contained iMac with an emphasis on beauty and design. It was described as the computer no-one knew they wanted until they saw it. By doing the opposite to what was expected – concentrating on design as much as functionality - Apple established a unique place in the market and went on to dominate it.

Sometimes, business solutions can also be unusual, if a little underhand. For example, in the 1990s passengers at Houston Airport frequently complained about lengthy delays in picking up their luggage. The airport invested in more staff and technology to try and speed the luggage delivery process up, but to no avail. Then someone had a brainwave. They simply moved the baggage claim hall further away from the terminal. This meant passengers had a much longer walk and their bags were there when they arrived. If they could not speed up the luggage, they would slow down the passengers. Complaints dropped immediately.

Without really knowing it, I naturally took my Dad's philosophy of examining problems and finding different solutions to them into my business life. It's like a subconscious gene I carry in me from him. Through all my working life I have tended to follow those principles. I tend to see solving problems differently and he taught me that through actions, rather than words.

One day in my second to last year at school there was an assembly, and I wasn't feeling great and wanted to stay at home. For some reason, Mum got me out of my sickbed and insisted I went in. They were reading out the names of the prefects for the following year and announced I was to be head boy. I was blown away. it was the last thing I expected. I was the first person in our family to be head boy and of course they were proud of me. My Dad never expressed it - it wasn't his way - but I knew he was pleased.

The reason I got the role was because for once I was working hard in lessons and I was involved in sport and music, I had been brought up to always be respectful to teachers and older people, and my friendships crossed the traditional school group boundaries. I left school with English, French and Maths O-levels. Oxford and Cambridge universities were hardly going to come calling but my parents knew I was intelligent, only occasionally did stupid things, and that I would be all right. For them, things were going well too. Dad's business was bringing in more money and he began spending it on things which brought us pleasure.

On a holiday in Devon, back when I was around eleven, we hired a dinghy with a 20hp engine and we had a great time fishing from it and motoring around. Back in London, he found someone who was selling the hull of a boat, just the skeleton really, so he bought it for £50. He rubbed the fiberglass down, sprayed it, built seats which my Mum covered with fabric, bought a steering cable, an engine, installed it and did the electronics. He built a boat. We called it *Sally Anne* after my sister who had just been born, took it to Shoeburyness, put it in the water and thankfully it didn't sink. That was our first experience of speedboats and water. We spent the next couple of years simply bombing about in second-hand boats. It was great fun.

It's another East End cliché but my Mum, Dad and grandparents, like half of East London, loved the Tendring Coast. There were more Londoners up there on a summer weekend than there were at home, so they went halves and bought an eight-berth caravan in St Osyth for £7,500. Dad then bought a proper speedboat, a 14ft Fletcher with a 50hp Chrysler engine. This was the start of us all learning how to waterski. We were mixing with new people, involved with the waterskiing and boating crowd on the beach, and there was also a skiing lake in the village itself. Dad then kicked it up a gear and bought a brand new 70hp Mercury engine for £2,500 to go onto the boat, which was a fortune in those days. It cost the same as his first house. It went like a bat out of hell! It would do more than 40 knots and was so fast you could ski barefoot behind it. We had the time of our lives on those boats for years.

By now, Dad was making so much money off the surveillance kits we upgraded to another static caravan right on the beach. For his thirty-sixth birthday my Mum bought my Dad a flying lesson for a tenner. She should have known better. Of course, he got the bug. Typical of his personality, he got his pilot's license, and then qualified for instrument and night flying. He couldn't get enough. His old mate Jim Laidler, who he had bought the Tottenham shop from, also got the bug, got his license and they decided to buy a second-hand, twelve year old, four-seater Cherokee plane for £12,000. Of course, Dad worked on it, re-sprayed it, and re-fitted all the inside until it looked brand new, and he would take all of us flying in it. I was temporarily working in his shop after leaving school, and we would go to Stapleford Airfield in Essex, jump in the plane and be in St Osyth in twenty minutes. We would fly over the sea at 50ft in front of our caravan, waggle the wings and Mum would get in the car and come and pick us up from Clacton Airfield.

From initially worrying about just putting food on the table, Dad was now successful enough to be enjoying life, having different experiences and mixing in different social circles. They were even going to the pub in the village. A shop then came up for the sale in St Osyth. By now Dad had his mate Phil helping to run the surveillance business in London, and it dawned on them they didn't need to live in Chingford anymore. They could work in the shop, they were getting money from the surveillance business - which was called Glideglen Ltd - and so they moved from the East End to Tendring, like East End families had been doing for decades. They bought a five-bedroom detached with a swimming pool for £42,000 and sold the terraced house in Chingford for £65,000. Even back then, London prices were astronomical compared to elsewhere in the UK.

For my Dad, buying that house, having a second-hand speedboat and plane, together with some money in the bank was success in life enough. To achieve happiness, he didn't need to take big business risks, borrow money, take on loads of staff and try to fit a siren to every police car in the country, or modernize each coach. He wanted a life he could control within the boundaries he was happy in. He had achieved a degree of comfort and wealth, raised his family and he was happy with his lot. For a lad with no education and crippling shyness, he had the determination to succeed in life and he did so. He knew even though I didn't have the best academic qualifications, I would be ok.

My Dad knew the person is what is most important, not their qualifications or the letters after their name. While education is a fundamental foundation of life, it will only get you so far. Being hardworking, emotionally intelligent, and streetwise can take you further than exam successes ever will. As Martin Luther King said, intelligence plus character is the goal of true education.

When my company employs people now, their educational qualifications are not the be all and end all for us. We just check they received a basic one. That is as far as it goes. We concentrate instead on their life experience, their attitude to the world, and how emotionally intelligent they are. EQ rather than IQ. If you want to join our management team, or answer the telephone, the process is the same. We do psychometric testing, personal assessments over a day or two, see how they collaborate with colleagues. Academic qualifications are not the answer to everything.

As if to prove it, moving forward 40 years to 2020, some of the biggest brains on the planet had no idea what was about to befall us.

COVID January 2020:

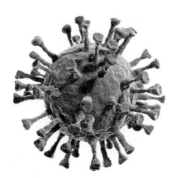

Crisis, what crisis?

Hundreds of thousands of people were about to die. The world was about to undergo a trauma which crossed boundaries and paid no heed to wealth, location, background or race. Like me, you probably didn't have a clue what was about to hit us. As subsequent chapters in this book will reveal, by 2020 I was running my own company. We will go through all the successes and disasters which led me to this stage in my life in due course. But COVID 19 – which you have also just lived through - represented a disaster for me, and my company, which was potentially far more financially costly than it was for most.

Was my company prepared? Every responsible company has contingency plans. HR departments love them. What if there is a fire at your HQ? What happens if your computer servers suddenly get infected with a virus? What happens if an angry mob of deranged customers suddenly storms into reception? My company had plans for all of those. I am sure we weren't alone in not having a plan for a worldwide pandemic breaking out which would shut entire countries down.

I am not sure when I first heard the words Corona Virus or COVID 19 as it was eventually renamed. Like the rest of the country, I probably read a few paragraphs in the newspaper about a new disease which had emerged in China, squeezed between yet another article about Brexit and a picture of a celebrity wearing a revealing dress. On December 31, 2019, the Chinese authorities told the World Health Organisation about the disease, but the announcement hardly hit international headlines. In the UK we were far more interested in Prince Harry and Meghan stepping back from Royal duties while bush fires ravaged Australia and President Trump's impeachment hearings rumbled on. Ignorance is bliss.

When more stories slowly emerged about the virus, no-one panicked. Headlines about massive health care risks are nothing new. I had survived the Salmonella crisis despite eating British eggs, and Mad Cow Disease had thankfully passed me by. Ebola, Hantavirus and other horrific diseases were things which happened in far off lands. Even unusual strains of flu were not a new threat. In 2007 bird flu had exploded, killing six out of ten people who contracted it. The world held its breath, scientists warned it could lead to a death toll in millions like the 1917 Spanish flu and then… nothing happened. The virus continued to kill chickens and to infect and tragically kill the occasional person, but as the years passed, the number of human cases subsided.

Then in 2009 came swine flu from Mexico. We were warned this could be another global nightmare. Start building a bunker. However, while it killed around 150,000 people across the globe, the death toll was lower than the usual winter flus which we have all learned to live with as part of modern life.

So, this COVID thing was surely nothing to really worry about? We're British! The rest of the world might get blighted by weird epidemics but not us Brits. We never have to worry about rabies, mosquitos or other foreign diseases. We live in a green and pleasant land where the most dangerous thing in the wild is a badger. The British government was advising against travelling to somewhere called Wuhan in China but that was ok. I, along with the rest of the planet, had no real reason to go there.

Anyway, back in 1980 I wasn't concerned about diseases, I was just worried about finding a job.

Chapter 2:

Low aspirations
and realisations

Nowadays, a lot of school leavers dream of being media stars, entrepreneurs or environmental activists. In East London in the early 1980s our aspirations were a little different. On leaving school, most of my mates just wanted to have enough money in their back pockets to go to the pub, get a motorbike and have a good time. They wanted to be plumbers, electricians, or carpenters. Most girls wanted to be nurses, secretaries, shopworkers or housewives. You might think those are sexist stereotypes, but it doesn't make it a lie. As a generation we weren't short-sighted, or lacking ambition, we were just products of a working -class environment where putting food on the table and paying the council house rent, or the mortgage, was the main priority.

Back then, I was the same. I had no lofty dreams. I just wanted a good job. Because I had helped my Dad install a kitchen in our house and dozens of other similar projects, I realised the prospect of doing joinery, plumbing and electrical work for the rest of my life wasn't going to get me out of bed every day.

What did excite me was doing something unusual, a job which most people didn't even realise existed. Forget being a footballer, fighter pilot or astronaut, I dreamed of being... a refrigeration engineer. My Dad had been one and had told me all about it. For years, every time we went to the supermarket, I was the only kid looking at how the fridges operated rather than at the food inside them. When I got a weekend job stacking fridges in Sainsbury's in Walthamstow Market, I didn't care about the produce. I was fascinated about the process which kept it cold. The physics and hidden engineering behind refrigeration was weirdly fascinating to me. I also knew being a fridge engineer would eventually bring some money in. My Dad had told me there were not enough fridge engineers to install and maintain them as it was a very specialist industry, which meant you could do a load of overtime and earn good money from it. I remember him saying, "You will never find a good fridge engineer out of work."

When he was doing it, my Dad would get involved in weekend work where a whole supermarket would expect all their refrigeration to be ripped out and new equipment installed and working by the end of that weekend. He and his colleagues would work from Saturday until the early hours of Sunday morning non-stop, get the job done and then have Sunday off, but still be paid for both days. That sounded good to me. I knew I would have to do an apprenticeship and I wouldn't earn much at first. I had mates who became plasterers and labourers and they were immediately earning £60 a week. I had the foresight (and guidance from my parents) to know if I made the sacrifice and invested in my future, while I would only earn £33 a week for a couple of years, before too long I would earn way more than most of my mates ever could.

Within a month of leaving school I went for three interviews. I didn't get the first two but the third was with Russ Nicholson, the service manager at Carter Refrigeration. Carter was a family-owned refrigeration firm with a turnover of around £150m. I told him about my experience with electronics and messing about with this and that and I got the job. I was made up, they had obviously seen my potential, my brilliance and been won over by my personality! In fact, Russ was desperate for apprentices and I happened to be the first candidate through the door. Life sometimes gives you a major boost which has huge long-term benefits and you don't even realise it at the time. Mine was being apprenticed to an engineer called Freddie Bird. Freddie was an Eastender, a bit of a rough diamond, a massive fella who had his own life challenges in the past but had got married, had a young baby, the penny had dropped and he had realised he had to change his life for the sake of his new family. He had a great work ethic, would take no shit from me and was the ideal person to learn from. He became my mentor.

I was also very lucky to get taken on by Carters. Their team of thirty-odd London engineers was the best in the business. There wasn't a really bad egg amongst them. Of course, there were some moaners and some were better than others, but they had all been trained under the old apprentice system where they were shown the right way to do things, and they all had a good work ethic. Everyone was accountable, everyone was conscientious and I was surrounded by people with superb working practices, so I came to think of excellence as the norm. Bad habits never crept in. It wasn't until later in life I realised there were more bad engineers in the industry than there were good ones.

I was lucky in a third way. I was part of the last generation who took part in the traditional apprenticeship process, which provided high-quality engineering training. For decades training had been at the forefront of every trade. You spent years getting on-the-job training and went to college as well. You were exposed to people with expertise and you learnt from them. Everyone at Carters had been through that process. In the mid-1980s, when businesses were feeling the economic pressure, the first thing they all did was cut the training. They were not to know this would badly impact the engineering world over the next forty years.

As well as working with Freddie, I was also attending Willesden College of Technology in Neasden, near Wembley, one day a week. The strange thing is, having been an average school pupil, I discovered at Willesden I had an insatiable appetite for knowledge. I had just come out of school and so had a learning mindset, but this was an adult environment and they treated you like a grown-up. In the mornings we learnt about the mathematical, physical and chemical theories behind refrigeration in the classroom, then in the afternoons we would be in workshops, doing practical work on this ancient old kit they had. When we went back to work the other four days of the week, we would then see the theories in use in modern equipment. It was brilliant, the best of both worlds.

Of course, I almost threw my career away. As an apprentice, one of the first jobs you are given (besides making the tea) is lagging pipework with foam-like insulation. Get a length of insulation, pour talcum powder down the inside, and then slide it over the copper pipe. It was mind-numbingly boring. After a couple of weeks my Mum came and woke me up for work and I told her I wasn't going in. It was boring, I couldn't be bothered to get the bus to meet Freddie at 6:30am, it was a crap job and I would just get another. She convinced me to get up, said I would soon start to enjoy it and drove me to meet Freddie so I could at least escape the bus ride. Of course, as a 16-year-old, I knew nothing about responsibility, sacrifice or commitment, and we had that same row every morning for weeks. It was her determination and, more importantly, her willingness to let me hate her for making me go to work, that kept me in a job.

For the first three months, Freddie did various maintenance and repair jobs while I mainly handed him his tools. Then one day we were sent to the Mayfair Hotel in London to install a new cold room in their kitchens. We only had one day to install it. Freddie was running around like a blue-arsed fly trying to get it all installed and he asked me to do one simple job, install a small solenoid valve in the pipework. The biggest enemies of refrigeration are air and moisture. If either get in, the whole thing is buggered. The industry goes to extraordinary lengths to keep them out. For example, you learn never to blow down a fridge pipe because that puts moisture in it. So, this solenoid valve came out of the box with two caps inside (called bonnets) to stop moisture getting in. I had never seen these before - in college, we had really old valves that were never packed from new. I lacked the emotional intelligence and maturity to ask Freddie what the bonnets were for, mainly because this was the one job which he had asked me to do and I didn't want to look stupid. So, I fitted the valve with the bonnets inside. Of course, that meant the system was never going to work, as the refrigerant gas couldn't pass through the valve.

After a full day's work, at about 6pm, Freddie tried to power up the system and, of course, nothing happened. He was mystified and then spent two or three hours tearing his hair out, wondering why it wasn't working, stripping the system down bit by bit. Of course, the very last thing he checked was the solenoid – thinking that's so easy even Jeff can't have got that wrong – and he found the caps were still attached. I had ruined his Saturday night, wasted both our time, but he just looked at me, cuffed me round the head, and explained the problem. I was lucky to work with Freddie.

Soon we were sent on to our first big job. We were part of a team of engineers installing all the refrigeration and associated equipment at a new Sainsbury's at Rayleigh Weir in Southend. My seventeenth birthday was approaching and I had always wanted to pass my driving test on my birthday, so I started pestering Freddie and Russ Nicholson to get L plates put on the van so I could practise my driving. And when I say pester, I could pester for England. I wouldn't stop until Russ eventually said "yes". It's crazy really, with all the insurance and health and safety problems it would cause nowadays, a firm would never even consider it, but it was a different time back then. There I was, sixteen, driving me and Freddie up the A127 to Southend and back every day with him invariably asleep in the passenger seat. Madness. I managed to pass the test on my seventeenth birthday. Sometimes pestering pays off.

We were at Rayleigh Weir for around six months. It was a big job with a lot of lagging. However, even while I was dying of boredom and covered in talcum powder, I was always watching the work the engineers were doing. The next basic task after lagging was pipe-bending. In a supermarket installation, it was an awful job - you were always crawling into ducts, under floor cavities etc. We had done some pipe bending in college so I asked if I could have a go. They let me, probably just to get me to shut up and stop pestering them. They gave me some copper and said, "Make ten bends like this."

Because of the attitude instilled in me by my Dad, to do jobs right, to use protractors and templates to check angles, to always measure twice, I was really good at it. Engineers were calling their mates over to have a look at my pipe-bending! They then allowed me to try brazing - welding together two lengths of 6m-long, 1 3/8" copper pipe. Refrigeration systems run under quite high pressure so if you get this wrong and the join fails it can be messy and costly, especially if it's under a cement floor. They let me start doing joins on the riser – the visible pipework on the wall which led to the plant room – because they knew if I got it wrong, they would have easy access to fix it. But I loved brazing too. I had done it at college, I was enthusiastic, my Dad's work principles still applied, and so they were also impressed with my brazing. When they pressure-tested the system, my sections held up fine.

They were giving me more responsibilities, praising my work and I thrived on it. Every single day my ambition was to impress everyone with my work. Attitudes like that get noticed. I was only seventeen but

I was working hard, being productive and contributing more than they could have hoped for. And suddenly, for the first time, I appreciated there was a career ladder I could climb. Being an engineer didn't mean just driving around in a van, fixing things - there was a whole infrastructure and hierarchy. I saw the industry had career progression: apprentice, junior engineer, engineer, senior engineer, chargehand, supervisor.

The measure of success is progress and I wanted recognition by climbing the ladder. Now, I know titles are less important than what you are contributing to a company, but at the start of careers they are seen as proof you are moving forward in life. People like measurable steps which take you on a journey and these are usually linked to titles and salaries. One day we were having a cuppa at work and I said: "I tell you what, I will be a supervisor by the time I am nineteen." The engineers, some who had been there for twenty years, fell about laughing and tore into me: "Get real Jeff... you are an apprentice... a kid... still in nappies.... no-one has ever got supervisor at that age.... shut up." I just repeated my vow. I would be a supervisor at nineteen. Some part of my psyche dictates that when I have an ambition, I need to achieve it. Becoming supervisor became my only goal in life. I knew to succeed I had to push myself and prove I could do it. No-one was going to just give it to me.

At Rayleigh, I also discovered one of the dodgy practices which is still common in the engineering sector today but which I would later abolish in my own company. Even though we were all working the same long hours, at the end of the week the supervisor would say how many extra hours he would allow you to put on your timesheet. Bill the engineer might be brilliant and hardworking and do three times as much as his mate Bob. Bill would work his socks off, get home knackered, sleep all weekend because he had worked so hard but earn the same as Bob who had taken it easy and was in the pub all weekend. The way they unofficially counterbalanced this was with the time sheets. They would say, "Bill, you put 55 hours down, Bob, you put 50."

This principle of fiddling the books to reward good performance was commonplace. Eventually, I would abolish all that but for now, I had a career ladder to climb and I needed one thing to do it - my own work van which would allow me to go to jobs on my own. But let's fast forward again to 2020 where the whole British economy was about to be driven over a cliff.

COVID February 2020:

Ignorance is bliss

As January turned to February, the biggest danger to the UK seemed to be the weather. Three storms battered the country bringing record rainfalls and the coverage of widespread flooding drowned out any early alarms ringing about this virus thing. British Airways had suspended all flights to China, but other airlines were still operating the routes, happily jetting off there and bringing people back to the UK. It couldn't be that bad, right?

Then in February, a trickle of British cases started to emerge. There was a minor outbreak at a Nike conference in Edinburgh, a few people returning from a ski trip to Italy were discovered to have the disease. Sadly, there was the first British death - a pensioner with the disease died on a cruise ship moored off Japan. Around 450 people a day die of cancer in the UK, and around 180 of heart disease. Aside from the awful human tragedies such deaths cause, the world keeps on turning and so it seemed with COVID. Nothing to see here, move on.

It was the same picture across most of Europe, a case here, a case there. However, in Italy there had been around 1,000 cases and around 30 deaths. As February dawned the Italian Prime Minister had declared a state of emergency for six months and quarantined 50,000 people in Northern Italy. The shameful fact is across the UK, most people's perceptions tended to be, "What on earth are they doing in Italy? It's just a bad flu. Italy has lots of old people living in big families, so they are more susceptible than we are, Italian governments have never been known for their stability, they just need to get a grip..."

Believe me, no-one in British business was losing any sleep over the virus. Back in 1982? Forget pandemics. Back then I was losing sleep over fixing compressors.

Chapter 3

Simplify to succeed

One lesson I learnt early in life was, "**If you don't ask, the answer is always no.**" This was bad news for poor Russ. Having pestered him half to death to get L plates on the van to pass my driving test, I now started constantly demanding my own van and my own jobs to be sent to. This was unheard of. No apprentice gets a van or sent to jobs on their own, it had never happened before. But I had a goal to achieve, and my pestering was shameless. Eventually Russ gave in. The career ladder might have been high, but I was on the first rung and moving upwards. My own van at seventeen. No-one could have been prouder. Of course, before long I crashed it. I was a boy racer with a heavy right foot and was not used to driving vans full of equipment in the back. When I hit the brakes, I didn't realise the extra weight, in the pouring rain, meant a longer stopping distance and so I ploughed right into the back of a lorry. The van was a right off. God knows how I wasn't hurt. I was terrified, that was it, job gone. Russ had put his trust in me and I had destroyed the van. You can imagine how I felt ringing him from the nearest phone box. You can also imagine his reaction. I was sure I would be getting the bus back to Chingford to tell Mum and Dad I had been fired.

Even when I realised Russ wasn't going to sack me, I was still devastated. Supervisor at nineteen? I would be lucky if I wasn't still an apprentice after this. For the rest of the week I was as miserable as sin. I had wrecked my own ambitions and had no-one to blame but myself. That Friday, I got off the bus and started trudging home. As I approached the house, I noticed a van parked outside with *Carters* on the side. Rather than sacking me, Russ had replaced the van and put his faith in me once again. **Little acts of faith and kindness like that can inspire people in business beyond measure. Sometimes taking a chance on people will pay you back massively.** Looking back, I think Russ took a chance on me because he saw something in me, a relentless passion and drive. He had received incredible feedback about me, and I think he just thought, "*This kid could be good, I just have to keep his feet on the ground.*" It was also indicative of the times and the firm. Carters believed in quality engineers, they trained people to be just that and supported individuals who showed initiative. Any company would die to have a workforce like that now but it's almost impossible. They hardly exist, which is indicative of modern training methods and culture.

I spent the weekend making that second van shine, fitting shelving, carpets, internal lights, a cassette tape player, a graphic equaliser. I sprayed the wheels, white to match the van, dropped the suspension, you name it. No-one has ever been prouder of a van than I was.

My second van with white wheels and loads of headlights. Inside, I installed a centre console and loads of other gadgets.

My Dad had fitted sunroofs to a couple of family cars, and I wanted the van to have one. The sunroofs came in kits. You cut a hole, the roof then dramatically collapses, you insert the sunroof, the roof then locks up solid and it's fine. So, I fitted one. I was proud as punch. Just make sure you cut the hole the right size or the whole thing is buggered.

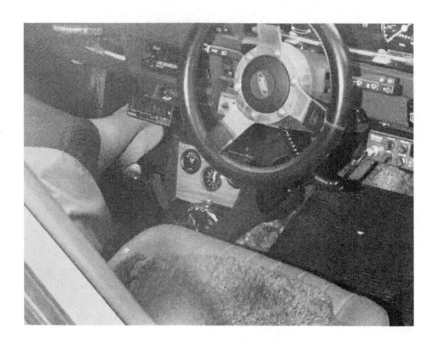

Every day, I literally couldn't wait to get up in the morning to drive the van and, more importantly, park it somewhere the other engineers could see it. Again, I wanted to stand out and be different. When I took the van to head office at Hanwell, West London, Russ saw the sunroof and said: "that looks good, but who gave you permission to do it?" I just walked off whistling. He knew no-one had given permission - he was the only person who could. But rather than shout at me, instead he asked if I could put one in his company Vauxhall Astra SI. I went to the local car accessory shop, bought one and fitted it. He was made up. One of the managers had just got a brand-new Ford Escort XR3i – in those days they were the absolute dog's bollocks - and he wanted a sunroof too. When I was fitting it, the roof collapsed as it always does, and he almost had a heart attack. He thought I had ruined his car.

Even the chief executive had heard about my van improvements and one day, when we bumped into each other in the car park, he asked to see it. Most vans were grotty and had equipment piled up inside, but mine was spotless. There was a rack for everything, custom-made straps, carpets. He was gobsmacked. Stupid stuff like fitting sunroofs and having a spotless van gets you noticed as well. In his position high up in the company, he would struggle to remember the names of most of the engineers, he had no reason to. But simply because I had shown pride in my van, he would remember me. Stupid stuff like that can pay dividends.

I didn't rest on my laurels though, I continued to nag Russ for more and more opportunities. There is a saying I saw later in my career which sums up my life: "To be an entrepreneur you have to bite off more than you can chew, and then learn very quickly how to chew it." That was me to a tee. I was forever demanding to be sent out on jobs on my own with no clue if I could actually do them. I could worry about that later. One Friday night my nagging paid off.

I was sent to an International store (an old supermarket chain) at Ilford to fix a large dairy cabinet. I walked into the plant room, was met with a maze of pipework, condensing units, switches and electrical control panels. I felt special and confident, they were trusting me to fix this on my own. The problem was I couldn't fix it. I was there for ages, prodding and poking, I just couldn't work out what was wrong with the bloody thing. The condensing unit – which was the heart of the system - would not run. The more I struggled, the more I panicked… "I have blown it, I don't know what I am doing, they are never going to send me out on my own again."

In the end, the manager wanted to close the store and I gave up and went home. I was devastated. My Mum was cooking dinner – usually it was sausage, egg and chips on a Friday – and my old man walked in and noticed I was crestfallen. He asked what was wrong. I said, "I have been given my first job, I can't fix it and I want to jump off a bridge." He asked me to tell him about the job, sat silently while I explained and said, "You have a problem with the control circuit. Get me a pen and a piece of paper and I will teach you about control circuits."

He drew a simple schematic explaining how it worked. Forget all the pipes and mysterious wires, he drew me a simple map of the entire process, what things did, and in which order. It was a genuine *Oh, my God!* moment for me. I could suddenly see how everything fitted in place and was connected. Despite all my training and education, it was a light bulb moment. It doesn't matter if it is a refrigeration circuit, the space station, our bodies, whatever. Everything runs according to a series of processes and reactions. Take standing up. To simplify it, our brain sends a message to our muscles, they engage, our knees bend, we exert energy to get upward motion etc. If we can't stand up where is the problem? Is the brain getting the message? Can our knees flex? Can we generate enough energy to achieve motion? Doctors look at every stage in the process to work out what is wrong.

The vast majority of engineering problems can be solved by similar investigations and logical deductions. Until my Dad drew the simple schematic, I had been learning engineering but not fully understanding the process. Another issue is we all, by nature, over-think things. I had been stood in that plant room, surrounded by all this equipment and machinery, half of which I didn't know what it did. I was lost, panicking, *What does all this stuff do? How do I know what is broken?* He explained everything with a simple line diagram a child could follow. Eureka. It was a life lesson I have taken with me ever since. **Simplify the complicated.**

I shot back to the supermarket at seven the next morning, found the problem and fixed it in less than fifteen minutes. Doing that one job successfully gave me momentum. Russ was soon confident he could send me out and I would get the job done. I had grown emotionally too. Now if I was stumped, I would ask for guidance. Going out and fixing jobs on my own meant I was considered a full engineer. Another step up the ladder achieved. By being on call to do emergency jobs at evenings and weekends I was earning good money, I was still going to college on day release and passing my exams. Life was great. A couple of jobs gave me ever-more credibility.

I got a call at three o'clock one Sunday morning when I wasn't even on duty. All the freezers at a Sainsbury's in Tonbridge had gone down and the store manager was panicking. In those days, if a store's freezers went down you had about six hours to fix it before the food had to be thrown out. The standby engineer had attended and told Russ the compressor was broken. There were usually two reasons a compressor went down, it was either seized, or down to earth. *Down to earth* is where the internal motor winding's insulation had broken down and the bare wires were touching the casing. These compressors were huge and weighed a ton.

Due to the risk of a compressor failure at Sainsbury's, there was always a replacement available in the plant room and a jack for changing it. However, the engineer said he couldn't change it on his own. Russ had lost his rag, called him a few names, and told him to piss off home. He called me, said "Show me how good you are", and I went out and changed it on my own. I might have broken my back lifting it, even with a jack, but health and safety hadn't been invented back then. The store manager was over the moon, thousands of pounds worth of stock had been saved, and I went home three hours later pleased as punch.

This was the plantroom where I changed a half ton compressor on my own at 3am.

I got a bit of flak from the original engineer for showing him up but, sod him, even at that young age, I didn't suffer fools gladly. I was building my reputation and he should have done the job in the first place. A month later, a similar thing happened. An engineer couldn't fix a fault, a compressor wasn't pumping, and Russ called me just to confirm the original diagnosis, as these compressors were extremely expensive to replace. The other engineer had just called it a write-off but I wanted to know why it wasn't working properly so, using the principles my Dad had taught me, I stripped it down and found it was just dirt on some of the unloading valves. I fixed it in an hour or two and saved the company £15,000 on the cost of a new compressor.

I loved the work, I loved the responsibility, and I knew by going the extra mile and always showing commitment and enthusiasm I stood out from the crowd. I was working every hour God sent, but it didn't seem like work because I loved it so much. For those reasons, having just turned nineteen, I was made chargehand. **In good companies, effort and skill which leads to results should always get rewarded. Effort on its own is not enough, it needs to produce something. If you are producing results and it is not recognised, you are working for the wrong company.** The new role meant I would be supervising other engineers and managing jobs rather than just working on them. Not so long ago as an apprentice lagging pipes, I had seen the career ladder and my ambitions to climb it had been laughed at. Within two years, I was very near the top. Those school mates of mine earning £60 a week? Financially I had left them way behind. From being delighted to get a clapped-out old van, I was now getting a company car. But not everyone was so happy.

My shiny new estate car, again souped-up.

The promotion meant I would be managing people for the first time which was totally outside my comfort zone. I had never done it before. How on earth was I going to do this? It was scary but I wasn't daunted. For some reason I have always been confident I would learn what I needed to achieve. I could have read books on management but instead I used examples from my own past. I had been managed well by some people, and badly by others, so I simply decided to try and copy the people I thought were good managers. Time gives you experience, and you eventually learn lessons yourself, but when you are thrown in at the deep end sometimes your own experiences are all you have to fall back on. And besides, I was naturally filled with self-confidence, which I know is an advantage that not everyone has. If I was on a plane and it was suddenly announced over the PA system the pilot had collapsed and they needed to someone to land the plane, if there wasn't an actual pilot on-board I would be the first to stand up and say, "If you get me a radio link so someone can talk me through it, I will get us down safely."

Managing a load of engineers would be easier than landing a plane but would come with more aggravation. Russ warned me what would happen. He said some of the other engineers, many of whom had been there for years, would be pissed off at my rapid rise. He was right, they went ballistic. By doing repairs other engineers had said could not be done, I had exposed them. Rather than admitting they could have done a better job, they criticised me for proving it. They bitched to their colleagues and a real atmosphere developed between me and some of my colleagues. It was lonely being ostracised - no-one likes to be on the outside - but it was also water off a duck's back. I didn't care. I didn't respect the people ignoring me. Sod them!

At one engineers' meeting, I thought I would be sensitive for once. I wouldn't turn up in my shiny new company car. Instead, I would park it around the corner so I wasn't rubbing their noses in it. Bearing in mind what subsequently happened, I should have roared into the car park and started doing car stunts. After the meeting as I was walking back to the car, one of the engineers I had embarrassed confronted me, saying, "You're an arse-licker, it's the only way you have made it to the top, blah, blah, blah." I was tempted to square up to him, but I just walked away.

single engineering firm had spent time and money hiding pipework away so no one could see it. I thought, *I am going to put the pipework where everyone can see it and I am going to make it look special.*

Freddie and me chatted about our projects and teased each other about whose would be best. We agreed not to visit each other's site until right before commissioning. When he eventually visited, some five months later, and saw my visible pipework he almost fainted. "What the fuck have you done," he cried. "You can't do that, they will make you rip it all out, it'll take ages, the costs will overrun. What the fuck have you done? You are meant to hide it, not display it!"

He was genuinely panicking. He wasn't slagging me off, he was worried for me! I reassured him it would be fine. Secretly…. I was shitting myself. Towards the end of most jobs someone senior comes along and does a snags visit, looking for things they aren't happy about and want changed. One judgement of your work is always how long the snagging list is. Sometimes it can be fourteen or fifteen pages. At Sainsbury's the company's head of engineering, Ron Filler, was that man. When Ron arrived, it was like a royal visit. Freddie's had been five pages, mostly minor stuff. I was worried mine might be one sentence: "Rip it all out and start again." He wandered in and stopped dead in his tracks, gaping at the pipes on the wall and the ceiling, muttering, "That's unconventional." The silence lasted minutes but felt like hours. He spent five minutes examining it and then called for a ladder.

Armaflex is a type of lagging around pipes and a lot of engineers get lazy and just push the sections together. At Carters we were taught the importance of gluing them together to create a true vapour seal. Ron goes up the ladder, checks they are all glued and solemnly declares, "Solid joints, Jeff." He then walks round, looking upwards, following the path of the pipes until they reach a junction where pipes are going off in different directions like tree branches. I made sure the pipes were spaced perfectly, at identical angles, and everything was totally symmetrical. He looked at this, reached into his pocket, got a camera out and started taking pictures of it. Eventually he turned around and said, "This is the best pipework I have ever seen. This is going to be the new spec for all Sainsbury's stores going forward."

I was delighted – and relieved. The word spread through Carters that Jeff Dewing had done it again. Oh, and my snagging list was one page! I remained at Carters for another three years. I loved it. I loved the role, the management aspect, the work, the money. I continued at college one day a week from 9am to 10pm getting the top level ONC qualification. My thirst for knowledge remained. I was happy. But in 1987, aged twenty-three, I left. The reason? Not every decision I made during my early teenage years had been a good one. Look ahead to 2020 and decisions were being made which would affect millions of lives.

COVID March 2020:

The unthinkable

In early March, the number of cases in the UK was continuing to slowly rise. Those who listened very carefully might have heard the first shouts of real alarm, but most people weren't listening.

COVID caused its first major UK corporate casualty as the airline Flybe collapsed into administration. For several years it had spluttered on through poor trading conditions, numerous changes in ownership and warnings of financial doom. Its demise was largely seen as an inevitable - but foreseeable - consequence of the increasing flight bans caused by COVID.

By March 8, the number of UK cases had risen to 273 with three deaths, but it was not until the following day the corporate world caught a cold. Suddenly, the stock market plunged eight per cent. Two days later it plunged another 12 per cent. Suddenly, the virus wasn't one item in the news, it was the news. Spain went into lockdown, but surely that couldn't happen here? It was inconceivable. Our economy had recently recovered from years of austerity and you did not have to be the governor of the Bank of England to know the damage would be catastrophic. However, by March 14, panic buying had started in supermarkets as idiots emptied the shelves of toilet paper, pasta and other essentials. Half the country condemned such people as panic merchants, but then decided they had better pop to the shops as well. On March 16, Prime Minister Boris Johnson advised people to stay at home if they could and avoid visiting pubs and restaurants. Tens of thousands decided the news was so worrying they had better drown their sorrows and go to the pub for a pint. Then the unthinkable happened. On March 20, the prime minister ordered all restaurants, cafes and pubs to close. On March 23, the UK entered lockdown. In the business world the initial reactions were the same. First came shock – *Oh, my God, what's happening?* Then came fear - *Am I going to lose my job, or in my case my company?* The important thing for us to do was sit back, keep calm and rationalise decisions before we made them. I wish I had done that in 2003. In the business world the reaction was the same. Panic.

Chapter 4

Frosty times

"Ten four for a copy, come in." Back in the early '80s the big craze was CB radios. The airwaves were full of amateurs saying, "Breaker, breaker, what's your 20?" It was fun, and not everyone pretended they were driving a big rig in Texas. Me and my Dad got the bug and started attending meetings in pubs where we would discuss the technology and meet fellow enthusiasts. At one of these I met a girl called Heather (her CB handle was 'Sweet Sugar'). To use the CB lingo of the time, "I was burning sixteen candles, she was burning nineteen." To those of you who aren't fluent in CB, that meant I was sixteen years of age, and she was three years older. If I had enjoyed the clichéd East End upbringing, she had endured a far harder time. She had missed a lot of school because she was looking after her older sister's baby, and it was an understatement to say her family home just wasn't a nice environment. We started dating and, after a couple of months together, I paid for her to move into a bedsit to get her away from her home life. My parents weren't exactly thrilled about us and subtly let me know they thought she wasn't right for me. But as ever, I knew best. My problem was a common one. **Sometimes in life you find yourself in a jam jar and can't read what it says on the label.**

The relationship initially went well, I spent most of my time at work and still lived at home, but we saw each other daily and were in love. In 1983, after my parents had moved to St Osyth, I got a mortgage and bought a little maisonette in Walthamstow and we moved in together. I was only nineteen years old. It was hardly a normal household, though. An old boyfriend of my sister's, Paul Sharp, showed a real interest in what I was doing, was struggling for a regular income (he was a bricklayer and labourer by trade) and was living in a dingy bedsit in Ilford. After a few months seeing his enthusiasm for what I was doing and the refrigeration industry, I made him an offer. I said, "If you are serious, I will train you to become a first-class engineer and get you a job at Carters." I then went on to name the conditions. He would need to live with me and

Heather and sleep on the couch. Monday to Friday daytime, he would come to work with me for nothing where I would show him the ropes. Monday to Friday evenings, he would sit with me and we would do the college and theory stuff. I told him it would take him a year to become an engineer. Was he committed?

He said "yes", and one year later he secured employment with Carters and did extremely well in his career. Years later, he came to work for me again. He had a great career and went on to have a good life. He realised **in life opportunities don't come along often and there might be sacrifices you have to make to achieve them but, if you are determined to succeed, most things are possible. However, you also have to realise sacrifice is always part of what leads to success.**

You can imagine what Heather thought about having someone live on our sofa and eat our food for a year, but I just had an insatiable appetite to help people. I am no saint but I have always wanted to do the right thing for others. The pleasure of knowing I had achieved my task in helping him achieve his goal was all the reward I needed. Heather eventually became pregnant. I thought getting married was simply the right thing to do. When I told my parents, they didn't say, "Congratulations, son," they said, "Oh dear."

We were married at Walthamstow Register Office. There was no honeymoon, just a small reception afterwards. My parents managed to bite their lips. On one of our visits to see my parents, we realised it was stupid living in the small maisonette in London with a baby on the way. If we moved to St Osyth in Essex where they lived, we could afford to buy a three- bedroom semi with a garage and garden for the same money. Obviously, this added three hours of commuting time to my already long days. We were fitting out a Sainsbury's at Pinner, so I would stay with my aunt who lived nearby, but increasingly Heather began to feel isolated. Understandable complaints soon followed about the fact I was always at work. Sarah, our daughter, was born, followed by Michael eighteen months later.

As a supervisor, I began to have a few weekends free, and started spending more time at home. This confirmed to me our relationship was far from perfect and maybe my parents had been right all along. This new spare time also meant I actually had the opportunity to get to know people in the area, and I started going out for the first time in years. Saturday was snooker night, Sunday was for darts. Admittedly, half the time I was meant to be playing snooker into the early hours I was at nightclubs in other Essex towns. My mate (who was my neighbour in St Osyth) was in similar circumstances to me and wanted to escape village life for an evening. We wouldn't go trying to pick up women but, to be on the safe side, in case I ever needed a lift home if my mate was 'indisposed', I always used to park my sign written van on a random street in nearby Jaywick so the driver would never know where I lived. That was a wise decision as one girl who gave me a lift subsequently spent about two weeks looking for me, knocking on just about every door in Jaywick.

Then one darts night in the village, I met Michelle who worked in the village convenience store. She was bright, engaging, funny and we would chat, laugh and flirt. Guess what happened next? One drunken night we had a snog. Drunk or not, when you are married kissing other women is not the best behaviour. It's even worse when you get a love bite, don't realise, wake up the next morning and your wife sees it. Her reaction was understandable. I went to stay in Pinner for the week as part of my normal routine and when I got back all my clothes were in plastic bags on the lawn.

I moved into my Mum and Dad's – who were secretly pleased we were having problems – and to say things went downhill from there is a bit like saying the *Titanic* had a design flaw. I had snogged someone. I was wrong. I tried to talk to Heather, and we might have eventually got past it, but she couldn't get over it. She wouldn't communicate, she couldn't escape her rage. Eventually we got divorced. Believe me, that doesn't even touch the whole nastiness and horror of it, but drawing a veil over this awful period in my life is better for all concerned.

The whole thing had two long-term consequences, one tragic, one good. The tragic? For more than a decade I had no real relationship with my two children. After the initial split I tried to see them but every time I went to pick them up it led to such vitriol and anger it broke my heart and it wasn't healthy for the kids. It was awful. I made the decision not to put them through that and the guilt of being an absent father lives with me to this day. It will never leave me. We lived in the same village and so I would see them a lot. However, trying to engage with them when Heather was nearby and have a relationship with them was impossible. Thankfully, we eventually reconnected when they were teenagers and I have tried to make things right, but nothing can ever repay lost time. Sometimes in life you do things for the right reasons but the repercussions last a lifetime. The separation was in no way down to them, they missed out on opportunities in life through no fault of their own, but ever since I have tried to be there for them and helped them when I can.

The second consequence was it pushed Michelle and me together. Phone calls about the crisis eventually led to us chatting more and more, we began to spend time together and soon fell in love. She was quickly pregnant with Kelly and lived with the baby at her parents', while I stayed with mine. Eventually, my Dad offered us the empty flat to live in above his corner shop in the village. We moved in there and have been together ever since. My personal life may have changed but professionally it was the same. Long hours, commuting up and down the A12 to work, but this time I realised it wasn't healthy for our relationship. I re-evaluated my life and decided to find another job locally. I applied for the job of engineer at Husmanns in Ipswich and got it. Carters had taught me so much and given me the greatest start in engineering anyone could wish for. They were upset I was leaving and offered me more money but I explained while I loved the firm it was time to try and make a new life.

Having achieved my dream of climbing the career ladder, when I joined Husmann I had to take a couple of steps down to work as a service engineer. I didn't mind, in fact the challenge of working my way back up stimulated me. Husmann was a massive American multinational firm. It had entered the UK market just a few years before, bought out a lot of refrigeration companies and now had around thirty offices across the UK. Despite their different sizes, culturally the two companies were largely the same. "Don't moan, get the bloody job done." Because of its acquisitions, Husmann undertook a wide variety of work, largely dependent on the needs of the surrounding communities.

In Ipswich, that meant there was a lot of agricultural work but it also had the contract to service the new local Asda in Ipswich. My attitude was joining a new firm wouldn't be a problem. I was a refrigeration expert. I had made supervisor at nineteen. I had incredible training, experience and knowledge. Bring it on! Within a couple of days, I realised I knew diddly-squat. I was totally out of my comfort zone. They worked in sectors I didn't even know refrigeration was part of. For example, a lot of their work was with bulk milk tanks, where milk is kept refrigerated, either on the farm, in lorries or at the factories, before it is bottled and sold. I didn't even know what a bulk milk tank was. They also serviced a lot of food production places where there were blast chillers on the line to keep the food cold while it was being processed. I had worked on supermarket fridges for years and never truly considered the refrigeration aspects of making the food which was actually put in them.

After a couple of days at the firm, I called in for my next job and was sent to a dry cleaner's at Martlesham Heath. I was mystified - what on earth did they need me for at a dry cleaner's? I said I didn't fix dry cleaning machines, I worked in refrigeration, but I was told to shut up and get down there. I thought it was a wind-up. When I arrived, there was a dry-cleaning machine in front of me. It looked nothing like a fridge. I had to ask the shop manager where the button was to turn it on and off. The shop manager was looking at me like I was an idiot and asked, "I thought you were the engineer?" I rang my supervisor at the office and admitted I did not have a clue what I was doing there.

He explained that every dry-cleaning machine has a fridge plant in it. As part of the cleaning process it helps to take the moisture out of the air. He told me there was a panel on the front, to unscrew it and the fridge unit was in was there. He talked me through how it worked and I fixed it. I was being sent to jobs where I had no initial clue what to do. I loved it. I asked to get sent to the weirdest jobs possible. Working at Asda was also an eye-opener. I had done most of my work with Sainsbury's, which at the time was the market leader. In terms of its refrigeration and the way they managed it, money was no object. When

I saw Asda's refrigeration systems I was thinking, "What is this shit?"

It was like comparing a Rolls Royce to a Ford Fiesta. I couldn't get my head around the difference in standards of investment, engineering, equipment, design and the ways it was used. I appreciated Asda was relatively new to the market and had a different economic approach, but blimey, this was nothing like Sainsbury's. Then I realised, "Does the system keep the fridges and freezers cool?" Of course, it did. It dawned on me in terms of supermarkets I had been operating in just one sector of the economic spectrum. There were cheaper ways of doing things than I was used to, and they worked.

When I had joined Husmanns, I thought I knew a lot, but I realised at Carters I had been working in a relatively small cage and now my wings were spreading. Husmanns used a national installation team for supermarkets rather than local refrigeration staff. When they were working at Littlewoods in Ipswich, I was asked to give a hand and supermarkets were, of course, my speciality. I had led bigger projects than this as a supervisor. I ended up leading the project. Word got back to the national installation manager, so he came down, did a site visit and offered me a supervisory role on his team. However, as it meant travelling all around the country and spending large periods away from home, I turned him down.

The Littlewoods project that I ended up running.

After nine months, I went to my manager and said I was really enjoying the job but couldn't live on the £14,000 a year salary. I said I had previously been a supervisor and I could do more, manage teams and budgets and, sadly, I would have to start looking for another job. Initially, they offered me an installation manager role within a fifty-mile radius, which included setting up a huge commissary at the US Air Force base at Lakenheath, which was about the size of ten UK supermarkets and was a five-year project. I didn't really know what a commissary was. I was flattered and curious but sensed working on one project for years would not be for me.

Instead, they offered me a joint service manager role supervising fifteen engineers. I snapped it up. Within three months of joining my salary rose to £16,000. **If you are working in an environment where your skills, commitment, talent and attitude lead to a major positive difference for your employer, but you are not eventually appreciated, recognised or rewarded, the joke is on you. Leave.**

Proud as punch at Husmann with another company car, complete with personally fitted sunroof.

Eventually, I got to see Lakenheath when I was asked to help with the commissioning. I had never seen anything like it my life. Fridges? There were thousands of them, all covered in chrome. They looked like Cadillacs. Some of the freezer cold rooms were the size of small supermarkets. A normal cold room had three evaporators on the ceiling - this had thirty-eight. Normally it takes a couple of hours to get a cold room to -20C, this took four days. The Americans did not do things by half. Under the fridges were corridors and ducts you could walk down. This was almost Star Wars stuff! One common problem with fridges is leakage of cold air, which is why it can be cold walking down supermarket fridge aisles. This leaking cold air is a massive waste of energy. The commissary system was designed so any leaking cold air was collected in the corridors and ducts underneath and then recycled to cool down the whole commissary. This would later be known as 'Heat Recovery'. I had gone to Husmann thinking I knew everything about refrigeration, when actually I knew very little. Husmann gave me far broader experience.

An interesting episode also occurred just before I left the firm. As an engineer you are always on the road and, if you have a heavy right foot, it can be easy to pick up speeding penalty points on your driving licence. I had six points already when I was allegedly caught doing almost 100mph on the A14 at Ipswich. That would be 6 more points, an inevitable driving ban and I would lose my job. Talk about panicking.

The police claimed they had caught me using Vascar equipment. To explain what Vascar equipment does, it simply uses a simple mathematical formula of 'Time over Distance equals speed'. Now as clever as this sounds, it is materially flawed. It relies on the police officer pushing the start button when they see a car pass a landmark and then pushing the stop button when the car passes a second landmark. From that they get the speed.

On this occasion, the police were parked on a slip road entering the A14 and were looking backwards over the top of a roundabout to see a change in tarmac colour.

This was their first landmark. They monitored me passing the landmark and pushed the 'Start button' and pushed the 'Stop button' as I passed their parked car. They recorded 98 mph and proceeded to pull me over and give me a ticket. Now I knew I wasn't doing anything like that speed, so later in the day, I returned to the exact spot the Police were parked to try and see what could have happened.

Whilst parked there, I could see a mountain of traffic and lorries travelling around the roundabout which frequently obscured me being able to see the change in tarmac. It then came to me that if they had guessed when I had passed that landmark (rather than physically seeing it), that would record a much higher speed because I would have taken less time to reach the second landmark.

As a budding photographer, I then went on to take loads of photographs of the view the police had from my car wing mirror.

After satisfying myself this process was flawed, I decided to take on the establishment and fight the charge in court. Due to the costs, I applied for Legal Aid but was declined due to my circumstances. I couldn't afford a solicitor, so decided to fight the case personally. When I attended court, the magistrate acknowledged that I was defending myself and went on to advise me on how to address the court and cross examine any witnesses. I was shaking like a leaf, especially seeing the policeman that had given me the ticket standing in the dock giving his evidence.

It was now my turn in the dock where I explained my position and my concerns. I then presented the photographs I had taken from my wing mirror which were then passed to the Magistrate.

In his statement the officer had said he had turned his head to observe the point my car had passed the mark, but then in court he admitted my photos from the wing mirror were similar to what he had seen. This discrepancy in his evidence – had he turned his head or looked in the mirror - led to the charge being dismissed and I was found not guilty. Now any police officer that loses what is deemed as an easy win will get tormented back at the station. As I left the court after being awarded all my costs, the officer said to me very quietly "you bastard, we'll get you, your card is marked."

Soon after I left Husmann, and my car went to a colleague. He got pulled over five times by the police in the next few weeks!

Anyway, enough about cold rooms and speeding tickets. In 2020, tragically many people's temperatures were rising.

COVID March 2020:

Frightening times

The dictionary defines panic as "sudden uncontrollable fear or anxiety, often causing wildly unthinking behaviour". When your company's biggest clients are in the restaurant and catering sectors, which the government has just ordered to close, a little panic is entirely understandable. The results of the lockdown on our business were immediate, and potentially catastrophic. The first thing our customers did was immediately stop paying any invoices. We would normally collect £6m cash every month but this money tap was turned off overnight. In the next couple of weeks, we would get just £250,000.

On top of that, as well as outstanding invoices which were not being paid, we worked out we were owed £6m for work we had not yet billed for. To cap it all off, we owed our suppliers something in the region of £10m, with no prospect of getting in any money to pay for it. To help make matters even more difficult, as international borders closed around the globe, I was stuck in Portugal where Michelle and I had gone to prepare to plan for the sale of the business.

Initially, like most companies, we were in shock the same as everyone else. We were speaking daily to our clients to find out what their intentions were but they simply did not know. They needed to look at the impact on their businesses, get further guidance from the government and examine their accounts and operations. One thing was certain though, we were not going to get paid for the foreseeable future. We didn't blame these companies, we had also shut our own cheque book. Out of such panic, one natural reaction might have been to give in to that "wildly unthinking behaviour" and start issuing statutory demands for the money. This would have forced companies to pay us something, or legally they would be forced out of business.

But, despite all our business models and plans having been smashed into smithereens in just a few hours, our management team soon calmed each other down. It was obvious that if we went for the jugular of firms owing us money, while we might get a few quid, our relationships with them would be broken beyond repair.

In those first few frightening days, the overriding principle we adopted was, *Communicate, communicate, communicate.* We contacted the financial directors of each of our clients and opened a line of regular communication. This would allow them to be open and honest about what their strategy was going to be and how they planned to navigate the challenges ahead.

Next, we wrote to all our suppliers explaining what action we were taking and why. We explained we were ceasing all payments to them for the next fourteen days, while we urgently assessed the situation with our clients and monitored the government responses. We said we would be back in touch with an update two weeks later. This also stopped every supplier calling us every day in the hope of getting some cash. We had given them clarity and ourselves some breathing space to think and strategize. We even gave our biggest suppliers the personal phone numbers of every member of the exec board and said, "Call us 24/7 if you want to talk."

We also started a policy of having video conferences with the exec team every day at 4pm where we would often talk late into the night, trying to plan for whatever the next days would bring.

When everything is falling to pieces, taking the wrong action can be far more damaging than standing back, breathing deep and communicating. Unthinking behaviour benefits no-one.

But how exactly were we going to survive this?

Chapter 5

Suits, Samaritans and the code to the future

A guy is at a job interview and is asked what his biggest weakness is. He says he tends to be a little bit too honest. The interviewer says, "I think that's a good thing, I don't see it as a weakness." The bloke replies, "I really don't give a toss what you think."

Jokes aside, I was soon to have my own interview experience, and tell a few un-truths during it. I am living proof that traditional interviews are largely a waste of time! Back in 1987, things were going well at Husmann. I was enjoying it and doing as much overtime as I could to bring in extra cash. You can probably guess what happened next. Michelle said, "We have a young baby, you are working a minimum of eighty hours a week, you are never at home and I need more support." She was right. One day she brought me a job advert cut from the local paper. It was for an air conditioning manager at Air Stream Ltd, a local air conditioning firm. I said, "It sounds great but there are a couple of minor stumbling blocks - I have never worked in air conditioning, nor have I ever been a manager. Apart from that it might be perfect." Michelle said, "Of course you can do it, you are always telling me you can do anything." I don't think she was being complimentary. To keep her quiet as much as anything else, I applied.

Air Stream Ltd was primarily an architectural louvre business – louvres are the horizontal slats you see on buildings which can either be aesthetic or are there to allow air in for *fresh air and extract* systems. In fresh air and extract systems, you typically have a fan at the other side of the louvre which draws fresh air in and an HVAC system (which stands for heating, ventilation and air conditioning) which heats up the air in winter or cools it down in summer. The third arm of Air Stream's business was basic air conditioning split systems, where on the outside of the building you have an aircon condensing unit, and on the inside a fan coil unit that would blow hot or cold air. The company was turning over about £6m, but only a small proportion of this – around £200,000 - was from air conditioning.

While I had never really worked on air con systems, I understood the mechanics and, through my design knowledge, I understood the principles of fridge pipes, heat loss etc. But air con technology was constantly changing and I hadn't really been exposed to it. Air Stream wanted to grow the air con side of the business and, at the interview, I told them about my supervisory experience, about my swift career progression and said not only could I install air con units, but I could also design air con systems for clients (a skill I had learnt theoretically while at Willesden College). If they had asked me to prove it there and then I would have been sunk - I didn't really have a clue. I would barely know where to start. They offered me the job. There's another perfect example of why traditional job interviews are fundamentally flawed - bullshitters can prosper.

I was chuffed. I had never had the word "manager" in my title before and the salary was £16,000, which was the same as my salary at Husmanns, even though I would lose out because of the lack of overtime. The job also came with a black Vauxhall Astra hatchback with a car phone – the car phone itself was enough to swing the deal for me. I turned up at work the first day wearing a suit and tie – which I had never done for work before – and started to learn things fast.

They wanted me to grow the air con side to £1m in turnover. How on earth was I going to do that? I had never been the public face of a company before, worked with clients, liaised with manufacturers, drawn up contracts and quotes or even dealt with office admin. I had never been a salesman. I didn't have any contacts. What on earth was I going to do? I had no clue. It was a major challenge but that always brings out the best in me. As the saying goes, bite off more than you can chew, and learn very quickly how to chew it.

I had to learn fast but that's what the entrepreneurial spirit is all about. When an inquiry was made, I would go out, measure up, do a heat-load calculation to see how much heating or cooling they required, do a design, source the equipment and supply a quote. If we won the

Holding Kelly, Michelle's and my first child. Not only had I become a father again, but also a manager.

job, I would then arrange subcontractors to install it. The poor 'subbies' never had it easy - my whole working life I had excelled at installations and so I would always go down there and say, "This was how I want it done, these are the standards I expect, and if you have any issues let me know but the work has to be first rate."

Our biggest client was a company called Cargill, one of the largest food processing companies in the world. Nowadays it has about 160,000 employees in seventy countries. In Essex they had a large site at Tilbury where they would import sugar cane and process it. There's a downside to that business - it absolutely stinks. It was horrific. It smelt so bad people would avoid going to meetings there. Some people have described the smell as "old man's socks" - after the old bloke has passed away wearing them and not been discovered for a month might come close to how bad it was.

Their air con needs were massive and constant. You could install a unit which might be expected to last a decade, but it would need replacing in two years. They would get a new portacabin on site and ask us to put a split air con unit in it. Two months later they would be finished with the portacabin and scrap it, then two months later buy a new one and need another air con unit. It was money for old rope. They were also buying so much equipment they rarely quibbled over cost. You could add thirty per cent to a quote with bated breath, but they would always agree, and the cheque would arrive in the post three weeks later. After a few weeks I was getting to grips with the job, I had learned most of what I needed to know about air conditioning and I had also identified a problem which was really holding the company back. Paperwork and filing systems are not the sexy side of entrepreneurship. **Worldwide business leaders rarely write books or lecture on how efficient their office admin systems are but, the truth is, in the real world a bad admin system can cripple a business.** At Air Stream they had a rack on the wall and a 'T' card system. When a call came in you would write it on the card and put it on the wall. When an engineer was assigned to it, you would write his name on the card and put it somewhere else. When the job was done you would write it on the card and file that somewhere else etc. Does that sound simple? Throw in quotes, invoices, new unit orders, new unit installations, emergency repairs, annual servicing, cards going missing, cards not being properly filled, no audit trails. It was absolute chaos. You might have an engineer drive one hundred miles to fix a system and there might be another job three miles away which needed doing, but because of the card system no-one would realise they were close to each other so a second engineer would have been sent to that job as well. I was trying to create £1m in turnover and the whole process was reliant on bits of card.

Then something happened which was to fundamentally change my life. My Dad had bought one of the first home computers - an Amstrad 1640. Home computers were so rare when I went round to his house and saw it I asked, "What's that?" He had to explain it was a computer. He showed it to me, inserted a 5 ¼" inch floppy disc, which had a publishing programme on it, did a bit of basic design and printed it out on a dot matrix printer. In modern terms what it could produce was ridiculously basic but before then everything had been done on typewriters. To put the technology in some sort of context, this thing was the size of a small suitcase and had 640Kb of RAM. The smartphone

The Amstrad 1640, the computer which would change my life.

in your pocket probably has 4,000 times more memory. This computer blew my mind. It was like having a magical device in your living room. He told me about the various programmes you could buy for it, word processors, databases etc. and let me have a play. I was hooked.

I walked into the computer shop and bought one for £900, more than a month's wages after tax, which I could ill afford. I put it on the credit card and told Michelle it had only cost a couple of hundred quid.

Because of the way I am, I spent hundreds of hours on this computer, working out how to write code and how to use it properly. I am the same even today. If I buy a new television, I can't just plug it in, sit down and watch programmes on it. I have to understand everything it is capable of. You know all those menus you stumble into when you press the wrong button on the remote? I actually go looking for them and spend more time understanding them than I do watching the TV.

That enquiring mindset is a real advantage in business. **Relevant knowledge is never wasted.** When you start a business, if you don't have a passion to learn everything about the trade, know what the competition is doing and thinking about future trends, you are in the wrong business.

Anyway, I bought a cheap £10 programme for the computer called Service Manager and realised, with a lot of tweaking, I could create an entire computerised admin system for Air Stream which would have everything we needed. When a job came in the right form would be on screen to be filled in, updated and then forwarded appropriately. There would be proper records, proper audit trails, it would solve all our problems.

For the next seven months I spent every spare minute I had creating a specifically designed system for Air Stream. I then spent months testing it again and again to make sure it ran error free. On the anniversary of my first year's employment I went to the two owners and said, "Can I have an hour with you tomorrow?"

I set it up in the boardroom and spent the morning showing them the system in its entirety. I told them I had spent nine months creating and perfecting it, and it would increase our efficiency by about ninety per cent. "Wow!" they said. "That's transformational, brilliant, amazing." They were genuinely astounded and wanted me to set it up and start training people on Monday. I said, "Fantastic!" but I needed one thing in return. I had spent £900 of my family's mortgage money on the computer and spent hundreds of hours of my free time designing the system. I didn't need the computer at home now, it would be based at the office, so could they buy it off me to reimburse the £900? They said no. I was dumbfounded. I politely pointed out I had built the system for free, the computer would be theirs, I was not making a penny profit but I had a big hole in my finances. They simply refused. I said, "OK, I am not going to fall out over this," and so took it back home. All my life I had responded to enthusiasm, but it felt like they had kicked me in the teeth. It was a sign of my growing maturity that, rather than react emotionally, which is always a dangerous thing to do, I went home and tried to put myself in their shoes. I tried to understand why they were reluctant to move forward.

Now, not every idea is a good one. Even apparently good ideas can have unforeseen consequences. To take things to the extreme, in the

1950s China's leaders were angry at the amount of grain which was being eaten in the fields by sparrows. They worked out for every million sparrows killed, they would save enough food for sixty thousand people. So, as only China can, the whole of society was mobilised on a massive, orchestrated sparrow killing spree. They killed hundreds of millions of them, the Chinese sparrow nearly went extinct. What they didn't realise was sparrows played a vital role in keeping locust numbers down. The locust population grew massively, grain production was devastated, and the country fell into a famine which killed millions of people from malnourishment.

As far as bad ideas go, that was right up there among the world's worst. But back in the business world, **every time someone says "no" to a good idea which has clear evidence and research proving it is beneficial and has no major downsides, ask yourself, *Why?*** The problem often won't be with the idea, but with them. The only conclusion I could come to was the owners at that time were reluctant to have a system operating in the company they didn't understand. Modernisation meant they would be losing control. They were happy to maintain the status quo, happy with a 'lifestyle business'. They were fine with their £6m turnover, they both got a new car every two years, took out a bit of dividend, the secretaries would bring them paperwork to sign in big leather binders. They were "gentleman businessmen", happy with the lifestyle the company gave them, and with no real interest in modernising and substantially growing it. It gave them the lifestyle they wanted and if it meant their systems were a little bit inefficient and wasteful so be it, at least they had got them to where they were. I had increased the air conditioning turnover from £200k to £1m in the first year but they seemed to think the computer was some sort of negotiation. They obviously expected me to take it into work anyway or accept a much lower figure. A few days later they even asked where it was. I told them it was at home and that was where it was staying. They weren't going to eat humble pie at that stage and ask me to reconsider.

But that Friday night at home I realised that although they hadn't given me £900 for the computer, they had given me something infinitely more valuable. They had given me the experience I needed to run my own business, and now they had given me the impetus to do so. I had gone there as a hairy-arsed engineer but now I was experienced at interacting with clients, I had learned how to write quotes, do designs, have a relationship with suppliers and seen how easy it was to get the equipment. I had managed teams of subcontractors, learnt the importance of back office staff and the business systems they work with. They showed me I had the capacity to run a business.

That very night I started planning to do just that. I mulled over the dangers, the opportunities and the challenges. In today's world, we call this a SWOT analysis (strengths, weaknesses, opportunities and threats). The thought of setting up a business didn't scare me, it invigorated me. I spoke to Michelle and I suspect most wives with babies would understandably worry about what if it didn't work, where was the money going to come from, and they would focus on the risks rather than the opportunities. But not Michelle. She trusted my judgement and said, "It's high risk, but I believe you can do it."

I decided I would spend the next six months planning and preparing. I wrote a business plan, put the software systems in place on the computer, designed all the stationary, a logo, and got a £20,000 loan from the bank via a government loan scheme. I also realised I knew nothing about accounting. Forecasts, cash flows and balance sheets? I didn't have a clue. Then along came another good Samaritan. The local accountant in St Osyth was a guy called Mike Fuller and I went and chatted to him. He was a workaholic, in the office until 10.30pm most days, including weekends. I said I want you to be my accountant, but I need to understand how it all works. I said, "I have a computer. I have Sage accountancy software, but I don't understand what any of it means." Would he help? Help? He turned up at the house three nights a week for about three months, from 7pm to 1am. He taught me everything I needed to know about profit and loss, cash flow, balance sheets, setting up sage, the works. He never charged me a penny, he just loved his job and loved teaching me. He was a really lovely guy.

He knew he was going to be my accountant and this way the stuff I presented to him was going to be perfect, but he did it because he enjoyed the mentoring role. He was incredibly professional and hugely competent as a small business accountant for people who turned over up to £500,000 a year. Over that size, I had some issues with him, but we will come to that later. Most people go to university for this knowledge, but I learnt it from a bloke down the road. **Never pass up an opportunity to develop yourself. As well as learning a new skill, it leads to a feeling of self-achievement and the desire to constantly improve.** All through my life from my Dad, to Freddie, to Russ Nicholson, people had seen something in me and gone the extra mile to help me for no personal or financial gain. Mike was another one. They passed on their knowledge because they felt it was the responsible and right thing to do and I benefitted enormously from that.

It also shaped the way I acted for the rest of my life. If I see potential in someone, I don't care what time and effort it will cost me, I will invest in them if they are prepared to learn. However, it was another person who was to subsequently give my fledgling business more help than I could ever have hoped for. But in 2020, the entire business world was in need of drastic help.

COVID Late March 2020:

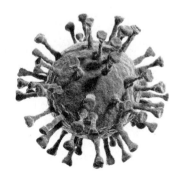

Communication

After the initial shockwave of the COVID economic earthquake had passed, along with the danger of the business immediately folding in front of our eyes, it was time to deal with the subsequent tremors. We continued to tell our customers who owed us millions, "We are here to support you, we are here to talk to you, we are here to work out all the things we can do to get through this together. Please don't consider us hostile. Whatever the truth is about your business, we would much rather hear it and work with you rather than be fearful you are hiding bad news from us."

The key to solving problems is firstly properly identifying them, and then methodically working out how to solve them. Because we choose our clients carefully and base our relationships on honesty and transparency, most of them embraced this philosophy. We were stronger together than alone. But we still had to act fast to protect our company's interests. We said to our clients, "We understand your financial position. We understand you need to retain cash in your business because that is the heartbeat of your company. However, to keep our own heart beating, and those of the suppliers we owe money to, we need you to drip-feed us the money we are owed."

We adopted a policy of accepting "little and often" payments. This meant while we were getting nothing like the sums we were owed, we were getting cash in every single week. One of our clients owed us £4m so we said how about you pay us £500,000 a week? They said they couldn't afford that, but they could manage £200,000 a week which we accepted. Ninety-five per cent of the money we received immediately went to our supply chain which meant they could survive too.

Of course, there were still periods of fear. The media was frequently running stories about the imminent collapse of many national restaurant chains including one of our customers, Pizza Express, which was meant to be in a £1 billion financial hole. They owed us a lot of money and that could have given us sleepless nights. However, because we had made it so easy and safe for them to talk to us, they told us the true situation. Pizza Express had kept £1 billion of debt on their balance sheet for five years because that is how their Chinese owners operate. It was their usual business practice. The owners immediately pumped £170m into Pizza Express so it had more liquidity and they started paying us £750,000 in regular chunks.

A couple of our clients in the DIY sector also continued to trade, which meant we were receiving money from them as well. Before long we had £1m a month coming in. From March 30 until June 30 we paid £7m to our supply chain. Few other companies managed to pay off their debts in such a fashion. To our customers and our suppliers, we were the good guys. But what would the government do next, and how could we care for our staff?

Back in 1990, I had no staff, but I was about to start my own business.

Chapter 6

Dirk, development and near disaster

Most new businesses fail within a year of starting. Thousands of broken dreams and shattered aspirations. That's a harsh reality. How was I going to ensure I didn't become another failure statistic? The brutal truth is it costs a lot of money to get a business going and it is much harder to generate cash than it is to spend it. I wanted to '**de-risk the risk', which is a policy vital to successful business. Every action has risks, but if you can find a way to remove them then you are on the road to success.** In my case, I realised Cargill was the key. I had a great relationship with the plant manager in Tilbury, a strange, scruffy fella called Dirk Hondsmirk. But appearances can be deceptive. He might not have been much to look at, but he had massive responsibility for hundreds of staff and, most importantly, he authorised the air conditioning cheques. He had an engineering background like mine and so when I went to see him I wouldn't try and seduce him with salesman patter, but would talk through the issues from an engineering perspective and present him with engineering solutions. We got along really well and one day, as we sat down for a cuppa, I told him about my ambitions and said, "If I start my own business, will you support me?"

It was a massive moment. With the Cargill contract I knew I could always pay the bills and put food on the table. I tried to appear nonchalant but my heart was thumping in my chest. Dirk said "yes". He knew I could do the work, he trusted me, so he would help me. What a relief. I could have kissed him, but believe me, that was never going to happen. When an opportunity presents itself, it is sometimes worth jumping in with both feet. I explained as a new business I would have no credit history, so no line of credit with manufacturers. They would expect payment upfront, which would be impossible for me. As well as giving me the contract, I asked for the first few jobs might it be possible for him to pay me in advance so I could actually buy the equipment? He agreed again. Talk about a result. If Dirk kept his word, he hadn't just given me a leg up, he had built me a ladder. I could immediately start making decent money with little risk. I suppose from his perspective it wasn't a fortune - he wrote hundreds of cheques every week - and he knew Cargill would get a first-class service. But for me, it was a game-changer.

As the weeks passed and I prepared to leave Air Stream, Dirk even became engaged about the business, asking when I was starting, what equipment I was buying etc. I spent a long time worrying if he would fulfil all his promises. He could have turned around at any time and said, "Sorry, there's an issue come up," and I would have been powerless. My business forecast for the first year was to achieve a turnover of £110,000. In the first twelve months alone, Cargill spent £700,000. Dirk wasn't just as good as his word, he was better than it. I also realised that running a new business was going to be lonely as well as difficult. An extra pair of hands could really help. I had previously convinced Air Stream to take on an engineer as we were too reliant on subcontractors. I had recruited an old friend of mine from Carters called Ian Smith. We were close friends, spent a lot of time together and had similar backgrounds. I knew he was looking to move ahead in life, he had a young family, and so I asked him if he wanted to be my business partner, 50/50, right down the middle. He agreed, but we soon realised that at the very start we wouldn't be able to afford two salaries, so he would stay on at Air Stream until we got some money in.

On Monday, June 4, 1990, six months after deciding to leave Air Stream, I left the company. It eventually went out of business four years later. Essex Air Conditioning was ready for business the same day. I had already deposited £20,000 into the business account from a bank loan. We bought a silver Ford Granada for me and a Renault van for Ian, both second hand. That was £10,000 gone. The company offices were in my kitchen where I had the computers set up. We were ready to take on the world. Dirk stepped up to the plate, gave us our first job and paid for the whole thing up front. With that money in the bank, Ian could leave his old job too. As for Air Stream, they should have been furious and chased me for taking their biggest client, but it took them about six months to realise Cargill had stopped calling them. They had lost their biggest air con client and not even noticed. Some people might say taking Cargill with me was ethically and morally wrong and, of course, I considered that. However, I believed Air Stream had never really treated Cargill with the respect they deserved. There had been one project where Cargill had challenged Air Stream on our price. I took it to the owners and their attitude was, "Sod them!". I pointed out they generated five times more money for us than anyone else, they were effectively paying for the owners' new cars every two years, and suggested they might want to show a bit of willing and reduce the bill. They showed a lack of class and respect, just as they had done with me about the computer. Sure, I took Cargill, but it wasn't making me lose sleep every night.

It was challenging stuff. I was the salesman, the accountant, I did the VAT, the payroll for the Inland Revenue, and project-managed jobs, while Ian would do the actual engineering. Even in those earliest days it dawned on me I had been naïve in sharing the business 50/50. I had set up and was running the business, while Ian was just an engineer. The longer this went on I knew it was never going to end well but for now I put the problem aside, there was too much to do. In the first six months we not only installed new kit for Cargill, we also took on their maintenance contract. The work was coming in so fast we took on six salaried engineers and a couple of apprentices. Every penny that came in was immediately going out on new staff, vans, salaries and kit. It was a whirlwind, exhilarating, everything I had hoped for. But I was about to learn some business lessons the hard way.

While we were winning work with Cargill, I was able to stop worrying about where the next client was coming from. So, I began to structure some marketing and direct mailing with a view to getting more "new end user" business, going to direct to individual clients where the profit margin was highest. This went well, and I started to pick up some great leads, mainly because we made our quotations easy to read and understand, and yet in the index, the quotes also had every piece of technical information the clients could require. No-one

Our new offices and fleet of vehicles.

else was providing such information back then. The quotations simply inspired confidence. Amazon do a similar thing now. Even if you are just buying a tin of paint, you get the basic details and then a long list of components, questions and answers, reviews etc., everything you could possibly need to know.

Then suddenly, over night, when the recession started to bite, the end-user market died and so I began focussing instead on opportunities in the construction industry. I had subscribed to a publication called Tenderalert, which publicises projects being offered by councils and private companies. Large jobs would often be managed by building contractors who would then use companies like ours to do individual elements of it. One such company was ENI Coward and we started doing some work with them.

Then the mother lode landed. Peabody Trust was a large, respected social housing company in London. They were moving into new offices on Westminster Bridge Road and gave the entire mechanical and electrical installation to ENI Coward to manage. The air con contract alone was a £150,000 job, twice as big as our previous biggest single job. We won it. Remember, our annual turnover forecast for the first year had been £110,000. This job showed we were moving into the big league sooner than we had dreamed of. We needed engineers to do the work, and on a project this size I wanted someone I could trust. Who better than my old mentor, Freddie Bird? I had heard that he had set up on his own but was struggling and only doing bits and pieces here and there. I called him, said I have a major job, and would he come and chat to me about it? He came to the house and couldn't believe the set-up. By now the office had taken over half the kitchen and there were computers and printers everywhere. It looked like space control at NASA. We drove down to the site in London, walked round the job and Freddie was like, "Jesus Christ, this is a massive project!" He couldn't believe this was the scale of jobs we were taking on. He wasn't hugely experienced in air con work but I said the principles were exactly the same as refrigeration and I would plan it and talk him through it like he had done so often in the past for me.

Driving home together, the car phone rang and it was another building contractor on the line. They had a £350,000 contract available and were asking me to pop in and chat to them about it. We were in the area, so we paid them a visit. I introduced Freddie as one of my engineers and we went through the project. I said the contract was worth £300,000, not £350,000, we talked about what I could do for them in design terms, and they said if the job came through the work was mine. Freddie couldn't believe it. He was open-mouthed in shock, kept saying, "This is a different world." He had been my mentor when I was a spotty apprentice. Not long ago, my main job in life had been handing this bloke his tools, and now I was answering calls on my car phone and doing £300,000 deals while I was driving home.

When we got back, we talked about the Westminster Bridge Road job, the timings, labour costs etc., and I said I reckoned it was about 1,200 hours' work, at £25 an hour, so that was £30,000. For two people, that was roughly three months' work without rushing things, and they would each make £15,000 or so - very good money at the time. Alarm bells should have started ringing when Freddie was strangely hesitant. He couldn't get his head round the size of the project. Freddie had been used to running huge Sainsbury's sites managing nearly 6,000 hours of labour. So why would he be nervous about such a small project? Was it because he would be personally accountable? Was it because he was now personally more at risk? Because it was Freddie, I said, "OK, I will pay you 1500 hours at £28 an hour." That figure was eating into my margins, but I knew how good Freddie was and having him there would be a weight off my shoulders.

He was made up. He couldn't believe I would pay him that much. He was getting three months of work at a good rate and wouldn't be scrabbling for jobs from one day to the next. Before he left, with a beaming smile on his face, I looked him in the eye and said, "Freddie, you know the rules… you work to the standard we always worked to. I haven't seen you for three or four years, but you know I expect the best. The pipework has to be shit-hot, all the lagging glued, the whole system pressure-tested. This job has my name on it, everything has to meet my expectations, and you know how high my standards are." "No problem," he replied.

It was a couple of weeks before I could actually get down there to see how he was progressing. I walked in and my heart sank. *What the fuck…* Look upwards in almost any commercial building without a false ceiling and you will see steel cable trays. These hang from the ceiling to support all the pipework and cabling, hiding it from view and keeping everything nice and tidy. The trays have a lip at the edge to keep all the wires and whatnot contained. A ten-year-old could work out what cable trays were for and how to install them. Freddie must have worked with hundreds of thousands of feet of these in his career.

On my job, he decided to put the pipes underneath and had attached them to the bottom of the tray with cable ties. It was a mess. I was gobsmacked. It was so stupid it defied belief. I was always one for taking risks and doing things differently but only when it was based on sound design, effective working practices and safety principles. I lost it: "I can't believe you have done this, it's a fucking stupid thing to do, we use cable trays for a reason. It looks a mess, if there's a fire the cable ties will melt and hundreds of feet of pipework will fall to the floor, containing hundreds of kilos of refrigerant gas at high pressure! It's never going to pass a safety inspection, it is never going to pass the snags check. It's a mess, it looks terrible. You will have to re-do it!"

Freddie explained he had done it this way because it was much easier to braze from underneath the tray, rather than having to work over the cable tray. I said it was the stupidest thing I had ever seen, and it needed to be re-done. Freddie said it would take two weeks and he wanted to be paid extra for it. I said, "What do you mean you want me to pay you extra for it? You didn't ask me permission to do it this way, you have done something stupid and it needs to be reversed. The client is not going to pay me extra because you have messed up, I am paying you more than the going rate already and I can't pay you more to repair the damage you have already done."

He just said it wasn't his problem, we fell out, and he walked off the job. He never got a penny and I had to pay new blokes to come in and start the whole thing again. I was devastated, truly gutted. It upset me for a long time. I had admired Freddie for years, spent countless hours laughing and joking and talking about life with him. I genuinely liked and admired the bloke. Half the things I knew about engineering he had taught me, and it had come to this. I felt awful, sick to the stomach. He could have worked for me on projects in London for years. I would have seen he did all right. I think it was fear and a lack of confidence that made him cut corners. I suspect he was cowed by the size of the job. Rather than breaking it down and saying, "OK, it's a kilometre of pipework and two of us have three months to do it, so we need to lay eleven metres a day, but let's call it fifteen metres so we have a bit of wriggle room", instead he was looking at a kilometre of pipe stacked up in the corner and panicking.

Remember, on my first individual job, when I was lost in a sea of pipework and weird machines, my Dad sat me down and talked me through the schematic so I could see beyond the mass of pipes? I think Freddie was in that mess, he had been overwhelmed by the big picture. I also suspect he knew I had always done things differently - like that Pinner Sainsbury's job - and he thought he would try and be different too. It was also a different environment for him. At Carters if he made a mistake, he might get fired, but there was a whole organisation behind him to take the blame and fix it. Here, he knew the job was just down to him and he rushed it. I wasn't only shocked at his work, but also at his reaction. **However well you might think you know people, in business or in life, you never truly do until you see them vulnerable. Whole new sides of their personalities can emerge and when they do it is important you maintain a level head. Never let the emotions caused by their vulnerability affect your decisions and make you vulnerable too.** I was about to be vulnerable myself. Through my career I had worked for other people, done a good job, gone home and got paid at the end of the week. I knew as much about theoretical nuclear physics as I did the legal subtleties of contracts or indemnities. We obviously had contracts at Air Stream, on most of our jobs a standard JCT80 contract was sufficient. These have been about since the 1970s in the building industry and in simplified terms they set out who is doing what, who is responsible for what and when it should be done.

When you move into much bigger projects, things get much more complicated. For the Westminster Bridge Road job, Peabody's contract with ENI Coward said Coward would pay massive penalties if the job overran the agreed schedule. ENI Coward passed that obligation onto its individual contractors. If we didn't finish our bit on time, I could have to pay tens of thousands in damages per week of overrun. So, you would sign the contract on the proviso you weren't prevented from finishing on time, weren't held up by other teams, could get access to the building etc. These were the sort of risks I had never worked with before. On this job there was also a collateral warranty contract. This meant we had to guarantee the equipment, pipework, and layout were up to standard, worked fine, and could never be called into question for the life of the equipment. For all these contracts you took out your own insurance to make sure if the proverbial roof fell in, you were financially covered. I had no real problem in principle with the collateral warranty contract, I knew the work was simple enough, but I thought I had better get some advice before I signed. I spoke to my insurance company who said, "Don't worry, these things never come into play, just sign it."

On major jobs like these you work on monthly valuations. You are buying tens of thousands of pounds' worth of equipment and forking out wages every week so you can't wait until the end of the job to get paid. ENI Coward would visit every month, see the progress and the equipment you had bought and pay you accordingly. At the end of the contract, they would keep five per cent of the fee for a year to make sure your work was up to scratch - this is called "retention". Michelle was nine months pregnant and about to go into labour with Hayley. This coincided with me putting in the valuation for the work we had done. I made a quick check that there were no problems, but I was told ENI Coward wouldn't pay me a penny until I had signed, and backdated, the collateral warranty. In truth, I thought I had, but I had only signed the JCT80.

They sent over another copy and when I was reading it a lightbulb went on. Under the terms of the contract, I would be responsible for the whole system and exposed to unlimited costs if something went wrong. I was fine with most of that, but the contract also included the Daikin air conditioning equipment I was installing. I had no problem being responsible for fitting them correctly, but how could I be responsible for them working properly when they had been designed and built in Japan? If these buggers started breaking down or catching fire, I would be legally responsible for them.

To make matters even more ludicrous, ENI Coward had insisted I use Daikin equipment in the first place. I phoned my insurance broker again who suddenly seemed a lot less confident about "these things not mattering" and suggested I took more specialised advice. *Great!* That was them sacked.

Someone recommended MKM insurance in Chelmsford. I called, told them the story and they had an expert at my office in Clacton in an hour. The first thing he realised was that they were not just asking for the standard "Collateral Warranty", they were also asking for "Professional Indemnity" cover as well, which also covers substandard work. This was a massive problem because he said no-one is going to backdate your professional indemnity insurance policy when you started the job already. For all they know there could be a massive problem with the work you have already done so why would they insure you for it? He also said you can't allow the Professional Indemnity to include the design of the Japanese air conditioning units, you can't be responsible for them. You are using them because they told you to, but if they start exploding like IEDs you are liable for them.

I was twenty-six years old and I was scared. I had spent £80,000 on this Daikin equipment, done a load of work, owed money to other suppliers and had staff to pay. And I could also tell how ENI Coward would react. They weren't going to pay me, they had me over a barrel, they had all the power, they knew I would be desperate for the money and would insist on the PI cover or keep the cash and kick me off the job.

I even spoke to Daikin and they agreed I should not legally be responsible for their machines and said they would contact ENI Coward. ENI Coward didn't care. I had to provide the cover. Thankfully, my agent at MKM used his personal contacts to find me an insurance company who would backdate the cover, and ENI Coward said fine, the cash would eventually come through.

A few days later I was in Clacton Hospital's labour ward as Michelle was having ten-minute contractions and in the process of giving birth to our daughter Hayley. Incidentally, if you ever want to know just how much strength is in a woman's hand, hold one while they are giving birth. Michelle was squeezing so hard I would need a hospital bed next. Suddenly a nurse came in with one of those "wheel-about" phones and said, "There is an urgent call for you, Mr Dewing." *Christ, I thought, if someone is ringing me in the labour ward this isn't going to be good news.*

One of my project managers told me he had heard ENI Coward was about to go into administration. They still owed me more than £80,000. If they went bust it would finish me. The colour drained from my face. This could mean my business was gone, my house gone, my dreams over. All the work I had done, all the faith Michelle had in me, all the people I had employed, it could be about to turn to dust. My daughter was being born, one of the most magical experiences any father can have, and ENI Coward had totally ruined it. They turned it into the worst professional day of my life. I didn't know what to cry about. Should I sob tears of joy holding my new baby and my wife, or tears of frustration as my whole company was about to go under? I was elated, but also crushed by fear at the same time. How would I support my family? It was the most stressful moment of my entire life.

The next day, as soon as Michelle's Mum came to the ward, I immediately made an appointment with Thomson, Smith and Puxon lawyers in Colchester. They said while ENI Coward hadn't gone into administration yet and no company wants that, there were three things I could do. Option one was a county court summons for the money they owed me, but it might take months to get to court. Option two was a High Court writ. It would cost me £500 to have one drawn up, but they would spend £500 defending it, and that would also take ages to get anywhere. The third was the nuclear option. I could send them a "Statutory Demand" to wind them up, which effectively said I feared they could not pay their debts. This demand would be officially published, telling the world about their woes and if they didn't pay me in twenty-one days their assets would be frozen and they would be forced into liquidation. It would cost them a fortune in legal fees to fight it. Of course, if they didn't pay, I would have shut the company down and lost the money anyway.

I was twenty-six years old and was suddenly waving a lethal legal weapon at a long-established and major company. A couple of years before I hadn't known dry cleaning machines had fridges in them. I asked the lawyer, "What should I do?" He immediately went into legal mode…. "I advise you on options, not on decisions. I am not risking what you are risking, I can't tell you the right way to proceed." I said, "Throw me a bone here, I understand you are playing with a straight bat, doing the lawyer's thing, but you know where I am at. There will be no recourse on you for any advice given, just tip me the wink, what would you do?"

With a smile he said, "Statutory demand, do it right now." It was delivered to ENI Coward the next day. I was terrified about what would happen. Two days passed with silence. My business was teetering on the brink, I had fired the legal nuclear missile and nothing had happened. Then I got a phone call, requesting my presence in their offices at 1pm tomorrow in Ipswich. I could hear the distaste and supposed superiority in this bloke's voice. It got my back up. I said I was busy tomorrow. That shocked him. "It's important," he stuttered. I said it was important for him, not for me, I was busy, but I was free on Thursday. In truth, my entire business rested on that meeting, but it was time for them to realise they no longer called the shots.

The butterflies in my stomach were doing cartwheels when I went to their offices for the meeting. There were mahogany floors and wall panels everywhere. The bloke's office had more leather than a farm full of cows. He even had a quill on his desk. It pissed me right off. He didn't help matters by declaring, "I want to record the fact you have acted disgracefully by sending a statutory demand and I want you to retract it." He obviously thought as he was a top dog at a major company, and I was a bloke who installed air con, he was in control. Big mistake. I said, "Let's get something clear, you promised to pay me twenty-one days after valuation. It is now ninety days.

"A few days ago, I was holding my wife's hand in the labour ward as she had our child and I get a phone call warning me you might be going out of business. That would cost me my company and my house. You ruined a day I would have cherished for the rest of my life, so don't talk to me about disgraceful behaviour.

"You have held me over a barrel about a contract where you want me to be responsible for equipment made in Japan, which you insisted I use in the first place. Even when the company itself said they would honour that part of the cover, that wasn't good enough for you. I don't trust you or this business as far as I could throw you, I am retracting nothing."

That was me off their Christmas card list. There was a period of shocked silence and he reached into his leather binder and handed me a cheque for £86,422. I literally ran to the nearest bank. In those days, cheques took three days to clear but you could pay a fee which checked they had the funds in the account and, if they did, would almost guarantee you first payment from it. I got paid. Three weeks later ENI Coward went bust. Other people lost their businesses as a result.

I said to Michelle, "We were lucky," and she said, "No we weren't, you created our luck." It was a decision which shaped my life. **In life and business, taking the initiative and making the right decision based on all the evidence before you is not luck, it is judgement. You also need to be self-aware enough never to make such decisions when you are emotionally vulnerable or acting out of panic. Take time, consider the options, think rationally and then act.** Dozens of companies they employed will have heard the same rumours we had but thought, *It will be ok, the money will come through.* Some might even have been proactive and spoken to ENI Coward. I am guessing they would have been told, "Things are fine, don't worry," rather than, "We are going down fast, mate, get the cash quick." I acted because I listened to my instincts and weighed the pros and cons of taking action, admittedly helped by a lawyer with a twinkle in his eye. And the main thing I learned from the whole episode? It wasn't about the paperwork and the contracts - lawyers will always make fortunes arguing over those - it was about understanding quickly who had ethics and who you could trust. Companies are like people. Some you are happy to invite round your home, some you put locks on the doors to keep out. If a total stranger came up to you in the street and said, "Lend me £50 mate and give me your address so I can send it back to you", you would say no. So why would you do massive financial deals with people you barely know either? Why would you buy hundreds of thousands of pounds worth of kit for a job because they promised they would pay you?

Choose who you work with carefully. Do due diligence on them, not just through records at Companies House, but also by talking to people who have worked with them before. You cannot find the truth about people's principles, behaviour and trustworthiness on a balance sheet, but often you can by speaking to people they have worked with in the past.

So, as ENI Coward crumbled into dust, we were doing well. Ian and I were both on decent salaries, there was some cash in the bank, we moved into new offices in Clacton. We were one of Daikin's biggest selling contractors, so they took us on a trip to a conference in Miami.

Being awarded a Contractor of the Year award for sales.

We were the entrepreneurs of the year in our eyes, kings of the air con world. The second year? It went even better. We won another major contract for the construction of Aspinalls Casino off Park Lane. John Aspinall was a legendary figure who held illegal casino nights for the upper classes in the 1950s, earnt a fortune, and then set up the famous Clermont Club in London where the original members included five dukes, five marquesses, twenty earls and two cabinet ministers. He also owned a zoo and allegedly helped Lord Lucan to escape justice after Lucan was accused of murdering his nanny. It's fair to say we didn't expect to see him helping out with the pipework.

It was a pig of a job. It was a listed building with posh wooden floorboards and no false ceilings. Running pipework was going to be a nightmare. Fate intervened again. When we were fitting out our new offices, I was introduced to two builders, Shaun and Phil. They weren't much to look at. Shaun was a skinhead who wouldn't hesitate to confront people in pubs if they looked at him in a funny way. However, as builders, these blokes were brilliant, different class. Going for a pint with them was dangerous but as workmen they were incredibly switched-on and so humble with it. They called everyone Mr This and Mr That. There wasn't a problem they couldn't solve and their standards were higher than mine – almost! I realised they were perfect for Aspinalls. They had the building skills we would need but they couldn't braze pipes. When I raised this problem, they said, "We will be able to braze by Monday."

They had the mentality that nothing was a problem. They did the job and it was perfect. The lads who worked with them soon adopted their mentality. Even the lead agent on site was saying, "Your blokes are brilliant, first class", and they ended up advising other contractors on the best way to do things. They loved working for us rather than fitting sash windows and other minor jobs, and they were workaholics like me. They were getting jobs done at twice the speed of everyone else. They worked for us for a number of years before eventually setting up their own AC company which was brilliant for them. That was another £180,000 job under our belt. We had used Daikin air con machines again and they were so pleased they took us on a trip to France on Concorde around the Bay of Biscay. The following year they took us to Japan for seven days and Hong Kong for four. Corporate hospitality? It's brilliant when you are not the company paying for it.

It's easy to imagine Ian and I were rolling in cash. The money was coming in but so were the overheads. We had eight vans, six or seven people in the office, engineers, builders, apprentices. Jobs like Aspinalls were great, and hugely important, but on building jobs the margins were a fraction of what they were compared to holding your nose and doing jobs at Cargills. Eventually we had to drop them as a client. Dirk had left and we struggled to get people who would go there, the smell was so bad. Peter Harris, one of my old contacts at ENI Coward, got in touch. He had been almost as angry at their behaviour towards me as I had. He said, "I have a proposal, I want to start a mechanical services business with you." Our air con business was based on DX (Dry Expansion), and used refrigerant gases. Another mainstay air con system uses water to either cool or heat. Buildings are either one or the other, fitting them takes entirely different skill sets, and the profit margins in water systems - known as mechanical systems - are lower.

He said an insurance firm was doing a massive refit of their offices, wanted to use a Versatemp water-based air con system and he thought, with the right backing, he could win the contract. He wanted to be a director of a new division, EAC Mechanical, with him owning twenty per cent of the company and Ian and me forty per cent each. We went over the risks and benefits, ringfenced the new business to ensure it would not jeopardize our success at EAC, and said, "Why not?"

Four weeks later, we won the £1.1m contract. You couldn't make it up. Who wins £1m contracts? It was off the scale. In profit terms it represented maybe £180,000, if we were careful. Peter was also sharp. At the time, interest rates were at fifteen per cent and he convinced the company to pay us £700,000 in advance for all the Versatemp equipment prior to the Christmas period. The money came through in the first week of December. We didn't need to pay Versatemp for sixty days so we pocketed the interest. That was a good Christmas.

It had been a cracking three years but one of my earliest decisions was still haunting me. Ian revealed he was getting pressure off his missus because of his hours. She was sick of him coming in at 8pm in his overalls every night, while every time she saw me, I was swanning about wearing a suit, driving a flash silver Granada and talking on my car phone. I was supposedly living the dream. I said, "You need to tell her I don't get the luxury of getting home every night at 8pm to get moaned at by my missus, because I am in the office until midnight every night. I haven't had the luxury of watching midweek telly with my tea on my lap for months."

Ian had lost sight of the bigger picture. Since we started the firm, for most of the time all he had to worry about was the one engineering job he was working on. I was worrying about everything else from the VAT to the salaries, the vehicle contract hire cost, the insurance, the collateral warranties, payroll, the whole shebang. Of course, he was consulted on all the major decisions, but he would then go back engineering while

I kept the whole ship afloat. Because starting a company was a big job and I didn't want to be lonely, I had been incredibly naive when I had offered him 50/50. At that age, as two mates, 50/50 seemed the obvious thing to do, but it was a decision made with little proper thought. The division of work and responsibilities was never properly discussed, or how the partnership might change as the business did. Before too long, it was obvious to my mind I was doing far more than fifty per cent of the work.

But again, I showed emotional maturity. I said, "Rather than have a row, assign your job to someone else, wear a suit on Monday and come into the office and work there from now on. God knows, I need a hand."

After three months behind a desk, he admitted he hated the work, the constant pressure, people wanting endless decisions day after day, having to worry about every aspect of the business, getting new deals. He was consulting me over every decision and adding little value whatsoever. Eventually, he just wanted to go back to working as an engineer. I could understand that. God knows, sometimes I wanted to do that myself.

I said, "OK, you can do that, but you must appreciate you can't be a fifty per cent partner because now you know you are not doing anywhere near fifty per cent of the work." I offered him 80/20. I suspect deep down he wanted to take it but his pride, and probably his missus, wouldn't allow him to.

Even though he realised he was doing a salaried job as an engineer and I was willing to keep his name in the business, he couldn't accept anything less than fifty per cent. **Temper can get you into bad situations. Misplaced ego and pride will keep you there.** Ego can be your enemy and can hold you back if you allow it. Research has shown in more than two thirds of business failures, the presence of someone with a major personal ego contributes to its poor performance or demise. Learn to recognise when ego is the inner voice speaking inside your head. It is always best to ignore it. In the end I bought him out. He walked away with a few thousand pounds. The partnership was over.

Years later, in 2020, it looked like the whole commercial landscape as we knew it might be over.

COVID late March 2020:

Breathing space

I have no doubt millions of words will eventually be written about how the UK government dealt with the COVID crisis. People far more intelligent than me will pass judgement on what the authorities did, and what they should have done. I can only comment from my own business perspective. First came a raft of measures to help keep businesses afloat. Companies were protected against winding-up petitions by creditors – an action we had already decided not to take – and firms which might otherwise have been declared insolvent and shut down were given a breathing space to get their affairs in order. Many sinking companies now had a life raft to cling to.

The Coronavirus Business Interruption Loan Scheme was introduced. The government guaranteed interest-free loans for twelve months to smaller companies with a turnover of up to £40m. While this was great public relations, in reality it was worthless to a lot of smaller firms because the application and approval process was so arduous and time-consuming. The vast majority of applications were subsequently rejected anyway. That raft you were clinging to? Now it's sinking.

A similar loan scheme was then introduced for larger companies like ours with a turnover of more than £40m a year. Under this, if the banks were willing to give you a loan, the government would guarantee it. The perception was the government was once more offering billions to businesses to keep them afloat. Hurrah! This was another fallacy. The offers were based on the banks' normal lending processes, which meant if they wouldn't lend you money before COVID, they certainly were not going to lend you money now. In truth, this made perfect sense. The banks and government were not stupid enough to lend millions to companies which might not have survived before the crisis anyway.

However, where the government did step up beyond my expectations was with the Furlough Scheme. They said where companies would have to suspend operations, the government would pay eighty per cent of people's salaries up to a certain amount. I did not get everything right during the crisis by any means, but I knew by mid-March such a scheme was inevitable. I was on a call to our exec team when I spelt out the reasons why. Unless the government did something very quickly, thousands of companies, including ours, would have no choice but to make mass redundancies. We would have had ten million people unemployed within weeks and the welfare state simply couldn't cope with that sort of problem. I told the board the government is going to come up with some way of paying companies to keep staff on, not least because every company has every employee's details and the payroll structure to ensure they can get money to them just as before.

To be fair, it was an obvious solution to the problem, but in mid-March the very thought of a government paying millions of people to stay at home and do nothing was mindboggling. But they did just that on March 26, with an initial three-month time limit. The government soon introduced other financial schemes to help companies, from new loan arrangements to business rates relief and a host of others. We had survived the initial crisis. Money was starting to come in and thanks to the furlough scheme, our staff were being paid. But our company had always been more than just about money. It had always been about creating an environment where people were trusted and could grow. We were a family, not just a firm. Caring for our staff was more than a cliché, it was at the very heart of our core values. How could we manage to do that? Principles were also at the front of my mind in 1994.

Chapter 7

Partnerships and principles

On another freebie trip to Japan compliments of Daikin, I drank lots of sake, ate lots of sushi and came back with a kimono and a new business partner. I spent the ten-day trip with a bloke called Chris Duncan. He had a small air con company called CSL, based in Romford, and we got along famously. He was funny, had a predominantly engineering mind like mine, and he had also gone through the experience of setting up and growing his own company. We shared our life histories, spoke about how challenging it was running businesses on our own, the loneliness, the pressure, the never-ending responsibility, the workload. We realised as well as being friends, our firms were compatible.

On the flight back I popped the question – "what did he think about joining forces?" He thought it was a brilliant idea. We spent the next couple of months discussing it, looking at the benefits of joining up and, to avoid the problems I had with Ian, putting in detailed plans for the division of responsibilities. Having done the due diligence, in the end I just went with my gut. We formed a 50/50 partnership, no money changed hands, just shares. He had a large office in Romford where he had workshop and storage space, his wife was also in the business and she was a talented saleswoman who could sell snow to Eskimos. She was winning work like you couldn't believe. The two businesses were roughly the same in terms of turnover and profit, he had types of work I hadn't broken into, like hospital contracts, and he also had more individual clients. Joining together meant further growth was easier, we had a bigger geographical spread, more engineers, more capacity and it should have halved our personal workloads.

It also solved a massive long-term problem for me - finding quality people. When the business was growing, I had shied away from employing people on salaries of £50,000 like mine, and instead employed people who were happy to earn £25,000. Then the realisation hit me, if I wanted the business to grow, and to attract people who matched my drive, enthusiasm and expertise, I wasn't going to find them paying roughly half of what I was earning. It's hard to find Porsches when you are paying Ford Fiesta prices. Eventually I bit the bullet and employed two people on top rates. They were earning roughly the same as I was, and I expected them to justify it. I saw this as the next step forward, a major injection of talent into the business at the cost of a lot of cash. Unfortunately, they both proved useless. With that sort of money, you expect to be buying vision, entrepreneurship, forward thinking. I might as well have stood on the roof, tearing up £10 notes.

One of the people I employed had previously been head of property for a major corporation. He was powerful, influential, and whenever we had worked for them, he had held us over the fire to ensure our quality, specifications and timings were spot-on. He was engineering-focused but was highly-enough thought of by this corporation to write multi-million-pound cheques. He played with a straight bat and when we did jobs for him, I was actually a little bit in awe of the fella.

After he was made redundant, I asked him to join us to oversee engineering and help grow the business. I soon realised he was out of his depth. He had no individual dynamism and, once stripped of his corporate identity, he was lost. He was a perfect example of corporate blindness. He had risen through the ranks at a major firm to a position he was comfortable in, could do the job, hope not to get noticed, go home every night and sleep soundly. In the world of private business there is no hiding. You have to fight for every contract, struggle for every penny of profit. You have to justify your salary on a weekly basis and there is no protection of a corporate giant standing behind you. When you get out in the real world, you can soon get exposed. He was useless and employing him bit me on the arse.

Do you remember Mike Fuller – the St Osyth accountant who gave me such a great start in setting up my business? Unfortunately, by the time the business was five years old and had grown, we really needed a chartered accountant to look after the books and Mike did not have that qualification, so we had to part ways with poor Mike. He was one of life's good guys and I will always be hugely grateful for the help he gave me. When I signed up with a new firm, part of its initial advice was that now I had a £4m turnover company, I should employ a full-time financial director. I needed someone with real quality, who was risk-averse, knew how to manage the accounts to our best advantage rather than the tax man's, and who had full daily oversight of our financial position.

My new accountants started looking for candidates, did their due diligence and eventually suggested one. He came to an interview, I liked him, he was highly qualified, had a great CV and he seemed perfect. He said, "I have looked into your business, I understand its structure, and the way you are accounting for it is all wrong. I will take on the job on one condition - you understand I know my stuff, I am the financial director and I need independence to do things my way."

I hadn't bought a dog to bark myself, so I said, "Fine, the job is yours, do it your way."

It will come as no surprise to learn my systematic approach to engineering had transferred to my financial filing. As well as information on our computers, I had lever arch files for every financial aspect of the business. They were all categorised and easy to understand. A few days after the new FD had started, I walked into the office and he was opening these files and just dropping the contents into two big cardboard boxes. There was more paper flying about than at a ticker tape parade. I was gobsmacked and said, "What are you doing? Those are all in order."

He said, "We have talked about this. I told you I like to do things my way, just leave me to it."

He then spent the next two weeks picking up bits of paper from these boxes and putting them in other boxes. I had a bad feeling about this, so I thought I had better make some quiet checks. I soon discovered he had been disqualified from being a company director twice in the last six years and was the FD for four previous companies which had gone into liquidation. I had paid my accountants to do proper research on him and they had given him the thumbs-up. It took me a couple of phone calls to discover you wouldn't have given this bloke control of your kid's piggy bank. He got fired and my accountants were lucky to escape the same fate. Instead, they got a right bollocking, and a demand for my search fee back. Those experiences had made me even more stressed and lonely. If even paying big bucks wasn't getting me people I could rely on, how was I going to grow? Joining forces with Chris was an obvious solution. It started off brilliantly, we won a huge contract at the SAS Hotel in London's Portman Square, mainly thanks to Chris and a piece of engineering genius.

We got the contract to install Daikin air con units in all the rooms. It was standard stuff; an air con unit was slotted into the ceiling at the end of each room's entrance corridor. You will have seen similar ones in hotels across the world. In the trade they are called mouth-organ units. However, when we looked at the designs, we realised the units supplied by the distributor wouldn't fit. They were too wide. Even then, as there was no space either side of the unit, there was no way anyone would be able to maintain them after they were installed.

It looked awful and was obviously a terrible idea. Trying to find a solution, Chris came up with the idea of using floor-standing air con units in the ceiling instead. These were much narrower, fit perfectly, did the same job and were half the cost. The only problem was they would need to be modified, or water would drip out of them. Chris designed a drip tray which could easily be manufactured and fitted, and we put forward our proposal. It was a perfect engineering solution. Of course, the distributor hadn't thought of the idea, he would lose money supplying cheaper units and so he refused to sanction it. It all kicked off but eventually we went over the distributor's head and he was kicked off the project. Because we had little faith in our team to do the job properly – which again shows the difficulties of recruiting the right people – Chris and I then spent every night and weekend for a month converting two hundred and sixty of these units. Really it was madness, that was time we should have spent building the business, but Chris wouldn't be persuaded. There was an engineering issue and he wanted to fix it and the bigger picture was forgotten. Still, it was a £250,000 contract, we had a good margin out of it, and it enhanced our reputation. We were proving we could solve problems, save clients' cash and get jobs done.

For the next couple of years things ticked along nicely, the partnership was fine with only the odd argument, and we were growing the business. I had realised Chris did not share my entrepreneurial spirit and desire for growth, but at last I had someone to share the burden with.

We were enjoying the success and even enjoyed some great Christmas parties.

Things were going well. Whenever that is the case, take your feet off the table because life likes to smack you in the mouth. When people ask how business is going, I always say "it's going well for now, but who knows which curveball is around the next corner". If your mindset is 'everything is going absolutely fine', you become complacent and unprepared for the next challenge you will face.

Our Mechanical Services division had got into trouble. It had failed to win any new major projects and for a long time we were just about paying the suppliers' bills, the relevant people's salaries and little else. Our view was if we didn't pay our suppliers they might go bust, but the country was never going to go bankrupt if we got behind on our taxes. We thought we would settle the tax bill when we won our next big job, but that job never came. It became obvious the division was like a cancer in the business and we decided to liquidate it. The official liquidator's report said because we had allowed a tax debt of £80,000 to build up, we had not acted properly as directors of the firm. We were hauled into a hearing and were both disqualified from being directors for a year.

It was obviously upsetting and embarrassing, but Chris went through the roof. He was furious. He didn't see why he should have been punished for it, he thought the division's manager should have been penalised and not us, and was angry because Mechanical Services had been one of the elements I brought to the business (even though he was happy to accept the £1.1m project it had brought). I understood his anger but, as joint owners, the buck stopped with both of us. We both owned the company, both got the benefits of doing so, but that brought responsibilities. We had failed to meet them and, quite rightly, had been punished for it. We had a blazing row, fell out and have never spoken since. He simply relinquished his shares in EAC and walked away with his side of the business. I was obviously sad and upset but I couldn't control how he should or shouldn't feel. You can manage many things in business, but you can't control people's illogical emotions. Again, you never truly know people until they are vulnerable.

In many ways it was a relief. While his personality meant he was always going to earn a good living, I also believed he didn't have the drive and vision to move forward like I wanted to. There was financially no impact on me from splitting up, I was still taking the same salary with the odd bonus, I was simply back where I started, on my own again. It was obvious partnerships weren't for me. I am sure Ian and Chris would have both said I was too aggressively driven, overpowering and too determined to follow my own course of action to allow a partnership to properly work. Chris had at least shown me that, while I was good at process, at detail, getting everything in the right place at the right time, he was better with clients. I am Marmite - some people love me and some hate me, and I had learnt to recognise when to step away from projects and let others take over.

Being banned as a director had no real effect. By now I had three people in the business who could run it. I was still an employee, and still the owner, so while I could give approval for expenditure as a shareholder, the ban meant I could not say, "We will pay this person now and another person then". Everyone knew the rules of engagement and behaved appropriately. And so, time passed, the business ticked over, it continued to make money. To anyone outside looking in, I had it made. I had a great business, we were living like kings, we had a big house, lots of cars, expensive holidays. Once upon a time my Mum had made all my clothes. Now I had a wardrobe full of designer suits.

But on the inside, I was bored and frustrated. I felt like I had the world on my shoulders and no-one to share the burden with, and the company had become a sort of "lifestyle" business I had once deplored for lacking ambition. Every time I tried to partner with someone it all went wrong and when I tried to grow the business through recruiting experts, my bank balance shrank. I was frustrated, bored and didn't see a way forward. My salvation came from an unusual direction. It gave me the best time of my life. And almost cost me everything. In 2020, a virus was costing lives.

COVID April 2020:

Furlough follies

In a crisis, communication is key. When the COVID disaster first broke, our immediate message to staff and suppliers was, "We don't know what is going to happen any more than you do. We are all going to have to hold our breath at the same time, for the same amount of time, until we get clarity into what is going to happen."

The furlough announcement gave us that clarity and it was a lifesaver. We could immediately put ninety per cent of our three hundred and thirty staff on furlough until the end of July. It took the fear away. Everyone had breathing space. The effect on everyone's mental health was immediate. For a rushed government programme, the system also worked surprisingly well. The scheme was up and running in April and, on April 22, we applied for £1m in salaries and got the money eight days later. It was a remarkable achievement.

What the government was far less successful in doing was communicating the furlough rules. In truth, these were quite simple. Staff on furlough could do anything which did not generate revenue. They could undertake training, email customers who had queries, respond to general enquiries and communicate with colleagues. But the message the government gave was so garbled people thought if they even turned on their work laptop the 'furlough police' were going to break down their door. This poor communication was hugely regrettable. We had to give countless reassurances people could still communicate with each other and, if any rules were inadvertently broken, the company would be liable to pay back the furlough money, not them.

There were other issues. The furlough scheme did not cover anyone employed after February 28, but we had eight new starters about to join us. We could have simply cancelled their contracts (as other companies were doing), but these people had left their previous jobs for us. How could we just cast them aside? We decided to continue to employ them, class them as critical workers and ensure they were paid. They were thrilled. We had shown them all the promises we had made about having different values to most companies were true. **Actions always speak louder than words.** They were part of our family, not just employee numbers on our profit and loss sheet. We even managed to help more people. The government also said we could furlough people who had left the company since December 31. A number of people who had recently left us and joined other companies had seen their new employers cancel their contracts. We brought them back into our business and furloughed them to make sure they had an income as well.

The biggest issue we had was over the staff who were still working. They were doing critical tasks for us but were being paid the same as those who were sitting at home watching Netflix. The amazing thing is not one person who was working complained, the only comments we received were from their furloughed colleagues saying this was unfair on those still working. They had a point. Some people were sunbathing for weeks at an end and others were working their socks off. Of course, we would not forget their dedication and when the time was right, they were rewarded for their efforts.

The furlough scheme got us all out of the fear stage and gave us some respite. So, that was wages taken care of. Back in 1997 it was all kicking off.

Chapter 8

It's not always a funny old game

Sometimes in life, you can take a few steps down a road and never dream where it will lead you. In my case, a bit of generosity led me to the best of times and dark depths of despair. When someone from the St Osyth village football team asked me in the pub to sponsor their kit for £350 I thought, *Why not? Give a little back to the community.* I had always loved football, I played at county standard at school until I was sixteen and I am a big Arsenal fan. Within weeks I was going to watch St Osyth's matches on godforsaken muddy fields, home and away. The football might have been amateur but I loved the camaraderie and the spirit. I had previously gone to night college to study professional photography, so I started taking pictures at their matches. Because the pictures were so good they were soon all over the back of the local paper. Not satisfied with just sponsoring their kit, I then bought them tracksuits as well and then, in a fit of generosity probably fuelled by too many pints, I lent them a £5,000 minibus complete with a fuel card. In financial terms it was a piss in the wind, but we were the talk of lower-level non-league football. While other teams were sometimes struggling to get eleven players, St Osyth were turning up to matches in their own minibus in matching tracksuits. The players responded and there was a great sense of unity. They would run through walls for us and, of course, we won the league.

Our success was noticed by nearby Clacton FC. They were a big step up, semi-professional, playing in Jewson Division One, but they were hardly going places. Their ground was crap, the pitch was terrible, there was a ramshackle stand for their fifty-or-so supporters to shelter in when it rained, and the hospitality suite was an old caravan. There was a turnstile, a pitch barrier made out of scaffolding poles, a changing room and an old bar with a hatch to a tiny kitchen where you could buy a burger - if the gas was working. The manager got in touch with me and asked if I was interested in doing something to help the club. I met the committee in the club portacabin. There were eight of them. There was a builder and his wife who washed the kit every week, a woman who worked as the tea lady on match days, a plumber who was paying one player's £130-a-week salary, another bloke who took the money on the gate and someone else who cleaned the changing rooms. They all had a couple of things in common. They all loved the football club and dedicated hours of their own time to making sure it survived. They were also united in the fact that as far as I could tell, they had no incentive or real appetite for trying to grow it.

They wanted me to put some money in and my blunt response was, "With the greatest of respect, I wouldn't put a penny on this table. You are all lovely people who are committed to keeping the club alive, and the town does not know how lucky it is to have your support. But there's no dynamism, entrepreneurism, or anyone wanting to start punching holes through ceilings to make the club a success. You are all doing a great job, but I am not going to invest when you haven't got a vision to improve the club."

Then I had a brainwave and realised I had said it out loud… "There is one thing I might do…. buy the club."

We then had a two-hour conversation about the club's background, its finances, the commercial deals already in place. We talked about where things could be improved, if they would still give their time to the club every week if I was the owner, and my vision for the future. A couple of them were under the misapprehension that their shares were worth money, but I politely pointed out the club didn't own its ground - the council leased it to them, it had no assets, was in debt and the Bahrain Royal family were not likely to drive up the A12 in a Rolls Royce to buy it. I asked them to give me a week or two to come up with a plan. The reason I suddenly decided I might want to become a football club-owner? I had loved my experience with St-Osyth, was bored by my business and had people who could run it, and the challenge excited me. I had also realised there were real opportunities to grow the club. I formalised my ideas into a professional business plan complete with architectural drawings. Clacton had no real advertising income but

I could leverage all my suppliers to provide it. I could see the club's biggest return was on food. I had a friend who manufactured cold storage facilities. I promised to build a big double-cold-room kitchen at the back of the clubhouse for £11,000, which meant we could have six people serving, churning burgers out like Mr Wimpy. I had plans drawn up for a new hospitality suite, converted from another cold-room. Another friend would do the groundwork for free, a friend in double-glazing said he would put windows and double-doors in and even build an apex at the top so it would look like a proper building.

I brought them a dummy programme, again packed with advertising from my suppliers and business friends, I did revenue projections, profit and loss forecasts, promised to resurface the car park, refurbish the existing bar into a proper sports bar in Clacton's colours, complete with a ten-foot projection screen, new carpet, new pool table, my old man would put alarms and CCTV up. They were gobsmacked. No-one had ever come to them with such a vision before. I bought the club for £30. I spent more than that most weekends buying rounds in the village pub. One of the biggest attractions for me? All the staff were volunteers. All the committee members were running the club and working for free. I had various revenue streams and next to no staff costs at all. If you can't make a profit when you have no staff costs something is badly wrong. In the first year I spent £30,000 fulfilling my promises.

One of the club's problems was because of its out-of-town location, you couldn't have a drink and watch the match as you had to drive home. St Osyth had stopped using the minibus I provided, so instead I got a volunteer to drive it round to pick people up from drop-off points every twenty minutes, bring them to the club, and take them back at night. The local taxi drivers were not too happy. I also noticed the bar was half a dozen-deep ten minutes before kick-off but would then be empty until half-time, before filling up again at full-time. I put an expensive camera on one of the floodlights so we could film the game and we put a feed straight into the big screen at the bar. From then on, some people never left the clubhouse. They got to stay warm, drink, and got a better overall view of the match from the screen than from the touchline.

The side's joint managers, Nick Nicolou and Johnny Kemp, were saying that if we were serious about moving forward, we were going to need these players, which was going to cost us X, Y and Z. I went to meet the players they wanted and sold them the dream. I said we were going to get promotion every season for the next three years and I wanted them to be part of it. Every player I met signed on the dotted line. It cost me a few quid obviously but all these signings were hitting the back pages of the weekly press as I was using my company's PR machine to drive the coverage.

The whole league was thinking, *Wow, this is going to be a powerhouse team,* and we were getting all this press about how big the club was going to be. I was telling everyone we were going straight for the Conference – the entry league to the professional national divisions – and there was a real buzz about the place. Before I joined, the kit sponsorship had been about £600. I got £2,500 and decided that wasn't enough. How could I increase it? Another brainwave. I got sponsors for the first half and different sponsors for the second. The players would change their tops at half time! That was £5,000 right there. I even got a different sponsor for the players' tracksuits.

When the team was playing at home, I got the players uniforms to wear - cream chinos, white shirt, Clacton tie and Clacton blazers. The players may have been semi-professional but they looked, and more importantly felt, like the dog's bollocks. I designed and had a new kit specially made by a manufacturer rather than buying it off the shelf. For away games we travelled by Colchester United's coach if it was available, or the best alternative we could find. The players were proud and motivated before they had even kicked a ball. Run through walls for us? These boys would build them for us first. I had an income stream from the gate, an income stream from the bar, income from the food, income from sponsorship. I had the local camera club using the camera on the floodlight to film and record the games and I was flogging fifteen videos of the match at £10 a pop. The club had previously earned about £150,000 a year in revenue, and the cash projections I had put forward assumed three hundred people would turn up. The first game was on a Tuesday evening, so I planned a massive firework show after it.

Seven hundred people turned up. *If you build it, they will come*, as someone once said. That night I watched people paying to enter, people buying drinks, eating burgers, buying programmes. If it was stationary, or moved, I had sponsorship for it. I sat there thinking, "My costs are X, my income is Y, blimey, I am making a fortune here." The first year I raised the turnover to £700,000 and re-invested most of the £160,000 profit back into the club. On the pitch? We kicked off in August and didn't concede a goal until March. Smash the league? We obliterated it. Of course, one of the problems of owning a football club is you can build the best facilities on the planet but you are still reliant on players. The consensus in football is players are selfish prima donnas but I wanted to change the traditional culture.

I supplied them with decent wages, the best transport, clothes and kit and I told them straight, they were expected to perform. Take training, for example. One of the problems in semi-pro football is sometimes the players don't turn up for training. They might have had a bad day at work, have to travel long distances and they just can't be bothered. At Clacton, the average player's weekly wage was about £100 and typically the players had three weekly commitments - two games and one training session, or one game and two training sessions. At Clacton, I made it easy. Each player was paid a third for each attendance. If they missed a training session, they only got paid sixty-six per cent of their cash. Miss two and they got thirty-three per cent. Because of that, we had one hundred per cent training attendance, which really helped with team bonding and performance.

I never tried to manage the team or become involved in the football side of things in terms of selection or tactics, but I engaged with the players at every level. Any issues off the pitch and the managers would send the players to me and I treated them all the same, preaching fairness, trust and accountability. I was at the ground forty hours a week, I loved it. The games were like a drug, I loved the press coverage, the atmosphere, meeting people. I had promised to deliver glory to

Clacton in my first season in charge and did just that. Everyone was on cloud nine. Then I shocked everyone by sacking the managers. It was a hard thing to do. They were employed to win football matches and they hadn't been beaten for eight months. The opinion around the league was I had made success easy for them by buying the best players. I never bought into that. Far bigger clubs across the world had given their managers squads costing hundreds of millions of pounds and it never guaranteed results. The managers deserved full credit for the success but in life, and in business, you always have to plan for tomorrow. **You might have an excellent team running your company today but you also need to be prepared for when it reaches the stage you want it to achieve tomorrow. Just because you can run a £5m business, does not mean you can run a £10m one. Every business owner or leader must know when to employ people who are better at running aspects of the business than they are.** I had people queuing up to be manager, but I chose ex-Colchester player Steve Dowman. He had credibility, a pedigree and had managed at a higher level. In the close season we built a big new stand, fifty volunteers turned up to help us, and then I unveiled the latest Dewing masterstroke, my latest sure fire hit to grow the club even further. I put together the biggest financial deal in the history of non-league football. Publicity had been at the core of our financial success. The club attracted huge interest, crowds attract crowds and attendances were at their highest ever level. How could I get more publicity? I went to the biggest independent radio station in the region, Dream 100, and said, "I want you to be our main sponsor. I want people to call us the Dream Team. We have a new stand with a massive space for a big advertising banner, we are on the rise and you can be associated with our success." They loved the idea but had no money. They might have been able to afford sponsoring the ball for a couple of games, but that was about it.

"OK," I said. "The full sponsorship package is worth around £100,000. If you give me daily coverage on the radio throughout the year, match updates live from the ground, adverts for our special events and feature us in your sports news, what would all that coverage be worth?" The MD ran some figures and said around £130,000. I said, "There you have it, let's announce a three-year deal and call it half a million pounds." The size of the deal made national headlines but not a single penny changed hands. I was canny enough to sign the deal early so we had the whole of the pre-season to promote the club on Dream 100, we signed half a dozen non-league superstars to the team and you could barely turn on the radio or pick up a paper without hearing about Clacton FC. This season was going to be massive. The crowds at the ground would make it look as packed as Oxford Street at Christmas.

We even got the model Caprice to promote us.

Show me the money! Show me the money! What a flaming idiot. I had scored a total own goal. Attendances plummeted to one hundred and fifty. We had just got promoted and we lost most of our supporters overnight. Why? People didn't need to go to the game when they could listen to constant updates on the radio. I knew the coverage might keep a couple of people away, but we lost about sixty per cent of our usual attendance. That's a lot of profitable burgers and pints left unbought. The deal was a financial calamity and I had no one to blame but myself. Another factor was there had been so much hype in the first year, people had come just to see what was going on. However, you have to be a die-hard fan to watch non-league football in the rain every week in the winter and so a drop-off was maybe inevitable.

Thankfully, on the pitch the dream team was doing the business. We started winning every game in the premiership and good cup runs in the FA Vase and FA Cup brought in £80,000 prize money which subsidised the lack of attendance. In the first year, our weekly budget had been £1,000. This had now doubled to £2,000 but in this higher league some other clubs were on double that. We finished third which was a blessing in some ways. Had we been promoted it was unlikely we could have gone up anyway. The ground and infrastructure requirements required in the Conference League would probably have been beyond us. The council was being difficult over supporting the sort of expansion we would have required and I knew that, had we been promoted, without investing massive amounts of my money on players' wages alone, we would probably have been relegated the next season anyway. I began to ask myself if realistically I had taken the club as far as I could, but, God, I was having fun.

Season three saw us win the East Anglia Cup for the first time since 1957. For a little club like Clacton that was a major achievement and to celebrate I took the team to London, booked them in Park Lane Hilton. We went to Tiger Tiger for dinner and then painted the town red. After another success, I took them to Dublin for the weekend. These were plumbers and plasterers being treated like professional sports stars and they responded with the kind of commitment and passion on the pitch other clubs could not compete with. However, season three's league campaign started badly when we lost the first four games. After two years of solid success this was a new experience for the club and I sacked Steve Dowman the manager.

I was actually more concerned about grumblings from the players than the results. In football speak, Steve had "lost the dressing room". Despite the high turnover of managers in football, it is emotionally no easier sacking people than it is in business. You are still affecting people's lives. Mickey Potter replaced him, but Steve Dowman would soon be back, paying us a visit.

He was appointed manager of Heybridge Swifts (who played in a higher division than Clacton) and, after a decent run, we drew them in the FA Cup. This was a massive local derby with £20,000 prize money up for grabs. We publicised it as David versus Goliath, eight hundred people turned up and we won the match. Steve got the sack the next day from Heybridge Swifts. He must have hated Clacton. We finished fourth that season. By then, the end of the road was in sight. I had always told the players, "You do your job and I will do mine," but I knew I would struggle to fulfil my side of the bargain if they got us promoted.

The expansion problems, never mind the cash it would require, would have made it a mammoth task. I was watching games and celebrating when we scored but thinking, *Oh God, if we keep winning, I am going to empty my bank accounts chasing a dream I know won't lead anywhere.* If promotion had happened, I would have stepped up and got it done somehow, but in some ways falling just short meant I missed a massive headache.

But what times we had. The bar was always full, we had created a social club where people would come to drink on a daily basis, not just match days, we had family hog roasts, fun days and became a real part of the community. It was the happiest time of my life, but I knew time deep down it was ending. In year four, attendances had not increased and the pitch, which I had spent thousands on improving, began to suffer again.

Combined with bad weather, this meant games were frequently getting postponed. That led to little money coming in to meet the weekly wage bill, so I started to take cash from the company. The postponed games were invariably rescheduled on a Tuesday night when crowds were much lower, so we didn't get enough cash in to meet our outgoings. I would then go back to EAC for more money. Not huge sums by any means - a couple of thousands here and there. But what had happened to EAC while I had been loving football life for four years? I had truly taken my eye off the ball and that led me to desperate times – in personal terms, even harder times than COVID would cause me.

COVID May 2020:

Home care

Most people at some time in their lives dream of not going to work. Instead of looking forward to four or five weeks of annual leave spread throughout the year, they imagine being at home for weeks at a time. Just imagine how relaxing that would be. People were now getting the opportunity to do just that, and even being paid for it. However, the furlough scheme also presented many people with problems. These included low self-esteem, stress, isolation, financial worries, anxiety and family problems.

Legally, as a company we could have said, "You are being paid, go sit at home and we will be in touch when all this is over." However, that was a million miles away from our company philosophy. Instead, our training team, who were on furlough, stepped up and implemented a whole range of programmes which looked after both the physical and mental wellbeing of all our staff. We immediately started a series of daily, voluntary, web-based activities. Staff could do anything from taking part in quizzes or exercise classes, to learning new computer skills. Managers were encouraged to have regular online meetings with their teams just to check everyone was OK. We wanted to make sure we did everything in our power to help people get through this terrible time. We even held an online company-wide talent competition with a grand finale. One of our engineers even made his van disappear.

The company now had money coming in, our staff were being paid and looked after. However, we needed to make sure as many as possible people had jobs to come back to. It was now time to start looking ahead to the future and how we would come out of this crisis at the other end. We knew many companies would not. But we didn't just want to survive, we were determined to come out stronger. But how on earth were we going to do this? We knew coming out of COVID in such a changed economic environment was going to be ten times harder than going in had been. We had no idea. Back in 2003, I had no idea what was about to hit me.

Chapter 9

The worst of times

How is it possible for someone to lose everything? It is remarkably easy, as I was about to find out. I had started EAC when I was twenty-four years old. I had dedicated my life, energy and soul to it. There had been giddy highs and a few lows, but the unavoidable truth was that by 1998 I had lost interest in it. The football club made me far happier than focussing on the business did. I had passed over day-to-day responsibility for running it to a strong colleague who saw it as an opportunity to learn and build a better life for himself. He had the enthusiasm and drive which had drained away from me. Unfortunately, he didn't have all the skills needed to make it prosper.

Of course, we had an understanding - if certain financial benchmarks were not met, he was meant to press a proverbial alarm bell. As it turned out, he was reluctant to press it and I had stopped listening for it. As matches got delayed, I would go to the company for cash, £5,000 here and there to tide the club over, small stuff for a company with a turnover in the millions. One day I went to get £5,000 and he said the company was struggling for cash. My immediate reaction was, "Why?" He said there been this problem, that problem, but he thought it could be solved if so-and-so happened.

With a sense of dread, I sat down and went through the books properly for the first time in months. It was worse than I could have imagined. It was obvious the company had about six months' life left, assuming I completely stopped taking cash out. Debts were mounting, the work was drying up and it would need massive focus from me to try turn things around. Even then, it wasn't guaranteed it was going to survive. The alarm bells were meant to have rung if the company got a cold. I was discovering it was already in intensive care. We had supplier debts, owed £30,000 to the Inland Revenue, the last VAT quarter had not been paid so we owed £60,000 on that, and in total I was back to being in a massive hole of debt.

I could have screamed and shouted at him, pointed out I was paying him a salary to avoid issues like this happening before they crippled us, but even in my fear and panic I had the maturity to know he was not ultimately to blame. I was. As much as he had been burying his head in the sand, I had dug mine deeper. I had allowed my happiness at the football club to cloud my judgement and, the truth was, it was my business, my name on the records, I was responsible for it. Whichever way you cut it, the blame was on my shoulders. A sense of absolute realism kicked in.

At the football club I had met a businessman – ironically, he was a liquidator - who had expressed interest in the club. He had recently helped to liquidate Cardiff City FC, he lived locally and when I expressed my doubts over my future at the club, he offered to take it over. I simply gave it to him. I didn't ask for a penny, not even the symbolic £30 I had paid for it. It had no appreciable debt, I had massively improved the infrastructure of the club and I could hold my head up high over what I had achieved while running it. There was a degree of regret but, even aside from my business troubles, I knew that journey had come to an end. With money I had taken from the business to support the club, and from personal investments in it, the whole thing ended up costing me around £200,000 in the end. Compared to the pleasure and experiences it had given me for nearly five years, I considered it money well spent. Sadly, the new owner struggled more than I had and nine months later he was declared bankrupt and the club collapsed. New owners came in, renamed it FC Clacton, and I was relieved I had not been at the helm when the end came. But by then, I had bigger problems on my hands.

I spent a month looking at the business and the opportunities of trading out of the debt. I brought in an expert and he confirmed my worst fears. He said, "You have six months to try and save it, but to do so you will need cash. During those six months your debts will continue to grow and there is no guarantee the company will succeed, so you need to make a decision now. You either go all-in and risk a far more costly failure, or you can throw in the towel and declare bankruptcy."

The thought of bankruptcy frightened the life out of me. I knew very little about the precise details, but I certainly knew for a businessman like me it was seen as the ultimate failure, the total reality you had royally messed up. It was a stigma you would carry with you for years. Mine, Michelle and our children's lives would be massively affected by it. And I had no-one to blame but myself.

I wanted to save the business but the writing was on the wall and, having lifted my head out of the sand, I could now read it. The chances of turning things around were too small. Bankruptcy was the only option. I raised a little bit of cash to pay off the suppliers I owed - I could not have lived with myself if my failures had put other hardworking small firms through the pain I was enduring - and then had to tell my ten staff their jobs were gone. The company was folding, we were bankrupt. It was heart-breaking. The company closed with debts of around £100,000 to the government. Because I had been banned from being a company director it wasn't a limited company. I was personally responsible for trying to repay all the debts.

The ramifications were almost immediate. In 1992 Michelle and I had moved into our dream home in St Osyth. I had spent a king's ransom turning it into a palace. At one stage I had spent £100,000 on just upgrading the front of the house and the gardens.

Our beautiful bungalow where the kids all grew up and which the taxman took from me.

At this point, as a registered bankrupt, it wasn't looking like money well spent. The house was taken from us to pay the debts, along with our cars and other possessions of any real value. Our bank accounts were frozen. It was a strangely cold process where everything I had worked for was simply taken away. I was devastated. I was on the floor, I was gutted. I had let myself down and let my family down. Michelle had been angry at me for a while for spending so much time at the club and abandoning the business and now there was nowhere to hide. **The lesson is if you don't passionately care about the business you are running, get out of it fast. If you are not doing something in life which gives you fulfilment, you will never make a success of it. Get out before you fail and have to pay the price for doing so.** The business certainly hadn't fulfilled me, I hadn't cared enough, it had become a chore, a noose round my neck and I didn't do anything about it. I had brought this on us and I had to be strong enough to try and drag us out of it, but it was crippling blow after crippling blow. I was going through each day weighed down with shame and embarrassment.

I had to sign on for Jobseekers Allowance. A couple of years before I had been running a football club and making tens of thousands of pounds a year. Now I was climbing the steps to the dole office to sign on for £70 a week. Walking through those doors was horrible, it was the most shameful thing I had done. We had been at the top, enjoyed it and we had lost everything. There was no further to fall. Thank God I am not prone to depression or I could have broken down and remained in pieces for years. Instead, I scrapped for work here and there, wrote a purchase order computer system for my Dad which I quietly had to ask him to pay me for and he gave me an old Toyota car so I could get about. For a couple of months, I was too down to think about a long-term plan to get out of this mess. I just did bits of work here and there to try and raise some money.

Just feeding the family became an issue. Once the food cupboard was totally bare, so we went to the cashpoint and there was £7.60 in the account. It would only dispense £10 notes so we couldn't even access that. My pride would not let me go to my parents or friends to ask to borrow a couple of hundred quid, so a couple of times Michelle and I went without to ensure the kids were properly fed. I had told my parents and friends the business had folded, said it just wasn't working out, and I hid the bankruptcy from them. I was ashamed. My Dad would have been devastated. Did he know? I will never know the answer to that, but he never raised it with me.

It showed me how even from an incredibly comfortable position, none of us are that far away from devastation. Before then, I had never personally experienced the financial difficulties which millions of people struggle with on a day-to-day basis, and many have it far worse than we ever did. We had lost everything, but we had a rented roof over our heads. Michelle and I could both look for work and if our situation had got worse, I could have swallowed my pride and asked for help. Not everyone has that safety blanket or the advantages we did.

Even now, decades later, Michelle and I refer back to that day when we had £7.60 to our name. We have used the experience to remain grounded.

Thankfully, we can enjoy nice things now, a villa in Portugal, a lovely home, cash in the bank. But every time we make a luxurious purchase, or spoil our kids, we remember when we couldn't afford to buy them a decent dinner.

It helps in life to have a fixed reference point to give your current circumstances relevance. When things are going great and you are tempted to splash out on that Bentley Continental GT (and believe me, I have been tempted), I just look back to those times and think, "do I really need to spend that much money on a car"? Of course, I don't. When deals go bad and an immediate natural emotion is to feel angry and devastated, remembering when there was no food in the cupboards puts it into perspective.

Looking back, I am not sure 'stupidity' is the right word for my failings. Certainly, there was a degree of it, but I was also inexperienced and naïve. Even though I was a supposedly successful businessman, I still didn't truly appreciate the impact bad decisions could have and how devastating they could be. But in retrospect.... it was the best thing that could have happened to me. I learnt the harshest of lessons and I have never been anywhere near that position again. Research shows the most credit-worthy people are those who have gone bankrupt and that's for a reason – it is so awful you will never put yourself through it again. Never again would I buy a house with a mortgage or get a loan.

But, like every nightmare, it eventually ends. Within a couple of months, I got a job with Denman Refrigeration in Reigate. Things were so bad the Job Centre had to give me money to buy a suit for the interview. I had to take in a letter to the Job Centre to prove I had an interview and it mentioned my starting salary, if successful, was £60,000. The eyes of the kind lady in the job centre went wide as spoons. I was asking for money to buy a suit but if I got the job, I would be earning three times as much as her. The company was owned by Mark Denton and Andy Blackman. I knew of them by reputation and I joined the firm in 2004 as Head of Contracts. Working for Sainsbury's was ninety per cent of their turnover and they had grown the business from zero to £35m turnover in just a few years. Coincidentally, when I joined they were paying off one of their old shareholders and guess who it was, Freddie Bird! It was a two-and-a-half-hour commute to work each day but I needed the job. The salary of £60,000 was more than I had earned before, I was on the board of directors, I had years of experience working with Sainsbury's and so I had fallen on my feet. We had gone from not having enough cash to buy food to being relatively economically secure again.

But, after a few weeks, it was obvious I was going to have a problem. Mark Denton was similar to me in many ways - he was determined and driven. However, I didn't like the way he sometimes treated people. I personally found him to be sometimes confrontational and occasionally arrogant. It was his company and he was going to run it his way – fair enough – but that meant the rest of us had no voice and had best keep quiet. We would have monthly board meetings with ten items on the agenda, he would tell us what we were doing about them and five minutes later, meeting closed. End of. We had no voice. I could perhaps have lived with that but when I thought he was being over-critical or confrontational, I could not stomach that. This was a multi-million-pound company, I was one of its senior employees, and things began to fall apart for me there because of a £6 sandwich.

One of the directors lived in Newcastle and he would fly down at 6am on a Monday, stay all week and return home on the Friday night. At one board meeting Mark became agitated – as he was prone to do – and started shouting about expenses, saying we were taking the piss. He pointed at this bloke and said, "You spent £6 on an easyJet sandwich! I don't buy sandwiches on easyJet, you can fuck off."

I have never been very good at being shouted at, and could never bear to see people being confronted, so I kicked off too: "Hold it there, this guy is on a flight at 6am to get to work and you won't buy him a sandwich, are you out of order or what?" He said, "Who the fuck do you think you are talking to?"

I said, "I am talking to you," and we had to be calmed down before things escalated. I am pretty sure most boardrooms do not see screaming rows about £6 sandwiches. That incident was one of many. When I considered he was treating people inappropriately I always confronted him about it. The values which had been instilled in me since childhood would not allow me to let things go. Another example... We were asked to go to a corporate golf day and one of our blokes had forgotten his jumper. It was absolutely freezing, and he said he would not be able to play. Mark told him to buy one from the pro shop, so he bought the cheapest they had and went out to play. Mark refused to allow him to claim it on his expenses. I bowled into his office and said, "What the hell are you deducting the money for the jumper off him for? I was stood there when you told him to go and buy it." He said it was none of my business. I said it was always my business when his actions clashed with my own set of moral values.

When one day he heard me being complimented by his PA saying I should be running the company instead of him, I knew my days were numbered. After all these rows about other people's expenses, the irony was I rarely claimed any expenses but major ones. Parking, entertaining, small stuff, I never bothered. I was being paid well enough. One time though I claimed £20 for a legitimate expense and was informed he would not pay it. On top of the rows, and his behaviour, I'd had enough. I wrote a resignation letter, put it in an envelope and left it on his desk. His secretary knew something was up, opened it and called Mark. He rang me and asked me to fly to Portugal where he was at a family event. We had a civilised adult discussion for once. I said I didn't agree with the way he sometimes behaved towards people and couldn't work in such an environment. It was his business, it was up to him how he ran it, but I couldn't stomach it. I was calling it a day. To be fair to him, he said, "I know you are right, I have some issues, help me solve this problem."

I said, "OK, let's start with a small step. If we are in a board meeting and you are behaving badly, I will scratch my nose which means, *Shut up*." He said he would give it a go.

The first board meeting went fine, he was like a new bloke, non-confrontational, reasonable. At the second meeting he started acting up, so I scratched my nose and he backed off. It was working, people noticed his change in behaviour, he was far more approachable. I was a genius, maybe my next job could be as a behavioural therapist. The next meeting was on a Monday and he had obviously had a very long weekend. I thought he was acting like an idiot and I was scratching my nose so hard it was almost bleeding. In the end I went and stood right in front of him, itching away until he told me to fuck off and sit down. I knew the end was nigh.

As part of the agenda, we were discussing pay rises for our four hundred or so engineers. Our view was the very minimum rise they deserved was linked to inflation, two per cent or something, which would cost the company about £16,000. Mark wouldn't have it, said, "No way, no discussion. Sod 'em." That night we were taking Sainsbury's out on a Christmas jolly. We went out to the Orange Club restaurant and were buying carafes of red wine at hundreds of pounds a time. The Sainsbury's team went home after the meal, but we carried on at some strip club. We all got drunk and the next morning, in reception, I totted up the bill. It was £17,000. We had spent more in one night than giving four hundred engineers a pay increase.

I knew it was all wrong and I told Mark in no uncertain terms. A few days later I was called to a meeting and he handed me a compromise agreement and said, "Go and get legal advice, you are finished here, we have taken your laptop and car, we have provided you with a hire car for a month and there is a cheque in the envelope for £20,000." That was a result bearing in mind I had been willing to resign for nothing a few months earlier.

I was glad. He was a successful businessman, but his personality meant I was never going to be able to work for him for long. My values of fairness and decency were more important to me than the job. None of us are perfect but I had been taught from childhood to treat people a certain way and all my life lessons had amplified those beliefs. But, unknown to me, something I had done at Denman was about to change my life forever. I rarely took sick days. I was the kind of "man up and struggle through type" who then infects everyone else in the office. However, a couple of years before, when I was running Clacton FC, I was really ill and was forced to stay at home for a couple of weeks. After a couple of days of staying in bed groaning, I recovered a little and was bored senseless. I was playing around on my laptop with Word and there was a button called 'mailmerge' I had never noticed before, so I investigated what it did. I discovered it was for setting up mailing databases. From my experience back at Air Stream Ltd, I knew a limited amount about code and setting up systems, but things had moved on dramatically.

In 2000 a web-based technology creating databases using HTML had opened up, and I realised the possibilities of it would one day be endless. This was my first experience with databases and so, being me, I learned all I could about them. Using the old dial-up internet I read articles on the web, watched videos which took hours to download, and learnt all about how databases could be created and linked to other business software systems. So, lying in my sickbed, I created a basic financial database for Clacton FC. When I joined Denman, I then built a system to help me manage my teams and their workload. They were amazed by it and, through trial and error over two years, I improved it, gaining new skills every week. Auxilia - another big air con firm - had heard about the system and, soon after I had left Denman, I was approached by a headhunting firm who said Auxilia wanted me to create systems for them. The owner was a guy called Keith Johnson who had sold a waste management business for £10m. He spent around £6m of it on a house and had bought Air Continental, an air con firm with a £12m turnover, and also the Peak Cooling Fridge Company in Wigan, which had a turnover of £15m. They wanted me to integrate the service divisions of both businesses using similar software to what I had created at Denman.

I met the owners at Paddington Station, shook hands on an £80,000-a-year deal with a seat on the board, and the company rented me a house in Cannock, near Birmingham, complete with a cleaner. For the next two years I spent almost every hour God sent creating and constantly improving a cloud-based database and management system. I would work from 7am to 11pm, go home to the empty rented house, eat something, get up and start again. I never stopped. I was like a machine. I was an absolute animal. The key to my success was none of the IT people who were creating alternative systems really knew what it was like to be an engineer, or how the industry really worked. They paid lip service to creating bespoke user-friendly systems but, really, they didn't have a clue. I had worked as an engineer for years and run my own company, so I knew what was needed. I knew the realities of the job and its various challenges, and so I was in the unique position of being able to code a system to precisely meet such needs. It might sound extraordinary, but there was literally no-one else in the industry who had both skill sets. Most people have to concentrate on one career path or another. Because of my unique career changes, and frankly my obsession with knowing everything about anything which interested me, I had managed to do both. I was building and perfecting systems which IT 'specialists' would take years to build, but they would build countless new models and for countless piles of cash.

It was hard work, but I enjoyed it. However, one strange thing about

Auxilia was they never produced full financial statements at board meetings. We would enquire and be told not to worry, "they would be ready soon". We knew what our own division's sales were, but we didn't know what our overall costs were other than salaries. We didn't know what the profitability was, but everything seemed to be fine, we all got paid, the suppliers never shut off their credit, we were acting like a company flush with cash. Keith was obsessed with PR and spent tens of thousands on the image of the company rather than the work itself. Our company brochures were like works of art. The reason we never saw the full financials was the profitability had disappeared. The company was in big trouble. The company faced going into administration, but Keith wanted to try and trade his way out of the hole. He asked us to go to suppliers who were unaware of our situation asking for more credit and I refused. My values kicked in again, I wasn't going to see other companies go to the wall to try and get us out of debt. The company soon crumbled, leaving debts of £8m. Everyone got shafted, every supplier got hit.

A company called Middleton then purchased the service and maintenance part of the business from the liquidators and wanted me on board, complete with my team, to integrate it into their existing business. I was appointed MD of their Service and Maintenance division and, thankfully, the new office was in Enfield so I could return to living at home. Within a month, once again I knew I had made a mistake. I might have been MD of my own division and on the board, but I needed authorisation to buy a pint of milk. It was another privately-owned business where the owners watched every penny rather than relying on their managers to run their own divisions properly. I could increase profitability tenfold, but God forbid I wanted to buy some pizzas for everyone in the office if we were working long into the night.

Things came to a head when a guy who had worked for the company for twenty-five years was retiring and I took the team to the pub late one afternoon for a quick pint to see him on his way. I had ensured the phones were being answered and it was just going to be a quick drink at the end of the day. The owners found out and had a fit, they were shouting at me to get everyone back to the office as they said I hadn't asked permission. I said I was MD in a business with a £40m turnover and I was surely empowered to buy someone a pint after he had worked for the firm for twenty-five years. I told the owners it wasn't working out but, after lengthy discussions, I agreed to stay on for a year to help bed my team in which I did for their sake, not Middleton's. I offered to improve their IT system, but they did not want to be dependent on me to run it, so we persevered with the garbage they had. I actually stayed for nearly two years. Remember how last time a sandwich had been the tipping point in my career? This time it was a phone. One of my engineers complained to me he had answered a work call up a ladder, in the rain, and had dropped the phone and broken it. The company deducted £250 from his wages. Cue another argument about their values, their business culture. This time the settlement when they severed my contract was £40,000. It was a touch.

I had earned £60,000 in a few years from being asked to leave companies. I am not totally self-unaware and of course I pondered if the problem wasn't the companies - what if it was me? Was I unable to work for someone else? Were my values unrealistic in the current climate? Maybe I was deluded one? But the more I considered things, the more I realised my values were the right ones. I knew these could be seen as disruptive, so perhaps my shelf-life in any organisation was going to be two years unless it was a very good company? If that was the case, then so be it. I would be conscious of my own failings, but I wasn't going to change the principles I based my life on. My concerns at these companies were never about business decisions - who was I to preach to anyone when I had made massive mistakes? - but I refused to tolerate people being mistreated. Even today I will go nose-to-nose with anyone if they are mistreating someone. I don't know why, it's just part of my DNA. Still, I had £40,000 in the bank, and then another agency came calling. It was time to join a business giant. Surely things would be better there?

In May 2020 things were getting worse as COVID infected tens of thousands.

COVID May 2020:

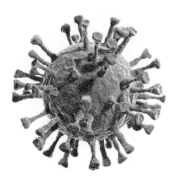

Secret meetings

While people were dying in hospital beds, for businesses the furlough scheme had been a lifesaver, but it had one critical flaw. The government had initially put it in place for twelve weeks until May 31 (they subsequently extended it until July 31). However, it seemed inevitable, like most companies, we would eventually have to make some redundancies. We knew there was no way, when the crisis eventually ended, our major restaurant sector and other clients were simply going to be able to bounce back into the same shape they had before. The truth is, in whatever sector you can think of, if you are running a £20m business with two hundred people, if it temporarily becomes a £10m business you can't keep two hundred people on.

The complication is because of legislation, if you are considering making more than twenty people redundant, it is a forty-five day process. We needed to know by the middle of May if furlough was likely to be extended past July 31. While we had enough cash in the accounts to pay our existing working staff until January, if we did not start the redundancy process in mid-May and furlough ended on July 31, we were going to start bleeding money because we would have wages and notice periods to pay.

It was at this stage myself and some other company leaders had a conversation with a senior government minister under strict Chatham

House Rules – this means you can take action based on a conversation, but can never reveal who gave you the information. I presume other ministers were holding similar consultations with business leaders across the country, but who knows?

We pointed out the redundancy date problem and the minister was apologetic but firm - the government would not make the announcement on any continuation of the furlough scheme past July by the middle of May. This put me in a tricky position with the board – did we wait, or start the redundancy process? I told them we would have to hold our nerve and trust furlough would be extended. With the virus still running rampant it was obviously too soon to for the country to return to normal life, and the government still had to protect jobs. To begin the redundancy process would also disrupt the business and cause a lot of emotional turmoil for our staff. We held fire. On May 22, the government finally announced furlough would be extended to October, and my call to hold fire on redundancies had paid off and enabled us to offer at least three more months of certainty to our staff.

With that breathing space, we could now truly start looking at the future. In 2009 I was doing the same.

Chapter 10

Bigger is not always better

If you are going to go, go big. That was the philosophy on my next job. ISS was a multinational corporation, the seventh largest facilities management provider on the planet and the biggest in the UK. They covered fifty-three countries, with around half a million employees and a £9 billion turnover. Of course, a lot of my previous experience was with companies providing services for facilities management firms, fitting air con etc., but what experience did I specifically have on the other side of the fence – managing FM firms? None. However, when has lack of experience ever prevented recruitment agencies trying to earn massive commissions by filling vacancies? By now, these agencies were running the world. Forget seeing a job advert and applying for it, now the market was all about recruitment agencies touting CVs around. It's an industry with few ethics and morals. If they can fit a square block in a round hole and earn their commission, they will do it, which is why I rarely use their services when looking to recruit.

So, what is facilities management? Modern businesses have premises with power, glass, lighting, heating, air conditioning and all these need to be maintained. Big businesses also need cleaners, security staff and other people to do work which is not really related to their core business. When businesses reach a certain size, it makes economic sense to contract these services out. That is what facilities management firms do and the industry worldwide is said to be worth about $2 trillion. In the FM industry there are two sectors which are materially different. Hard services are lighting, electricity, air conditioning etc., the physical aspects of the buildings. Soft services are personnel, from cleaners to landscapers to security staff. The two are materially different. ISS offered both as part of its portfolio.

The job they needed filling was European Operations Director, which included management of their mobile division. ISS looked after hard services for thousands of clients across Europe. At the centre of the web was a huge help desk with people taking various calls from clients saying, "Our boilers are not working," or, "Our shutters are stuck". ISS had four hundred-or-so engineers on the ground in the UK to tackle such problems, plus a huge supply chain of companies throughout Europe to do the work for them. As part of their contracts with these companies, ISS also did scheduled maintenance. My job - despite the fact I had never worked specifically as a managing agent in FM or for such a major corporation - was to ensure the technology and operational infrastructure was in place so that all the work was covered, and, as head of operations, to ensure it ran smoothly and profitably. My first thought at the initial interview was, *How am I going to look after sixteen countries when I barely speak the Queen's English?* But, as ever, my policy was, *Bite off more than you can chew and then learn how to chew fast.*

In truth, I wanted the job. For years I had worked in companies of varying sizes which were all owner-managed, and I wanted to see a different side of the coin. ISS was a business giant and I wanted to experience what working for such a corporate firm would be like. In my naivety, I thought, *If they are successful enough to employ 45,000 people in UK alone, they are going to be like a well-oiled machine, a Rolls Royce of industry, purring along powered by organisational excellence, business acumen and good practice.* Their premises certainly suggested as much: three floors of an eighteen-storey tower block on Canary Wharf, polished floors, glass offices everywhere, shiny chrome, designer desks. Their meeting room had more hi-tech kit in it than a nuclear submarine. I was thinking, *Wow, this is amazing, it's a different world, I will have some of this.* It took me about a month to realise that in your average multinational, I believe things are more chaotic and messed up than you could ever imagine.

One of the reasons they gave me the job, at a healthy £90,000 a year, was because of my operational experience, together with my experience in database technology. When I joined, they were just in the process of buying a systems platform which would oversee the whole operation. They wanted me to ensure it was fit for purpose. I knew from past experience that to do my job successfully, there were a number of things

I needed to control and I had built my systems around these. I met with the company that ISS had contracted to ensure their new system could do everything we needed it to. I gave them a list of about seventy system requirements so it could run the business properly. We went through it carefully and it could deliver about eleven of them. From past experience I knew systems designed by IT experts rarely worked in the real world, but this was a total shambles. So, I went back to ISS and said, "This system is almost useless, it doesn't have half the capacities we need and will actually make life more complicated. We should pull the plug right now."

I was told to just somehow make it work. The reason? Saving face. For months, ISS had met with the software company and discussed the deal. The software company had told them the system could do everything they needed, whether it could or not, and ISS had given the thumbs-up. It had been approved by a long list of managers and committees, the cost put in the budget, clients had been told about their new game changing software. If someone now had to report they had messed up and wasted everyone's time and money, there would be consequences. I had only been there a couple of months and I was telling them they had been sold a pup. As you can imagine that didn't go down well. *Just make it work,* was the message. I said, "OK, let's get it working as best we can and I will backfill the areas it doesn't cover with my software skills." After months of work, I managed to cobble something together which just about fit the bill.

But if you want an example of multinational corporate madness, I can do much better than that. While the software itself only cost around £60,000 – peanuts for a firm the size of ISS – the real financial cost was paying a team of consultants £800-a-day each to prepare and configure it. Before you knew where you were, you could have spent a million pounds on consultants in a matter of months. One day I noticed a sharply-suited consultant from the software company on one of our terminals, so I introduced myself and asked him what he was up to? He said, "I have a list of all the assets ISS looks after throughout Europe – lights, fire alarms, boilers, extinguishers – and I am inputting them into the system." I asked how he was doing it, and he said, "I have about ten spreadsheets, with 25,000 lines on each, and I am keying them in one by one." I almost fell off my chair. That would take him months and we were being charged £800 a day for his "expert" consultancy services. I knew the same information could be imported with some simple code, which would take me a day or two to create. For once, I was almost speechless.

When I asked why he wasn't just importing the databases he said he was only doing what he was told. I called the software company and asked what on earth was going on and they said it was a great idea to import them automatically, but ISS had not suggested that! "Well, why would they?" I shouted. "You were the experts guiding ISS."

I was working in cloud cuckoo land. The software company had sold ISS a system which was not really fit for purpose, ISS had refused to dump it because someone would lose face, and we were paying £800 a day for a consultant to do a job for months when anyone with any systems' knowledge knew it could be done in two days. The software company knew it could be done quicker but then they wouldn't earn £800 a day. Once my blood pressure had gone down a little, I candidly asked the bloke why he was doing this? He was a business consultant, intelligent, well-qualified, but he was inputting data line by line when he knew there was a better way. His answer was the saddest response any employee can give: "I know it's crap, I hate it, but it pays the bills."

Please, for the love of God, if you are doing a job to simply pay your bills, please, please find a job you enjoy. This is the foundation of one of the most valuable life tools you can adopt – the Ikigai principle. In those circumstances it says you can only have a fulfilling life if you are doing something you love and you are having an impact doing it. No-one else at ISS apparently cared enough about that £800 a day to look into it. When I raised it, I was told, "Well done, that's why we employed you, make it work."

I had only been there a few weeks and one aspect of multinationals had already slapped me across the face. In owner-managed companies the owners often worried so much about every single penny that it damaged the business. In multinationals, I found saving face was often more important than good decisions, and no-one looked after the pennies. On a global scale, those pennies mount up to millions. But that's OK, these big companies can just pass those costs onto the clients. So, we imported the data electronically. It covered more than a million pieces of equipment all over Europe. You can imagine my thoughts when I then learnt the data was eight years old and out of date. I started looking outside for bridges I could jump off. I hardly dared raise this latest debacle, but when I did the answer was predictable: "Just make it work." But, in the grand scheme of things, this problem was a pebble in the shoe compared to the major flaw of the facilities management industry.

I realised the whole industry at that time was based, to a large degree, on false promises and I will forever be grateful for ISS for revealing it to me, because without them I would never have set up Cloudfm and started changing the industry. As the saying goes, "The truth had set me free."

Now I need to carefully point out these criticisms are about the industry as a whole. ISS has hundreds of thousands of employees and a fair few of them are lawyers. I can do without being sued. ISS is a massive company and its size and longevity are testament to many of their clients being content with the services they offer. They employ some great people and I have nothing against them. I am sure their culture and working practices are different now to what I personally experienced many years ago.

The issues I identified with the FM industry in general are common to many other sectors across the globe. The problem? There is a fundamental flaw in the industry itself. To win contracts, everyone has a tendency to over-promise. If you are putting services out to tender, some which can be worth tens of millions a year, some FM companies won't just promise you the earth to win the contract, they will offer to polish it three times a week as well and be there in forty-five minutes if it breaks down. Until I later set up Cloudfm (which we will come to), if you wanted to win a contract, everyone was making such exaggerated claims over what they could potentially achieve for clients, you would never win a contract without matching such claims.

FM firms frequently sell companies levels of service which they know they will struggle to fully comply with. They are not alone in this… every company says its products are better than the competitors. For example, say an FM company has a massive client worth £12m a year, or £1m a month. They might, as part of the contract, need to perform five hundred routine maintenance tasks a month on top of any emergency work. In reality, more often than not, the contract will not be worth the paper it is written on. These firms will compile reports saying we achieved eighty-five per cent, or ninety-five per cent, of our targets. This alone is staggering. Sure, operations might be affected by the weather or other issues, but surely companies need to be meeting one hundred per cent of their obligations because that is what they have been paid for? It gets worse. How much real supervision do you think there is by the companies who pay FM firms to manage their affairs? The answer is very little. As we have seen, big companies can be as ineffective as anyone else and these things simply don't get checked. And if you are meant to have done five hundred inspection visits but you have really only done three hundred, what do you do? I know people at FM firms other than ISS whose actual job it was to alter the numbers. They were paid to sit at a terminal and fix the books. Failed to make engineer visit figures? Just add a few, no-one will know.

At ISS, I was part of a team which won a massive contract with another multinational company. They had sites in thirteen countries. As part of the contract, we were promising to have a qualified ISS engineer visit them onsite twice a week, Monday and Thursdays, at 9am. As the individual who had to manage this process, I knew we didn't even yet have an engineer in the whole country. Of course, we could try and subcontract a local engineer to do the work on our behalf, we did that all the time. However, we couldn't supervise them closely enough to promise they would be properly qualified, would do the work to our standard, turn up as promised, or that we could even find one. When I raised such issues, I was told not to make a fuss, this was a big contract. I sat in meetings with senior figures at ISS where we would have lengthy discussions about how to try and fulfil contracts which most of us realised might not actually be practically achievable in the first place. We would have meetings with prospective clients where I would tell the truth and say, "Meeting that part of the contract is going to be a real challenge for us." I would then be heavily criticised by some of my colleagues after the meeting for being too honest. "That's not how the facilities management sector works," I would frequently be told. The fact was, I needed to be less honest to survive.

After a while I would sit there in the twelfth-storey restaurant, eating a gorgeous subsidised lunch, surrounded by bright, engaging, clever and lovely people in their best suits, gazing over stupendous views of London, wondering if I was working in some strange, perverse alternative reality. I was the elephant in the room who would point out we were making promises we knew might be almost impossible to fulfil. I was the weirdo who told the truth. The truth? What a nutter! Yet again, I was a disruptor. I wasn't blind to the fact that again I was the spanner in the works. My values wouldn't fit. I was generally liked and respected by my colleagues, and most people agreed with my observations, but when I walked through the offices they could have been murmuring, "dead man walking". I knew this was only going to end one way but all I could do was try and be an influencer. I would never have taken the cash and just shut up - it was totally alien to my nature. I would rather have worked for nothing until my savings ran out, trying to change the system for the better, than blindly follow the herd. But in a multinational organisation, at my management level, I might as well have been trying to turn back the tide.

I would tell colleagues there is a better way of doing this. We didn't have to be afraid of humility, greater honesty and transparency. We could sit down with clients and be honest about what we could realistically achieve, and what the true cost would be. They thought I was mad. It was me against the world. I was at ISS for a couple of years and after six months friends at the company were saying, "I admire your bravery, but you won't last long." They weren't telling me anything I didn't know, so

I started making plans for when the axe fell. In December 2010, I was called to a meeting and there was Derrick Hidden. I had known him since my Denman days. He is one of the best people on the planet. A gem. A former Royal Navy engineer, he is naturally calm, an incredible hard-worker, reliable and a genuinely nice, easy-going guy. As part of the meeting, I took him through the system I had helped set up and improve at ISS, and afterwards we went for a coffee. He immediately asked if I had ever thought of going into business with someone? He said he was tired of working for other people and wanted to use his experience and selling skills to start a business, but he lacked the systems, technology and innovative approach to run one and thought I could bring my know-how to the table.

We talked more over the next couple of months and by February 2011 we agreed to set something up. I had been burnt in partnerships in the past, but I also knew how lonely and difficult it was running a business on my own. We could see our skills complemented each other. For example, while I had the software experience and the entrepreneurial spirit, in terms of winning clients, Derrick had the ability to keep knocking on doors until they opened and doing that just wasn't for me. More importantly, we both knew what chaos the FM industry was in and I was burning with a vision to revolutionise it. It might have existed for decades and be worth $2 trillion worldwide, but I knew a sizeable chunk of the FM industry was largely based on unrealistic promises. I didn't just want to change it, I wanted to rip it up and start again.

I knew I had the knowledge, ability and passion to change things and I had this vision of forming a company based on four simple principles – integrity, empathy, freedom and humility – and the benefits they could bring. Those principles don't sound too unreasonable but when I talked about them, people looked at me like I had come to work dressed as Ronald MacDonald.

Based on the systems I had set up for Denman, Auxilia and ISS, in 2006 I had created a holistic system, messing about in my garage, to manage the FM process. I thought it looked great but I needed something to test it on. So, I had set up a company called InformLive (a special purpose vehicle), and approached the charity Age UK to look after its FM affairs. In 2006, it had six hundred shops across the UK, was spending £3m a year on FM, and had a team of eleven people running it. I approached them, explained what the technology could do, and they signed up. InformLive initially had one employee, my wife Michelle, and we charged them a £30,000 a year management fee which was her salary. We then looked after their FM twenty-four hours a day, seven days a week, and they were able to re-deploy ten of the eleven staff that previously ran the estate. In the first year we saved them £1.1m, reducing their spend from £3m to £1.9m, and continued to maintain that saving for the next five years. The technology and processes worked and were an overwhelming success!

I then brought in my daughter Kelly to assist her Mum and teach Kelly the business. She had been the manager at a huge Yates bar in Colchester for the previous few years and hated the unsociable hours. She had learnt a lot about people, management, and human behaviour. She was cool and calm in all situations and it was a pleasure to watch her develop.

I knew I had the knowledge, enthusiasm and drive to help change the FM industry, and I also had the software to do it. But to properly understand the changes I wanted to make, it helps to know more about the madness that the FM industry was suffering from. You could fill a library with the rip-offs and faults, but in the next chapter we will just look at a couple of fundamental ones. In 2020, the world was still mired in turmoil.

COVID May 2020:

Looking ahead

Let's forget business for a second. During this time when we were looking ahead at balance sheets and the future of the company, around the UK, thousands of people were dying. That was something we never forgot. The human cost of the virus was horrific and while, thankfully, my immediate family escaped such tragedies, our wider business family did not. We did not lose anyone on our staff, but two colleagues lost relatives and others lost friends.

When we knew this had happened, we had support systems in place to help those affected as best we could. Family must always come first. However, it was obvious our working landscape would radically change after the country began to lift lockdown restrictions. The entire casual dining sector was on furlough, which was the only thing keeping businesses afloat. In May, no-one knew what might happen when this life support was eventually switched off, and it was our job on the senior team to look at all the possible alternatives. What would we do if businesses stayed closed until December? Which of our clients would survive? How would we? When, and if, restaurants and other stores did re-open what would their capacity be? There was talk of a two-metre social distancing rule which would have meant most restaurants and other establishments could only operate at thirty per cent capacity. There was no point in most re-opening at all like that, they would simply lose money.

Thankfully, we got the word from our secret politician that if the impact of the virus continued to decline, pubs and restaurants would probably open in July with a one-metre system in place. This would allow them to return at seventy per cent capacity, which could be profitable. It was a game-changer for the industry but we were not naïve enough to believe things would go back to normal. Every restaurant company in the country was looking at its books, knowing savings would have to be made. Would customers want to go out? Was there any point in keeping restaurants open which had low profits before the epidemic? Would some major chains simply collapse anyway?

The senior exec team and I spent weeks on countless video conferences, calculating endless worst-case, medium-case and best-case scenarios and how we would have to react to each. We played out every possible scenario. What would our incomes be, our expenses, our cashflow? How could we best tailor the company to meet these new demands? We went through every possible scenario and made plans over how to best deal with the outcome. I named the way we tackled this as **The 5 Rs** and it is applicable in many times of crisis.

1 Resolve: Take immediate steps to secure and protect the business. Get a thorough picture of where the company stands financially. Communicate with staff, keep them in the loop and engage positively and clearly with suppliers, customers and stakeholders, from banks to business partners.

2 Resilience: Tighten the purse strings, stop or renegotiate payments where appropriate. Get a clear insight where the company balance sheet will be three or four months down the line. Work out the best, mid- and worst-case scenarios for how the company will be affected in the longer term. Communicate, communicate, communicate.

3: Return: Start planning on how the company will return to operations, which in COVID's case included the right health and safety environment being in place. Look for new opportunities for short-term revenues, make sure staff have the right priorities and tasks in place and everyone is ready to re-engage with customers and suppliers. Have contingency plans in place to meet all their differing needs.

4: Reimagination: Reimagine what the next "normal" will be and what the implications are for everyone involved with your business. What are the opportunities and threats and how will you tackle them?

5: Reform: Think radically. Would a whole new business model better meet the new reality? What can you do to make sure you rise stronger from the crisis?

Time spent in preparation is rarely wasted, even if most of our calculations would prove not to be required. It may be a cliché but if you **fail to prepare, prepare to fail.**

England rugby world cup winning coach Sir Clive Woodward and I.

I was once talking to Sir Clive Woodward, the England Rugby Union coach, who was at the helm when England won the Rugby World Cup in 2003. England's fly-half, Johnny Wilkinson, kicked a drop goal in the last minute to win the match. I said, "How lucky was that?" and he answered there was no luck, Wilkinson had practised and trained for that type of situation for months and months. The most professional people train for all eventualities, however unlikely it is they might happen. So, that's what we did, we prepared. We produced a shelf-load of different solutions to match the various scenarios over what state the industry would be in when business re-started. On the shelves we had solutions already in place.

Ultimately, we had two options. We could tinker and tamper with the company and try to respond to different scenarios as they arose, or we could look upon the crisis as an opportunity to make long-term material changes which would benefit us, whatever the future brought. The truth was we had entered the crisis as a £60m business. If our customers lost sixty per cent capacity, suddenly we were a £20m business, whatever happened. We knew our staffing levels were unfortunately too high and our business structure needed amending. We were unanimous: it was time to make major changes. We wanted to keep as many people on as possible but there was always the risk we would not be able to do that - the situation was entirely out of our control. We knew people would feel exposed and at risk but we could only do what we could do and there were always going to be people hurt by it.

Chapter 11

Beginning the revolution

Let's pretend you are running a major telecoms company. You have suspicions that, despite their £10m contract, your FM company is failing to fulfil its obligations even though you are getting monthly reports claiming they are spit-shining all your equipment so hard you need sunglasses to look at it. They tell you they are doing three-monthly maintenance checks on your phone masts, as per the contract. You decide to spend a few quid on a consultant to check. He discovers half of the phone masts have bird's nests growing on them and are so covered in bird shit it is obvious they haven't been visited for years. A quick look at your other dusty and unmaintained assets proves the FM company is either lying to itself, or to you. In terms of ripping off customers, that's nothing. Here's a couple of real-world examples I am aware of, none of which were linked to ISS.

Engineers would be sent to a job and would say a compressor has broken. Under the typical terms of their contract, they would charge for the replacement parts, plus ten per cent, and then £35 an hour for labour. They would quote £1,200 for a new compressor, add the ten per cent, charge them six hours of labour and give them a bill for £1,520. In reality, however, the compressor would only cost £400. If that's not bad enough, because the client had no competency or system to check these costs, and they didn't have the capacity to police every quote, they were unaware the compressor was only six months old, still under warranty and would be replaced by the manufacturer for nothing. The company had been charged £1,520 for a £210 job. Sound bad? That happened all the time. It was typically how one company made its margin. They had to lie. They only won the contract by giving a price they knew they could never make money on.

As for those hourly repair rates, they are also hugely flawed. The market sets the hourly rate they will pay for engineers. If they set this at £30 an hour, you might be the best engineer on the planet but if you ask for £40 an hour you will never get a job. The other issue is the client can set the hourly rate, but what they don't know is how long that job should take. A good company will do it in two hours and cost them £60, a bad company will do it in four hours and cost them £120. The problem is the good company is not making any money working quickly at £30 an hour so they would say it took them four as well. The industry worked like that for decades, charging for more hours than were worked.

Another example? In the air conditioning and refrigeration world, you hate the peak of summer. It is when all the equipment breaks down because it is poorly-maintained, gets dirty and when the weather gets hot the machines can't cope. If you can imagine, you have just enough engineers to meet the normal demand, so in summer you are screwed because you would need four times as many people. As soon as it gets really hot, every single client is then screaming blue murder because their air con or fridges are failing. An engineer can normally attend and repair three or four breakdowns a day. But now they would have to do twenty visits a day to meet demand. So, the company sends an engineer, tells them to spend five minutes there, say the compressor is broken and needs replacing without even really looking for a fault. This means the engineer can do twenty jobs in a day and buys the company some time because the clients know it takes a while for a new compressor to arrive. The engineers would then eventually return a few days later when the volume of calls is lower, fix the real problem, which might be something tiny like a blocked filter, and charge the company £1,500 for a "new compressor". It's theft and its commonplace.

A third example. When you are quoting for air con, you do a heat-load calculation. Simplified, you work out the size of the room and how much cooling power you need. You always base this on the hottest period of the year, so all the client's air con needs are covered. If you need 25 kilowatts of cooling, you install two 12.5 kilowatt units and however hot the weather gets, you have matched the room's needs. But as everyone is quoting as low as possible for the job, you need to find an edge. So, you quote for two 12.5 kilowatt units but you only install two 10 kilowatt units which are twenty per cent cheaper. You know the client is never going to refer to the model number of a Japanese air con unit to see what its capacity is. The two 10 kilowatt units will work fine for ninety per cent of the year, except during the hottest couple of weeks. If they fail, the client complains, and the engineer goes out and says, "There's a fault with the drain pump. Don't worry, we will replace it for nothing, but it will take a couple of weeks for the part to arrive." In fact, there is nothing wrong at all, the machines simply can't cope during the hot spell and the engineer is just buying time for a few weeks until the weather cools and the machines run fine.

Those are three real world examples of typical unethical behaviour from different companies and, believe me, they are just a drop in the ocean. This sort of dishonesty is like a cancer in the industry. Even at a massive firm like ISS we used to joke we needed to take three things to meetings with clients - a laptop, a PowerPoint presentation and a Yellow Pages to shove down the back of your trousers so your arse didn't hurt after they spent two hours kicking it. About ninety per cent of meetings were simply the client telling you how shit you were, the lies you had told, what a bad job you were doing and threatening to pull the contract. And the sad thing is, they were right.

Back to your telecoms firm. After shouting down the phone at the lying FM company, quite rightly you decide to cancel their contract, give the FM firm the boot and tender for a replacement. Now the old company could not do the work for £10m, but all the companies tendering for the contract will tell you they can do it for £9m. Their sales team will sit there and assure you they have the capacity to do the work for less because of some bullshit about "strategic strength, added value or international infrastructure". In truth, the FM company doesn't hugely care about the details of the contract - it could be the most onerous one in the world - they will barely have looked at it. They just want that £9m contract for their commission, their company's turnover and their bonuses, and to give their company the illusion of growth. Perhaps most importantly, they are desperate to win new contracts because their poor performance means they keep losing other ones.

The company promises your contract will be staffed by a dedicated, independent team whose sole responsibility will be to ensure your needs are met. That all sounds perfect, so you sign them up. After all, you are going to get a better service and save £1m. Happy days. The first thing the new FM company does is look at its own costings and knows it has cut so many corners to tender at £9m it will struggle to make a profit. So, that dedicated team? Forget it. The work gets lumped onto a team already struggling to meet its obligations with another client. The FM firm told you it had access to a top team of contractors. Some companies will bill you contractor time by the hour, so if they work one hour ten minutes, you get billed for two hours. Your new company boasts it will charge you by the half-hour, or even the quarter-hour. But none of that solves the fundamental problem the contractor only gets paid for time worked, and so some do everything in their power to be "flexible" with their time sheets. If they are getting paid by the half-hour, how many engineers do you think break sweat to get the job done in twenty-nine minutes?

After a year, you look at how things are going and discover the work so far has not cost £9m, it has cost you £13m. You ring the FM company and scream, "You have hung me out to dry, my CFO is going to sack me, you have totally screwed me over."

The FM provider hits back and says when they started work, they noticed huge parts of the original contract were not accurate in terms of the work which needed doing, so they had to spend more money. The account might be £4m over budget but it is your fault. In reality, however, you probably won't find out after a year, the massive, or maybe that particular, shock comes further down the line. Initially, you are told things are running to budget but suddenly you find massive overspends occurring. The reason is the accountancy process the FM firm uses is still in the stone age. You suddenly start getting unexpected bills for work done twelve months or even two years ago. What do you do? You have another screaming fit, get the lawyers involved. You cancel the contract and start the exact same process again. You go out to tender, firms promise the £9m contract can be done for £8m and the cycle goes on.

The golden rule in life is: **if you want different results, you need to do things differently.** You cannot do the same thing over and over again and expect a different outcome. That is just simply unintelligent.

The traditional FM relationship is stuck in a cycle of self-destruction. Clients procure services the same way but expect different results. And it is not just the FM providers doing things the wrong way. Client FM managers tend to focus on the detail, not the big picture. They might have a £20m contract but rather than worrying if they are wasting millions of pounds, they obsess about a dishwasher which has broken down three times in a week. **Even as intelligent people, we still stupidly focus on cost and not value.** The FM companies waste time and money constantly fixing the same problems again and again without coming up with solutions. A constantly broken dishwasher is a perfect, tiny example of the massive issue facing traditional FM companies and their clients. The FM company never bothers to find out why it keeps breaking down, which is probably something simple like cutlery keeps being thrown into the bottom of the machine, which is where all the mechanisms are. They remove the cutlery and declare victory, rather than finding a solution to stop the cutlery hitting the machinery.

My vision was to change the industry from the bottom up because doing things radically differently is the only chance you have of getting a different result. How would we achieve that? My vision for Derrick's and my new company was to do things very differently from day one. We were going to tear up the template and do things the right way. That cycle of self-destruction? Procure the same old way, focus on the detail, fix the same problem time and again? We simply step away from it. Then, from the outside, we look in to see what everyone is doing wrong. We look at the root cause of problems rather than obsessing about the issues themselves. We look at long-term solutions and abandon short termism.

This change in emphasis begins at the very start. If your telecoms company sends us a tender document, it goes straight in the bin. Instead we ring you and say, "Sorry, we don't do tenders. If you insist on it as part of your company rules, then we are the wrong people for you. We would suggest you go and talk to the other companies and do things the same way you have for twenty years. When it all goes wrong again, you know where we are."

The reason we don't tender? When a company puts its services out to tender and says it has ten thousand assets, no-one ever checks how many assets it actually has because it's too expensive to do so! The client's information is usually the worst on the planet. It changes daily, stores shut down, others open, kit gets swapped out. The asset list is always wrong and if you tender on that basis, the first day you start work you are buggered. They say they have ten thousand fire extinguishers to safety check and in fact they have twelve thousand. Your budget is out of the window and you start shouting at each other.

The intelligent companies then ask us, "If you don't tender, what it is you do instead?" We say, "OK, we need all your FM data, and not the data your current FM provider has given you because that will be wrong. We don't even want your own data because that is probably worse. We need to sit down with your accounts team and look at every single transaction you have paid out of your bank account for FM services over the last couple of years." You can guarantee the company won't have that data compiled, so we sit down and go through their purchase ledgers so we both know exactly what they have spent, what they have spent it on, and only then we can agree what their true FM costs and assets are. We do this consultancy work for free and with big clients, this process can take a few weeks to a couple of months to complete. They are inevitably shocked at the outcome. From that data, we have an indisputable set of figures from which everything can be measured. We can work out their average job value and give them precise figures on what the contract will cost.

Simply by working through that process, seeing our professionalism and the clarity we have given them over their own operation, they begin to feel extremely confident in our knowledge and experience. This quickly generates more openness, we can talk about areas of the business, and deal, we both feel vulnerable about, and the end result is a foundation of trust before the contract is even signed. We have rarely gone through this whole process and not won the client's FM business. That clarity also means we have never had a disagreement with a client because, from the first day we start working with them, we have agreed a baseline of work and cost which we agree to do as a starting point. Another difference? We advise the new clients that the period of mobilisation is non-negotiable, we will not start the contract early under any circumstances. What inevitably happens in the rest of the industry – and what happened to us with one of our early contracts before we knew better - is when FM companies discover they have lost contracts they stop supporting the client. The new FM company then gets a call saying, "We are in the shit, our existing FM supplier has walked away, things aren't getting fixed and we need you to start next week."

Most companies say, "OK, we will step in now," but they haven't got enough staff, the whole relationship starts off badly and the client starts complaining about the service it is getting. We refuse to mobilise early. This will also allow us to recruit the necessary staff to meet the contract and fully train them. This is a line in the sand and we will not cross it. By refusing to get involved before we are ready, we prolong our relationship with clients because from day one we provide exactly the service they require. If we are ready to sign a contract, we approach that differently too. Traditional FM companies might win a three-year contract. In the first year they do a decent job but in the second year they start getting paranoid, worrying if the client doesn't renew after the next year they might not have made any money, and so they start cutting back on their investment. Work starts to be prioritised, they might concentrate on ensuring the client's premises are legally complaint with health and safety, but they start cutting cut back on routine maintenance. Because of this, the work and the relationship start to crumble and year three ends up being a shit-show for everyone. The client is unhappy, sacks the FM provider and the cycle starts again.

At Cloudfm the intention is to always be transparent from the very start. We say to the clients, "You are currently spending £10m a year on FM and these are your requirements. Based on the data we have put together and agreed upon, in the first year we will spend £9m meeting these obligations, in the second year £8m and in the third year £7.5m." And here is the killer touch. We tell them if we don't meet those targets, we will give you back the difference. If in year one we spend £9.5m instead of £9m, we will write you a cheque for £500,00. We guarantee how much they are going to spend. The clients love this because, all of a sudden, they perceive all the risk is shifting from them to us. But we know, because of the data, exactly what needs to be done and what it will cost. Obviously, there are caveats and white lines which have to be followed. If a hurricane sweeps through central London and destroys fifty of their restaurants, obviously the FM spend will go up. A more realistic caveat might be if they have an oven with a six-year life expectancy but which is fifteen years old, we are not going to be penalised for having to go and fix it every day if it keeps breaking. The client will be advised on the first visit that this kit needs to be replaced or will have to be excluded from the baseline measurement.

All clients want three things,

- Budget certainty
- Quality
- Legal Compliance

When I meet potential clients, I stand up on stage and make a controversial statement. I say, "I have never met a client in my forty-year career that wanted to cut costs." They sit there and look at me like I am an alien, thinking, *What on earth is he talking about, everyone wants to reduce cost?*

After a pause I will say, "What every single client I have worked with in forty years has wanted to do is to control cost, because if you can control it, you can increase it, keep it the same or reduce it."

Everyone chases around chanting, "Reduce cost, reduce cost, reduce cost," but they are chasing the wrong rabbit. To manage things properly, you have to control your costs and we are the first people to have given them the ability, through technology and culture, to allow them to do this. That three-year contract cycle? At Cloudfm, we seek to extend contracts right after the first year which means we can always focus on investment. It also helps that we know after the first year the clients will be astounded by the differences we have made. We want long-term, mutually beneficial partnerships and so we tell our clients our contracts always follow a similar cycle.

Year one we call 'Control'. Here we do the work we have agreed is required, get proper hands-on control of the operation, save the client money, and amass the data we need to see where things can be improved. In year two, which we call 'Learning', we have built up a forensically detailed picture of the business and its culture. We then start to put together feasibility studies on where the client can invest some of the money which we have saved them to improve their infrastructure. Year three we call 'Excellence' where all that data and knowledge is put together to help clients achieve excellence in every facet of their FM business.

Cloudfm was set up to be revolutionarily different. That's a claim made by every single FM company and you normally only find out they are deluded when they are twelve months into a contract and you find they have failed. The industry is based on broken promises. The difference with Cloudfm is we actually do what we say we will do. The key to this process is our technology and the total transparency it gives both parties. In the old days, if something went wrong in a shop, you would call your FM provider and a contractor would turn up eventually, fiddle about and six months later you would get a bill for the work they had done, with details of the job scribbled on the back of a fag packet. With our system, when the problem occurs, it can be logged onto our system directly from any computer or an App or via our helpdesk. If we promise an engineer will be there in four hours he will be, or on the rare occasion he isn't, you will get a call explaining the delay and given a new time of arrival. When they arrive, the engineer will log on the minute he steps through the door and then update the system in real time on the problem he has found, if the machine is in warranty, what needs doing to it, the cause of the fault, how it might be prevented, how long the repair took and he will log off the minute he leaves. You will be charged for his time by the minute. If he needs to order parts for a repair, the system will tell you which parts are required, when they will arrive, where they are from, what they will cost and when he will return to install them. From the second something goes wrong, right through to paying the bill, the client gets total visibility over what is happening and when. And that visibility is total, everyone sees everything. The contractor, the client, ourselves. We all look at exactly the same data. If a fridge seal goes in a restaurant, typically there are more than fifty steps and checks that the repair process might go through from someone originally recording the problem to the bill being paid. We share all that data and do it for more than half a million jobs a year. That is why the rest of the industry is in such a mess - no-one can control the data flow like we can or give clients the visibility they need and want.

Another problem in the industry is auditing. Traditionally, it relies on sample testing. The client might have one thousand fire extinguishers which need compliance checks. The FM company says it has done the work, but the client doesn't have the time, or money, to go to every job to ensure it has been carried out. So, instead, they will do a sample of fifty and cross their fingers over the other nine hundred and fifty. Because at the core of our work are monthly maintenance visits by our own engineers, we offer one hundred per cent audits. As soon as our engineers get on site, they know through our technology all the jobs which have been done by independent contractors since their last visit. They then go and look at the job and score its quality and even take photographs of it. They also speak to the manager to ask, "Were you happy with the contractor's conduct and behaviour and how quickly they got the job done?" Every job is marked out of one hundred and if it scores less than seventy a report is immediately sent to whoever supplied the contractor. You might think this means we are constantly falling out with suppliers and contractors but it's not the case. If we bring new suppliers on, we usually find out within a few weeks who is failing and normally it is about culture and attitude rather than competence. We sometimes get contractors who are not very good but have a great attitude and if that is the case, we will teach those companies how to improve their performance.

And backing that up even further? Our data cannot be edited, it can't be tampered with. Remember how the big boys were simply editing data to make it show they had done far more work than they had claimed? Our data can't be altered by anyone, deleted by anyone, or hidden by anyone. As a spurious example, if the engineer wrote on the job report the site manager had been an unhelpful idiot, the big firms would edit the paperwork because they didn't like the phrase "unhelpful idiot" and didn't want to upset the client. In our world, once he has typed "unhelpful idiot" it is there in real time for the world to see, it is there forever and no-one can delete it. What we will do however is educate the engineer not to say "unhelpful idiot" but instead say the site manager was "not too helpful".

To control your costs, you also need up to date financial reporting. Most companies send clients summary monthly operational and financial reports (referred to as MI reports) which is where a lot of the data tampering comes in. Our financial data is reported weekly and comes straight off the technology. It is not altered by a human being. If the client wants to see why £80,000 was spent in week twenty five, they simply click on it and it shows them precisely where every penny was spent. If £3,000 was spent at your Keswick site, click on that and it will show you what the problem was, when it was reported, what the engineer's name was, how long he was there, what work he did, where the parts came from and what they cost, when the bill was submitted, when it was paid, together with the report by our maintenance engineer who then checked the work. Total and utter clarity.

And the other important thing about our technology? It does exactly what we say it can do. As Cloudfm became increasingly successful, the industry language changed. Everyone else used to boast about the size of their business, the coverage they offered, value engineering and spout every other business buzzword they could think of. *Value engineering* and *value added* were the biggest favourites. It was all nonsense. Now, every company in the FM sector makes the same technology promises we do but not one of them can deliver on it. Their technology inevitably isn't up to scratch or used properly. Their data can be edited to fix the books. But, most importantly, their mindset is still stuck in the past – "Win the contract and we will worry about the rest later." Of course, we have to be realistic and candid. This culture has been massively influenced by the clients and the market. This is because we have created a world of 'cost down' from dawn to dusk.

The other massive advantage of our data is that it also shows our clients how they can actually save money and get huge returns from their FM spend. For example, our data will show they are spending £100,000 a year on cleaning drains. We then carry out full feasibility studies into how to solve the problem. We will then say if you spend £200,000 installing proper grease traps, you will never have blocked drains again. The client might blanche at the extra spending – we understand that – and that is why we underwrite such projects. We simply say to the client, "If spending that money does not save you £300,000 over the next three years, we will write you a cheque and reimburse you the difference." Needless to say, we never have to write out cheques because our data shows us what the savings will be. But technology is just half the solution, you need people and the right culture. How are we different? Again, it starts from day one. Every time we win a contract, we organise a conference for everyone involved in the FM work we will be managing, the client stakeholders, the suppliers, the contractors, the bloke who sweeps the floors. They all receive a ten-page document in plain English setting out our standards and how we expect them to work. We call this our SLD (Service Level Document)

We tell contractors their work is going to be checked on our monthly engineer visits, we explain exactly how they have to use our technology and we incentivise good performance and penalise bad. This approach was born out of my upbringing. I was always taught, and life has shown me countless times since, **if there is no consequence to bad behaviour, bad behaviour will continue.** Think back to being a child. If you screamed and shouted every time you wanted a biscuit, and you got a biscuit as a result, there would be a lot of screaming and shouting going on. Instead, I was taught the only way to get a biscuit was to ask politely. I have taken that simple principle forward from childhood to business. Bad behaviour has to have consequences.

Those four-hour call-out windows? If the contractors fail to reach the job in four hours, they pay a three per cent penalty charge. If they were going to charge us £100 for the job, they can only charge us £97. Losing £3 doesn't hurt them, but it pokes them in the side, reminds them of our standards. If they hit the four-hour target ninety per cent of the time, they receive other benefits, such as faster invoice payments. Any engineer worth his salt wants to maintain their professional reputation. As for the ones who are consistently late, we have the precise data to show why we no longer want to work with them.

At our headquarters we even had our own engineers' academy. For example, if a restaurant chain becomes our new client, we will build replicas of their kitchens with the special equipment they use. We then train all our engineers and our contractors how to use the equipment and how to fix it. Remember how I was once told to fix a dry-cleaning machine and didn't even know how to open it? If a contractor or engineer of ours walks onto a site, he will know what equipment is there and how to repair it. First fix rates are a common measure in the FM industry, which is basically if something breaks down, how many times does it get repaired on the first visit. The industry average is sixty-six per cent, ours is eighty-eight per cent. We also train people on customer service and to have an appreciation of the client's business. Our contractors don't walk onto a site, suck air through their teeth and say, "Who last fixed this oven, mate? It's a botch job, going to take me four days to get a replacement part," and saunter out again. Our contractors and engineers appreciate we are in a partnership with the client and it isn't just a broken oven, it's a damaged cog in the whole restaurant production line and, without it working, the client has a massive headache. Having that knowledge, and that attitude, is crucial.

The revolution even carries on when the job is complete. Invoicing is a massive problem in the industry. We have taken over contracts where the company is still receiving invoices from its old FM provider two or three years down the line. One received a consolidated invoice for £900,000 nine months after the contract had ended. This places the client's finance teams under immense pressure, consumes a huge amount of time and attacks the client's current budgets. Our solution was simple. All of our contractors have to agree if they do not invoice within seventy-five days of completing the job the cost is written off. Our technology constantly reminds them the invoice needs to be submitted. If we are approaching seventy-five days without receiving it, they get a deluge of emails and phone calls. It not only protects the clients from receiving uncontrolled invoices months down the line, it encourages the supply chain to invoice much quicker and stimulates the contractor's own cash flow. Yet again, it's a win/win and all about control. The client knows what has been spent, why, and by who. They have control over the process.

Those are just a couple of basic examples of how we intended to do things differently and these differences extend to almost every part of our operations. From day one of Cloudfm, I vowed never to go to a meeting needing a *Yellow Pages* in my trousers. I didn't need to - honesty and accurate data was enough. The rest of the industry pretended everything was perfect and lied when it wasn't but we had a completely different outlook. I didn't want to just make money and create a firm we could sell in ten years' time for £100m - I wanted to change an industry. But first we just needed to set up a firm, and win clients, to prove it to. Years later, in 2020, we were struggling to save the very thing we had created.

COVID late May 2020:

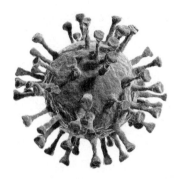

Engineering a solution

In my heart, I am still an engineer. It's how I started, and our team of one hundred and thirty engineers was at the coalface of everything Cloudfm had achieved. Because we employed the engineers directly, unlike most FM firms, customers got clarity of service and the monthly engineer visits created stickiness which helped us to retain our major clients. However, with huge uncertainty over how business operations would return in the months after lockdown, keeping one hundred and thirty on the payroll was simply not feasible. Engineers need to be kept busy one hundred per cent of the time or losses soon mount up. Something had to change.

The company had two divisions, Integrated Services (the main part of the company), and Shared Services (the engineers).

We had long known the profit margin in Shared Services was quite low but, while we were constantly growing, this had been acceptable. However, now we were examining every facet of the business and seeking growth after the crisis, it was time to look at its future. We asked ourselves what would happen if we sold Shared Services to a third party? We would get some money – much less now COVID was still in full swing compared to a couple of months before – but, more importantly, we would lose control of the engineering service we offered customers that created such a great offering. In the long term, that could put the whole company at risk.

However, we did know we were employing a number of highly-skilled people who had sought, and received, great business experience as they looked to grow to new roles in the company. Could some of these people be budding entrepreneurs?

The solution dawned. What if we fished out these people and helped them establish their own businesses rather than working directly for us? These people had been on leadership courses, engaged with clients and suppliers and were looking to develop their skill sets. If we helped set them up as independent companies with guaranteed work from us, they would then be reliant on us, and would know how we operated and the high levels of service we require and within the culture we had all developed.

We could also solve the problems which normally prevent people from setting up their own business. These are the fear of not making enough money and losing their savings and their house. New companies do not know who their clients are going to be, if they can get credit with their suppliers, how they are going to afford vans, where they can employ other engineers from. These are all major barriers to starting a business, and our proposal overcame all of them. It was similar to the help I received when I started my first business and got help from Dirk at Cargill. We would help them set up in their own companies, guarantee them an income, would act as guarantors for their creditors when they needed to buy equipment and we could also provide them with the engineers they would need from our staff by moving them to these new companies, while maintaining the terms and conditions of their existing contracts (known as TUPEing).

From our perspective, we knew the people leading these firms had the skills to do it, we knew they would work their socks off and their engineers would constantly be kept busy working on jobs for us as they wouldn't want to pay them for being slack. We also worked out it was costing us £48 an hour to have an engineer on the road, but if we moved to this partnership system, the new company owners could earn more money than they currently did, but at a cost to us of £38 an hour – a saving of £10 an hour. It was a win/win. Of course, it wasn't an easy process, there were long consultations, we had engineers from Cornwall to the north of Scotland and Ireland to look after. We had to look at how clients would react, and the administration side of things was horrific. We also had to check with all our suppliers to make sure they were happy to provide equipment to these new customers with our guarantee. It was a monster job but in the end it all made sense.

With those savings spread across our entire engineering department, we had created an impressive margin which was not there before while, most importantly, we kept the same control and level of service because these engineers knew our culture, rules, standards and working practice. Of course, we could have tried to do this before, but the fact is when you are successfully sailing a ship across the Atlantic with a valuable cargo, you don't stop it in the middle of the ocean and try to rebuild the ship. However, COVID created the environment where we had to make such major decisions. There were many more to follow. Just nine years earlier I was setting up the business we were now trying to save.

Chapter 12

A bumpy start

My end at ISS was profitable and relatively painless. A new boss came in and demanded I stopped raising potential issues in meeting our obligations to clients. I said I had a problem doing that, she said she had a problem with me, and I walked away with a £40,000 cheque.

Derrick and I said, "OK, let's do this," and I started thinking up names and came up with iCloudfm. I would like to say I had seen into the future and realised one day much of the world's data would be centrally stored in 'the cloud' and could be linked to any machine on the planet. However, neither Apple nor Microsoft had even revealed the concept yet. My thinking was more along the lines of we were aiming high and our vision for the FM industry was so out there most people would think we had our head in the clouds. Anyway, I liked it, registered the name and iCloudfm was born. As you can guess, a year or so later when Apple launched its own iCloud they had a few issues with our name, and that's another story.

From the very start I had a vision of the principles the company would hold – largely based on all the bad practices I had seen before. These were, and still are, the bedrock of our success.

Integrity: We would be entirely trustworthy and do what we said.

Humility: We would always admit to clients if we got something wrong and work with them to fix it.

Empathy: To actually listen to clients and understand and truly care about their needs.

Freedom: The freedom to explore new ways of doing business, the freedom to fail, and the freedom to try new things.

The plan was for Derrick to continue to work for his employer (SGP) but start contacting prospective clients, while I would go to my villa in Portugal and enhance my technology which everything relied upon, and rebrand it to the new name. I already knew the barebones were in place and worked because it had been used by AgeUK, Denman,

Auxilia, Middleton and then ISS, but it needed a major upgrade to work with far bigger clients. Derrick and I agreed iCloudfm would start trading on January 1, 2012, and in June 2011, Derrick started knocking on doors and we started having meetings with prospective customers.

Derrick and I at Silverstone in 2016.

Initially our approach was as revolutionary as our vision for the whole industry. Similar to what many energy companies do now, we would say to prospective clients, "We will save you money and then go 50/50 on the savings." This was great in principle. Say a company had FM costs of £10m, their eyes lit up when we said we could do the work for £5m. But when they realised that they would then have to write us a cheque for £2.5m reality dawned. They said no finance director on the planet could stomach writing a cheque for £2.5m even if we had saved them £5m. Entrepreneurially, the idea was a no-brainer with yet another win/win outcome, but doors were shutting in our face every single time. We didn't understand why they could not see the benefits but soon realised this approach was never going to fly. We went back to the drawing board and formulated our new approach. This came in the form of an AJV (Average Job Value). This totally ignored prospective client's asset lists, which we knew would be wrong, and instead we learnt how much the companies had been spending over the last three years on FM to keep their buildings open. We would then look at how many sites they had and how much work had been carried out. Crudely, this gave us the AJV - total Client FM spend, divided by the number of jobs carried out. We would break this down into separate categories and analyse how much contractors had been charging companies for certain jobs. No-one had ever carried out this type of detailed analysis before signing a contract and every single time it would reveal their AJV was always sky-high, say £350. We would offer to charge them £300 per job instead. Their eyes invariably lit up.

We also decided we would not approach firms whose FM costs were less than £4m because, with smaller FM spends, the client management team would struggle to let go of their control and their expectations were almost always unreasonable. In addition, it did not meet our philosophy of securing a small number of large clients. To change a £200 billion industry, you would need to consistently demonstrate material benefits to get people to stand up and listen. Working with companies with a smaller spend would not help us do that. We were pitching to people like Clarks Shoes, Whitbread, and were punching well above

The fabricated office we set up in Wokingham to impress potential clients.

our weight. Derrick still had a full-time job and our technology was not finished. We had no real infrastructure behind us and no offices other than a room we could borrow on an industrial estate in Wokingham and set up to look like we had a real business operation.

I was working from my shed in the garden. Canary Wharf seemed a long way away.

I left ISS in June 2011 and said to Derrick I was going to Portugal for three months to stay in a villa which we had started renting for next to nothing. I would try and perfect the technology, rebrand it all to iCloudfm, and get it up and running properly by January 2012. I had a little 6mg internet line in the villa so it was a painful process, but I knew I could get it done. I had been in Portugal for three weeks when Derrick phoned me up and said the clothing retailer Republic was interested in our new company. We held a series of meetings and despite not really being ready, signed a contract to take control of their FM operations on January 1. We were delighted: *Bring out the champagne!* Before our company was meant to start trading, we had a national retailer in the bag. It was the first concrete evidence we had that our plan could work. It was a massive weight off our shoulders.

A few days later - and this will come as no surprise to you now - Derrick called and said, "Republic are in the shit, they need us sooner. Their existing FM provider has thrown its toys out of the pram and I have agreed we will start the contract on September 1." That was typical Derrick, take the money and worry about it later. I was screaming, "You are having a laugh, aren't you? We have promised them transparency and we haven't even got a system yet." Taking the contract early flew in the face of all the principles we would later stand by, but this was our first ever client and we hadn't even really started the company yet. As for our technology, thankfully my philosophy was to build the bike while you are riding it and, in the time I had left, I managed to cobble something together which we could improve upon later.

Unfortunately, I had a major problem. Every FM company is utterly reliant on a fifty-two week planner so it can schedule its planned preventative maintenance – to stop things breaking - and compliance work. Every fire system needs to be checked twice a year, your contract says you have to maintain air con twice a year etc. Creating such a planner should not have been rocket science - it's a two-dimensional grid. On a chart you have the assets on the left, the week numbers across the top, and dots going across saying which PPM needs doing when. I had years of experience with code, I had set up countless systems, adapted one for a multinational company, but I simply could not get this sodding planner to work in the way I wanted it to. I was tearing my hair out. I had done a crude work-around, but it just wasn't effective. It was a bit like having designed and built an ocean liner but somehow, I could not get the lifeboats to float. I had already talked to my friend Andy who looked after my servers and who was also an experienced coder. He would say, "Try this script, try that one," but we could never come up with a solution. It was killing me. One day in early December 2011, my younger brother Paul rang up and said, "There is a bloke in the village called James Blackman and he does what you do – sits in his dressing gown all day writing code and messing about on computers. He is looking for work, so do you mind if I put you two in touch?"

I said, "No problem," and called him, and we soon realised we were doing the same sort of work. Having previously worked as a software consultant in London on £400 a day, he had set up his own company and designed the software system for a charity. The charity had subsequently gone bust and he was out of work. We met up the next day and I told him about some of the other problems I had experienced with my software which I had solved with Andy's help. He knew all about them. It turned out Andy lived next door to him and had been constantly popping round asking him for advice every time I had a problem. I said to James, "I have a challenge for you. I need to get this planner built properly," and he said he would have a look at it and get back to me. He came round three days later, fired up his computer and asked, "Is this what you meant?" He had built the entire thing in three days. He had smashed it out of the park. I knew there and then he was the answer to our software issues. I had self-learnt programming and solved almost every problem I needed to with code. But I was not naive to the fact that my architecture would need to be replaced within the next few years and was not going to be scalable. James was the real deal, he had studied computer science at university and understood how to build scalable systems.

I already knew with a business based around technology we needed an expert full-time in the role. I said I would love him to join the business but there was a slight problem – we couldn't afford to pay him. I explained no-one was being paid a salary yet, but he could have a ten per cent share of the company. I forecast by February the following year we could pay him £25,000 a year, and by July this should have risen to £45,000. He was so mesmerised by the business and our plans to change an industry that he went home and presented the idea to his wife. You can imagine her reaction, no salary for six months and ten per cent of a company worth nothing. What an amazing opportunity! Thankfully, he convinced her, got a five-month mortgage holiday to help make ends meet, and joined the company. Working from home, and my shed, he immediately started improving the software and we still use newer versions of it today. We managed to pay him the salary we promised a few months later, and his share of the company eventually rose to twenty-five per cent.

The deal we came to with Republic was relatively simple. They had one hundred and twenty-one clothing stores and we did an analysis which showed historically they spent around £1.5m on FM a year. We said we would reduce that figure and charge them an average job value rate, on the condition that if the amount of work rose sharply, we would let them know. Part of the contract was a £150,000 management fee, which they paid in monthly instalments. Our profit margin was about ten per cent on every job, which was lower than most in the FM industry, but we could live with it because we were trying to win our first contract. And besides, as Derrick was a salesman, he would often sell at any sort of rate, which at times caused me some headaches.

Republic was delighted. For the first time, they had incredible visibility and control of their FM spending. They could see what needed doing, how fast it was done and how much it cost. Every single store could log into our software and see the system in operation. Nothing like it existed in the rest of the industry. It worked, our system worked! No sooner had we begun the contract than realised the contractors we brought in to do the work were ridiculously slow at invoicing us. On October 15, we had been carrying out works for Republic for six weeks, and still not received a single bill from any of the contractors. The reason this was a problem was because without contractors sending us bills, there was no mechanism for our technology to charge the client.

I then had to work fast on my technology to change it. We would charge Republic what we knew the bills were eventually going to be (these are called *accruals*), rather than on the invoices we had received. When the invoices eventually came in, the system would check if there were any differences and adjust the next invoice to Republic accordingly. Thankfully, Republic was happy to work in this way, and by Christmas 2011, we had nearly £600k in the bank and had still not received a single bill from a contractor.

We had opened our little office in Langham barns and here I am with Michelle and our three daughters who were running the whole operation.

Month after month passed with no contractors' bills coming in and suddenly, we were swimming in cash. By March it had risen to £900,000 and even we realised the situation was getting ridiculous. We were urging contractors to invoice us so we could pay them but they were always so slow. As part of our transparency and trust principles, Republic was aware of this but when a new finance team came in they said, "We are not going to continue this way. This reconciliation process is too painful for us. We will now only pay you when you have received invoices from your contractors." They said it was deal-breaker and we didn't want to lose our first contract.

One of the things hindsight teaches you is when to walk away. If contracts change, identify the risks of change and make sure you investigate every possible outcome before you agree to them. De-risk the risk. The problem for us with changing to this method is that we were now offering credit. A contractor would do a job, we were beholden to pay them, but even when we got an invoice and sent it Republic, sometimes we were waiting up to thirty days for payment. Sometimes they would push this out to forty-five days. Instead of having £600,000 in the bank, we were now sometimes going into the red. Then, the inevitable happened, the biggest worry for any new business. In June 2012, Republic went bust, owing us £250,000. We had heard whispers for some time they were struggling, and I had said to Derrick we need to pull the plug right now. However, he said, "Everything will be fine, my contact at Republic said everything would be OK." It wasn't. Great, nine months into our new business, our first client had gone bust owing us £250,000 and we would soon have contractors banging on our doors to get paid. I had been in a similar situation before and it had cost me my business and my house. I was devastated. We had put so much time and effort in and we weren't just back to square one, we were on square minus 250,000.

Thankfully, there was a glimmer of hope as we were in advanced talks with Pret a Manger. The problem was they wanted a comprehensive FM agreement, which I hated as it went against all of my principles in terms of changing an industry. What this meant was their historic FM spend was agreed at £1.4m, so they would pay us £1.4m to cover it. The catch was, if we ended up spending more than that, it was our problem. Furthermore, we had not been allowed to review their financial spend as forensically as we would have liked, which was totally against our principles and approach.

If someone had suggested such a contract to Cloudfm even a couple of years later, we would have politely laughed them out of the building. With a £250,000 hole in our balance sheet, I said to Derrick, "This is a very bad deal, it lays us open to all sorts of costs. We are never going to make £250,000 profit from this," but the alternative was to close the doors, shut the business and walk away. That was not an option for me as we had a £250,000 debt to our suppliers. I have done many things in life but leaving suppliers who trusted me in the lurch has never been one of them. Countless companies declare themselves bust, shaft their suppliers, then re-open under a different name the following month. These are called 'Phoenix companies'. I won't say what I call them. Instead, we approached the suppliers, agreed extended credit terms with them and decided to take the deal with Pret to keep our firm going, on one condition – we insisted we were paid quarterly in advance. That first advance of £350,000 was in our bank the first day of business and we could start making inroads into our debt. We knew how many visits Pret had required in the past, what the cost had been, and if they didn't mess us about, we could make it work. We trusted them. It was a bad mistake.

Within a couple of months job request lights were flashing up on our portal like a fruit machine. The volume of work was almost double what it had previously been. We had just managed to avoid going bust with Republic, now Pret was feeding us a shit sandwich. We continually said to their FM management team at the time, "You are being unreasonable here, you know you are logging double the jobs you were before, and this is unsustainable." Their response could be summarised as "you signed the contract, this is not our problem, we don't give a shit, stop bothering us and get it done." When we further queried why the work volume had doubled, they would tell us it was because the weather was hot, it was cold, or unseasonably mild. It was just bullshit. We were subsequently told a couple of months after our contract began, someone had contacted the branches and said, "We want all the fridges to be absolutely pristine. If you even think a seal might be about to go, don't wait, call out the FM people, don't worry about the cost, we are not paying for it. If you even suspect the air con might be out by half a degree, pick up the phone, it's a free service."

It wasn't reasonable, it wasn't a partnership, we were being shafted. I am sure those running Pret now would never dream of acting in such a manner and their culture is totally different. We later learnt we had also shot ourselves in the foot as well. We had been led to understand by the Pret team we were dealing with at that time, in the previous year they had spent £1.4m on FM. Through acquaintances, we eventually spoke to the company which had the contract before us and they claimed Pret had actually spent more than £2m. As we have discussed before, **do your due diligence before you sign a contract, not after it. Speak to clients already working with companies to check you want to work with them.**

One of the principles of Cloudfm is everything is based on trust, and they betrayed it. We would never sign a comprehensive agreement again, we dropped Pret as soon we could, and if one of the FM management team from those days called me now and told my PA I had won the lottery, I still wouldn't pick up the phone. I am sure they run their business in a completely different way nowadays. But even though we were being screwed, by Christmas we had managed to trade our way out of trouble. Every supplier we owed money to had been paid and I began to sleep a little easier at night, despite paying off the contractors meant we had a £250,000 hole in our balance sheet.

To survive, we simply needed to keep winning contracts. Derrick came in one day and said he had won a contract with Guardian News and Media and I immediately had visions of us caring for their massive London HQ. Result! Sadly, he had only leased them our technology to run their own FM department. When I asked how much had charged them and he said £5,000 I thought "that's ok, £5,000 a month will help" but sadly, he didn't mean £5,000 a month, he meant £5,000 a year. To say I wasn't happy would be an understatement but, to be fair to Derrick, we did later earn a couple of hundred grand doing various projects for them and acting as consultants. He also got the same deal with Central Hall, the largest conference and events hall in central London, and came back proud as punch having got £24,000 a year. These were fine, they were bringing in revenue and he was banging on doors and hustling like I would never have done, but they were not exactly the sort of multi-million-pound contracts we were meant to be winning.

The next company to show an interest was Poundland. This time I spoke to Derrick and said I needed to be the one who took the final decision. We had been screwed by Pret, we were taking too many risks. Derrick had unbelievable strengths, but this was all new to him. I had more experience in understanding the pitfalls of contracts and I insisted I had to have the final say. It soon became clear Poundland was never going to be our salvation. Their procurement guy at the time was insisting on a contract which was completely ridiculous. There were conditions like they would have sixty days to pay our invoices when we wanted seven days as we were deep enough in debt as it was. Even worse, they insisted on procuring and managing the contractors who did their work, which meant we would have no control over their working methods or costs. It was a £6m account and all we would earn would be a £150,000 a year management fee. It was a complete waste of our time. We were going to get all the headaches and all the hassle looking after their hundreds of stores for £1,000 a month profit. In addition, we were never going to influence the service delivery and quality when the contractors could play us off against the client, with whom they had a contract. I said we need to change X, Y and Z in the contract to make this work and they said, "No, it's our way or the highway." I was happy to take the highway. I then went to Portugal for a couple of weeks and Derrick rang and said, "Guess what, I have signed the Poundland contract."

I was massively impressed. I said "Wow, you got them to agree to X, Y and Z?" and Derrick said, "No, I signed it just as they wanted it." I started banging my head against the villa wall!

Financially, in my mind it was a poor decision, and he should never have signed it without my approval. However, he was my partner, he was as much at risk of losing everything as I was, and I eventually began to calm down. The only real benefit I saw was it was a household name, and it would show the industry we were growing. I had to rely on the principle that 'people breed people'. In other words, with this level of credibility, more clients would be happy to come on board. While we hated the people at Pret, it was a great brand to have in recognition terms. Poundland was a nightmare, but it was another big name and whatever the problems with the contracts, we were at least getting national customers.

It was at this point I brought in Natalie, Kelly's younger sister, our middle child. Natalie was driven and very confident. She had a solid head on her shoulders and had her Dad's quick-thinking brain. Both Natalie and Kelly were running the helpdesk and I put them both on a three-year ILM Diploma course in Facilities Management.

By now, we had about seven people working with us full-time and the shed was getting cramped, so we rented a lovely little office in Langham in a converted barn for £20,000 a year. We felt like we were going somewhere. The next contract proved we were. Aurora was a clothing firm which had a number of brands including Karen Millen, Oasis, Coast and Warehouse, and three hundred shops. It was a major account, and they were introduced to us by their head of FM, a nice South African bloke called Brent Nell. Previously, their FM provider had employed twelve engineers who worked full-time for Aurora who paid their full-time salaries in advance. With management fees on top, this aspect of the contract alone totalled £675,000. Aurora did not believe they were getting value for money from their FM provider who wanted them to pay for more engineers. Initially, Aurora simply wanted to license our software for £150,000 to supervise their FM account. We went to see the FM company and they said, "We are a £600m business, we have more infrastructure and technology than Cloudfm will ever have," and they laughed at the idea of our software managing the account. Aurora called their bluff and said, "Use the software or we will give the whole contract to Cloudfm." They said, "Fine." As part of our new contract, the twelve engineers Aurora were paying for joined Cloudfm under the TUPE transfer scheme and it was a great deal for us. The engineer payments brought immediate cash into our business and we reckoned our annual profit from the contract would be around £600,000.

Just as importantly, it was the first contract we had won as a mature company, based solely on our technology and our principles of trust and transparency. Pret's FM team had exploited us and Poundland had wanted someone stupid enough to take on their contract. But Aurora had seen how we wanted to change the industry, they believed in our philosophy and it was a relationship based on trust and honesty. The first problem was the engineers. They hated our technology and didn't want to be monitored because it meant we could check if they were working eight hours a day. Our technology showed on average they were working a few hours a day for their full-time salaries, and they were doing other work for different people on top. No wonder their previous FM wanted to recruit more engineers. They thought the reason that work was not being done was the engineers were rushed off their feet. They were, working for other people. Eleven of the twelve engineers left after a couple of weeks. We employed six new engineers and said to Aurora we were confident with our system, and with them working at capacity we could improve the service they were getting with fewer engineers. And they didn't just have to take our word for it, our system meant they could check on it themselves. It was symbolic of our relationship with Aurora that they said, "OK, if that's the case, and you continue to save us money, you can keep the cash which would have been spent on the five engineers you do not need to employ."

That decision embodied everything we had started to change in the industry. Rather than lying and cheating and fiddling figures, we had a proper relationship based on trust and mutual respect. We were in a proper partnership, rather than our two companies battling to exploit each other. We were also following a policy to keep a low profile in the industry. We were a small outfit based in a barn in the countryside and the longer we went unnoticed by the big boys, the better. Even with the contracts we had won, we were still only turning over a couple of million quid a year, so we were hardly giving the competition nightmares.

The principle of monthly engineers visits for routine maintenance was at the core of our success. Brent Nell - who had seen what we were doing at Aurora - thought this approach had real opportunities of changing the industry and wanted to come on board. Derrick and I set up a company called RMT (which later became shared services) to run these engineers and Brent Nell joined us on an £85,000 salary with a view to eventually becoming a thirty per cent shareholder of RMT if he met certain targets. He then said he needed to employ someone to help him, another South African he said he had known for years, and was going to pay him £30,000. He was a lovely bloke, but I was chatting to him one day and he said he had only known Brent for a short time and they had met at a train station. Because they were both South African, Brent had offered him a job! Then I learnt Brent had also set up a business doing events on boats on the Thames and he was getting the PR company Cloudfm used to do all the brochures. Derrick and I called him in, said he was being paid £85,000 to build our business, not his own, and that was the end of Brent. Surprisingly, his new South African mate stayed on for a few years and did a decent job. In business, as in life, you have to kiss a lot of frogs to find a Prince.

Here are all my daughters, including my eldest Sarah from my early marriage.

But our next contract put us firmly on the map. In November 2012 we had started talking with the Gondola Group which included the Pizza Express, Ask, Zizi and Byron Burger chains. They were a well-respected national company with a £10m FM spend. We were desperate for their business and, just as importantly, we wanted our relationship to embrace everything we stood for, even beyond what we had achieved with Aurora. We never tendered for the contract, we did the free consultation work based on their purchase ledgers, and spent the next six months talking with them. Securing them was vital. Pret was still bleeding us dry but thankfully the contract was coming to an end and we couldn't rip it up fast enough. The Poundland contract was still as painful as banging your head on a desk and the Aurora contract had only just started bringing in cash. We were skint. Without Gondola, we were again facing going bust.

In June 2013, Gondola signed the contract with a start date four months later. All the cash would be passing through our account, the work was based on average job value, we were making a healthy margin and, crucially, we would be saving Gondola money. It was a game-changing moment in the whole industry, even if people didn't realise it. It was the turning point of our business. It was celebration time. We took the entire team out for a champagne night out none of us will forget. I knew we needed bigger facilities and found office space at Oyster House in Colchester. When I showed the space to Derrick, he thought I was mad. It was about the size of a football pitch and could comfortably accommodate about seventy people. At the time there were seven of us. I said, "Look at our business plan, things are going to take off, Gondola is about to get started and, trust me, we are going to need the space."

He wasn't happy, so I just had to put my foot down, and we took the space. I even got the design and print company we used, called Green Square, to move in as well. That helped us with the new rent payments we were about to commit to. Green Square had started at roughly the same time as us, we had a great relationship and, what also helped was when clients visited us, the place looked busier and people naturally thought the Green Square team was part of Cloudfm. When Gondola came onboard, within a couple of months we soon burst out of that space and needed more room.

Around this time, we also got a letter from Apple saying we could not use the name iCloudfm and they were going to sue us to death. I told our lawyers to tell them they could shove it up their arse because I had thought of the name and legally registered it before they had. I was ready for a fight. I could take a bite out of Apple! Our lawyers laughed at me. They said it would be like taking on a 1,000lb gorilla in the jungle, but far more painful, and with much less chance of success. Pointing out we had about £30 in our bank account, and they were on their way to becoming the most recognised brand on the planet, it was not a battle we were going to win. iCloudfm therefore became Cloudfm but I still like to take a little credit for creating the Cloud phenomenon. Steve Jobs and Bill Gates, an air con engineer from Essex got their first!

As for my family and business life, my daughters had been working with me for a while, and as the business began to grow at pace, so did Natalie. However, as Natalie's role grew within the business, Kelly faded into the background and simply kept a low profile. I was pleased with how Natalie was developing, but at the same time, worried about Kelly.

As for Gondola, our relationship became a textbook example of how the FM industry should work. Let's take one of their divisions. Their FM cost was £6m a year and we saved them £500,000 the first year and an extra quarter of a million pounds for the next two years, while at the same time improving their FM service. But that was just the start, the key to a proper relationship between an FM company and its client is that both benefit massively from it. It is the complete opposite from the traditional relationship of chaos, dishonesty and exploitation. But if they were spending £6m with us and we reduced their costs by £1m in three years, how could we profit from that? By December 2019, with the same number of restaurants, the same cook lines, the same assets, the same management team, they weren't spending £5m, with us, they were spending £14m. Our system allowed them to see where every penny of their FM money was going. They weren't stumbling in the dark like most companies where FM spend is constantly out of control. We were able to demonstrate not just where the money was going, but how they could spend money to save much, much more. As part of the deal, they received monthly maintenance visits from an engineer specifically trained on their equipment lines. But as well as doing scheduled preventative maintenance, making sure all the ovens were working properly, that the building and equipment regulations were being met etc., they would also do everything from fixing cracked tiles to changing lightbulbs. Our engineers knew we were in a partnership with them, and if they could help in any way, they would. If a door squeaked, our engineer fixed it.

As well as adding to the customer experience by ensuring each restaurant was in pristine condition, this constant care meant the restaurants had to be refitted far less often. That saved the company a fortune. That level of service was again based on trust. When we first approached them with the monthly maintenance proposal, we said that level of service would cost them a million pounds. Naturally, they were a little reluctant - no company wants to spend that sort of money. But, based on our technology and mutual transparency, we were able to say, "We know this will save you £1.5m a year in having to pay for reactive breakdowns. If we expand our maintenance agreement, your bottom line will benefit." And here is the key, we trusted them and so we said, "If you don't save half a million pounds through this, we will write you a cheque for that amount." Within a year they saw the benefits. They realised putting in place proactive measures to stop problems occurring, having pristine premises, and properly working equipment, all led to overall cost savings, greater footfall and return visits to their restaurants. Their sales went up materially. Good facilities management helped them sell meals, and it can have the same positive effect on any business.

Another of our clients had previously been spending £8.8m a year and carrying out 17,200 breakdown repairs. In four years with us, we saved them £13.3m. Of those savings they reinvested almost £5m with us, improving equipment and infrastructure. Rather than spending money on constantly fixing knackered old air conditioning or lighting, which they could not afford to replace, the savings we gave them meant they could afford to do it and still save money on their old total FM bill. That meant their sites were far more comfortable and better-lit. After five years, their number of annual repairs had gone from 17,200 to 5,900. We were showing our clients how, working in partnership with the right technology and culture, we could be of substantial benefit to their business.

After years of struggle, Cloudfm was now doing well. Of course, there were challenges. I was constantly fighting pleas for us to bid for contracts the usual way and step back from our principles to make a quick buck, but I refused. I hadn't entered the industry just to make a few quid, I was going to change the industry. And slowly, other FM companies started to adapt to our technology, working methods and our use of language and customer approach, if nothing else. Occasionally we are called in by companies to work on a consultancy basis and to check how their FM providers are doing. A national organisation with two hundred buildings got in touch to look over their existing FM suppliers' work because they were worried about their safety compliance. Compliance sounds dull but it is important. It is what stops your company killing people. You have to be compliant in meeting fire regulations, health and safety legislation etc. If you think you are compliant in fire safety you sleep well at night knowing the emergency lighting works, the alarms work, your fire extinguishers are full and have been properly maintained. If they are not and a fire breaks out and your customers or staff get charred, you and the chief executive are going to live with guilt for the rest of your life, go to prison and the legal bills and fine could bankrupt your business.

We did some research and said, "You have a problem. Your FM firm has been co-operating and given us what information they have, but they don't realise their whole system is a mess. We estimate your buildings are forty-four per cent compliant, when the FM company is telling you they are ninety-four per cent compliant." As you can imagine, the shit hit the fan. The only saving grace was in one of their buildings the fan would have been broken. The FM provider said we were talking out of our arse, so we said, "OK, let's just sit down round a table and go through it."

We explained our software and its capabilities and how we had used it to prove they were failing to meet the contract. The FM provider said, "That technology is nothing new, we have similar software, but we are a multinational giant and ours is the best on the planet." So, Derrick said, "OK, let's play a game. I will show you mine if you show me yours. I can see you are talking with real passion and you honestly believe in your software and systems, so demonstrate it to us. When you are done, I will show you our findings. We can decide if we agree with each other or not, or if we just have to agree to disagree."

They opened the software, Derrick picked a building at random from the client's list and said, "OK, take me to the fire alarms," and the bloke says, "No problem." The fire alarms were highlighted as being compliant. So, Derrick says, "So show me the certificate." The bloke clicks a button, up it pops, and the certificate is out of date. The building is not compliant. The bloke is embarrassed and says, "OK, pick another one." I almost felt sorry for him. We picked five and each building had faults which meant it wasn't compliant. We then picked five of our projects, from emergency lighting in Luton to PAT testing in Penrith and every single one was marked as compliant and had the certificates to prove it. The client went on to sue the FM provider for £12m. For a number of political reasons, we had no interest in this FM contract, but we said we would assist them in trying to find a replacement. We sat in on the interview panel and five companies came in. Each talked about trust and transparency and how much visibility their software gave their clients. It was an almost out-of-body experience. Everything I had been saying for years, and been called mad for doing, was now being repeated to me, almost parrot-fashion, from the competition. That compliance problem example was not an exception. On three of our clients, we found compliance at thirty-three, forty and forty-four per cent. Once we had got them off the floor after they fainted, we gave another example of our honest approach. We didn't promise them the earth. If you tell the regulatory bodies you are ninety per cent compliant when you are forty per cent you are in big trouble. However, the authorities also understand you cannot be forty per cent compliant one day and one hundred per cent the next, you just have to show you are improving compliancy. We told the clients we would rapidly improve their compliance but just as importantly, for the first time they would actually know how compliant they were from one minute to the next. When they have this knowledge, they can then plan on how to improve it. Within a couple of years those same clients were ninety-three, ninety-five and ninety-six per cent compliant. Those are incredible high figures for any industry. If they wanted to be one hundred per cent, they also had all the information they needed to achieve it, it was simply a case of if they wanted to spend the money.

We had started a revolution. We were making money, we just needed to continue to grow. But businesses are not just about technology, they are also about people.

COVID early June 2020:

Win win

With the engineering side of our operation entirely restructured, it was time to look at other areas of the business.

Our helpdesk predominantly takes calls from clients who contact us with issues, and then the desk acts as middlemen between the clients and the engineers. Every FM company tends to have a help desk, typically staffed by young people who have been highly trained but are on low salaries.

But as we have always shown at Cloudfm, just because everyone has a help desk does not mean it is right. With our metaphorical ship still marooned in mid-Atlantic, we challenged ourselves to say, "What do these people actually do?" Analysis showed a typical job was taking them up to seven calls to rectify. The help desk staff didn't understand the technical aspects of the equipment, they were not offering advice to the client or the engineer, they were simply passing information from A to B. Essentially, they were administrators. We asked ourselves how would we restructure this service if we were starting the business right now?

We also realised we still had about forty engineers looking for roles. Again, the solution was obvious. Why not bring in some of those engineers to work on the help desk? They have technical know-how, knowledge of which machines are on site, can communicate properly with the client to identify the root causes of problems, and can add value in transmitting that information to engineers so they can do the job right first time. It saves us money and gives the client a better service.

The problem was engineers earn basic salaries of £30,000, plus overtime, much more than help desk staff. Few engineers would be willing to take a major step back financially when they have a mortgage, and bills to pay. I said, "Never mind, we are offering a better service, we will take the financial hit. These engineers have expertise, experience and life skills and they will be adding real value to the business, but in a different arena. They deserve pay that recognises that." We swapped engineers over to the help desk and maintained their salaries. Again, it was a win/win. Our clients would receive a better service and because of our next series of changes, we could save substantial sums.

Sadly, we did lose some of these younger people and one of the by-products of employing young people is when things get tough, they can get very emotional. A couple of them wasted no time in going on social media and business sites saying we were a terrible company for making them redundant. They just didn't comprehend we were going through a worldwide pandemic with economies collapsing across the globe and they couldn't accept the fact changes were going to have to be made. As an example of the real ethos of our company, a couple of years ago I got a letter from one of our employees who was worried sick.

She had recently returned to work after having a baby and her Mum, who was caring for the child, had been diagnosed with terminal cancer. She had gone to our HR department for advice and they had told her the best thing she could do would be to leave her job and get state benefits, which meant she could be at home to look after her baby. Technically, they might have been correct, but when I found out that was our advice, I blew a fuse. I rarely lose my temper, but I was struggling to keep it in check. That was not Cloudfm's culture. Within two hours we had set up an account with a local nursery and we paid for her child to get full-time care while she was at work. That meant her Mum could rest and the girl wasn't constantly stressed about her childcare. The upside was this girl become super-effective because we had looked after her and done the right thing. One of my senior team said, "I don't agree with what you have done as it sets a precedent for others."

I rarely, if ever, use the veto I have to force decisions though, but I said, "OK, here is a new rule I have just written. If someone has had a baby and comes back to work and their mother, who is looking after the baby, gets diagnosed with terminal cancer, well in those circumstances we will look after their childcare. There's your sodding precedent and I am happy for it to stand."

That is the 'care without caring' culture I believe in. **Sometimes doing the right thing must override the possible consequences.** Mandy Hickson, the former Royal Air Force pilot who flew forty-five missions over Iraq, gives a perfect example from her life. One day she sadly learned her grandfather was about to pass away within hours at the other end of the country. Her superior officer told her to take an RAF jet and fly to be with him. Such a trip was not officially part of her training, or schedule, but he said: "I am telling you to go. I have sanctioned it and I will deal with any problems which arise, on my shoulders be it. Don't worry about anything other than going to see your grandfather."

That officer was potentially placing his own career in jeopardy by sanctioning such a flight, but that is what care without caring means - putting others before yourself when circumstances demand it. That is what I, and Cloudfm stand for, whatever enraged teenagers might write on Facebook. Talking of social networks, rewind a few years and Derrick was brilliant at building his own.

Chapter 13

Partners and promises

Be careful who you get into bed with. That's a lesson for business life, as much as your personal life. While I was charting the progress of Cloudfm in the last chapter, I left out the tsunami of decisions, good and bad, which we took to try and develop the business. It brought us people who benefitted us beyond measure, and one millstone round our neck which cost us a million pounds to remove. To avoid legal action, I have changed the names of some of those involved.

When you are setting up a business, new clients are key. You might have invented the best product on the planet, but you need to tell people about it. One way is to spend money on marketing but that is difficult when you don't have any cash. Another way is to network yourself to death. And Derrick loved networking. Almost every day he was at events in London making contacts, getting our name about and hoping to meet people who could be useful in the future, who might know clients we could go for and, as we sank further into debt, who might want to invest in the business. This was another area Derrick excelled in, but which left me cold.

One of the people he met we will call East End Eddie. He was about seventy-five, well-spoken with a Cockney twang, always smartly dressed in a pin-stripe suit and £250 shoes. He claimed to know everyone on the planet. If you said you were looking to buy a one-armed monkey from Macau, East End Eddie would say, "You need to speak to Bob in Beijing, here's his number." Derrick loved this bloke, so I went to meet him and within ten seconds I was thinking, *You are kidding me, this bloke is just a wide boy.* I checked him out and he had liquidated about three thousand companies and gone bankrupt fifteen times. He was an absolute nightmare. Anyway, he introduced us to a guy called Frank Hodgson (and that's his real name). Frank was supposedly a serial investor with lots of money. He lived in a huge, rented apartment in Mayfair which cost him £15,000 a month and he appeared to be a class act. He looked loaded, talked the talk, had more art and sculptures in his flat than the Tate Modern, and had companies all over the world. He had apparently managed to get every big businessman in the country on his speed dial. If you mentioned sugar he would ask if you wanted Sir Alan or the chairman of Tate & Lyle.

He loved our idea of changing the FM industry and wanted to invest. Bearing in mind we had a financial black hole in our accounts, this was music to our ears. But life is never simple, and he wasn't willing to simply hand over a cheque. Instead, he said, "I am not going to give you any money, instead I am going to bring a guy called Mark Chappell into your business. He has reshaped one of the big water companies, reshaped one of the energy giants, and he has the contacts, know-how and network to make Cloudfm a £100m business. I will pay his expenses for twelve months to work with you, but I want twenty-five per cent of your business. In addition, I have a wealth of contacts in the investment world. My skill set is raising funds for investment, I will sort you out." I was quite succinct. "Thanks, but no thanks," and we politely left the meeting. Derrick and I retired to a nearby café and for the first time in my life I saw Derrick spitting mad. He was convinced Mark had the keys to unlock all the doors to our future, and Frank could unlock investors' cash. I said we needed money, not "Miracle Mark" turning up for twenty-five per cent of the business. For all we knew the bloke might be an idiot. In addition, one of the golden rules of life is **you don't value what you don't pay for,** and Frank wasn't going to be paying a bean in strictly cash investment terms. But Derrick was adamant, and I could see this ruining our partnership. In the end, I said, "OK, the business is currently worth nothing, so twenty-five per cent of that isn't much. If you feel so strongly, we will take Mark on, but on your head be it."

Soon after, in walked Mark, having driven down from his twenty-acre estate in Yorkshire in his brand-new BMW X6. He wanted to look at the books and present us with a business plan. He confidently said, "This can be a £100m company in seven years." I didn't want to point out I knew that anyway, and off he went. Around the same time, we were given the opportunity to present our business model to a group of people we had been networking with. Derrick and I prepared our presentation and it went down a storm. There were thirty people in a room at the European School of Language in London and, at the end of it, everyone was pumped up and ready to reach for their cheque books. We talked to them all over the next couple of months and three quarters of them disappeared. However, I grew to like and respect Andrew Frith, who was a major player in the NHS, and a chap he had introduced us to called Chris Gallop. Chris was an ex-Deutsche Bank big-hitter, tall, ramrod-straight, plummy-voiced and well respected. He is the sort of bloke who used to run a continent when England had an empire. They both agreed to join Cloudfm's board, on no salary or even expenses for twelve months, in return for one and a half per cent of the business.

Mark Chappell also wanted to bring someone in, a chap we will name Redundant Richard. Mark then said he wanted the executive board to be made up of him as Chairman, Chris Gallop as Managing Director, me as Chief of Operations and Redundant Richard as CEO. Derrick had fought to get Mark into the company and now Mark had removed him from the executive board. That's irony for you. In Mark's business plan we were all on salaries of around £250,000. That was a joke as far as I was concerned as we couldn't afford to pay ourselves salaries of £35,000. We raised our concerns with Mr "twenty-five per cent Frank Hodgson" and I said, "I am not comfortable with the way this is going. Mark is changing the board, the business plan is unrealistic, and we are losing focus of the business." Frank said, "Let me give you some advice. When you are a shareholder like me, you need to let the board do its job, sit back and wait for the money to roll in. Stop worrying."

Derrick was nodding his head sagely, drinking this in, but I was sat there thinking, You are talking out of your arse. I didn't think the people he had brought in were having a positive impact, I thought they were more of a distraction. At the next meeting we had one of Redundant Richard's first proposals as CEO. He wanted to make sixty per cent of our people redundant. Bear in mind we only had about thirty people working for us at the time. His justification was that, based on his expertise and brilliance, he should be earning a salary of £300,000 but we obviously could not afford that. However, if we made all these people redundant, he might be able to clear £100,000. That was enough for me, I stood up and sacked him. Derrick was open-mouthed, saying, "What are you doing?"

I said, "It's simple. Redundant Richard, you are fired."

Mark had brought him into the business, so he was furious, but he wasn't the only one. I said, "You are all living in cloud cuckoo land. You are behaving like this is a FTSE 100 company, but we don't have a pot to piss in. There is no money. In fact, there is less than no money, there is a big hole in the balance sheet. We have got people who have joined this company and this board without a penny in salary or expenses. They are willing to work hard and one day, who knows, they might earn a fortune, but if you want to earn £100,000 a year by sacking people you are in the wrong place."

A couple of months later, Mark also left the company. Frank had stopped paying his expenses, we started having disagreements about the future direction of the company, and we were even rowing over his expenses, which included things like him staying in Claridge's Hotel the night before meetings in London. I could barely have afforded to buy an afternoon tea there. Mark and I had further rows over the future of the company and so he left. So much for Frank Hodgson's first method of justifying his twenty-five per cent of the business.

Still in need of investment, we next met two sheiks who wanted to invest. They were willing to give us £450,000 but they wanted ninety-five per cent of the company. You don't have to be the CEO of Coca-Cola to realise that that percentage was madness, but when you are in debt and you face losing everything anyway you will contemplate anything. We would be running the company for someone else on a salary but at least we would have made a big chunk of cash. We discussed it with Frank who said not to do anything hasty, he would put us in touch with some investors. It turned out like a Guy Ritchie movie. The first bloke to appear was this Russian man in a chauffeur-driven car who had a bodyguard. It was scary as soon as he walked into the room. His proposal could roughly be translated as, "I will give you £400,000 for a hundred per cent of the business, or I kill you." We couldn't get him out of the office fast enough and were praying he soon forgot about us and turned his deadly attentions somewhere else.

The next two weren't much better, although they didn't come close in terms of sheer terror. We said to Frank, "Who are these guys? They obviously have money but none of them are being rational or reasonable, they all want everything for next to nothing." And to be fair to Frank, what he said was true. He said, "You are the ones not being rational or reasonable. You have a business worth less than nothing because it has a £250,000 debt, so what do you expect people to pay for? Your business has potential, but so do a lot which fail, and no-one is going to hand over boxes of hard cash on just a hope of success."

We pointed out we had brought him into the business to solve problems like these, but in my view, he had no answers. To my mind, we had given a quarter of our business away for nothing. That left us with the sheiks. I said we would take the investment cash for fifty per cent, they insisted on ninety per cent, but they did own a lot of care homes we could FM manage for them which would be a £10m account on its own. Derrick wanted to proceed. He was terrified of being in debt and so we began negotiating and doing the due diligence. I got them down to seventy per cent of the business for £400,000. I then went on holiday at the end of August 2013, on my first ever cruise right at the time we were about to go live with our biggest ever client – Gondola. I gave the matter some real thought for a couple of weeks. I knew the business was going to be fine with Gondola onboard and I rang Derrick and said, ""I have been thinking about this constantly on this cruise. I have given you latitude, tried to follow your desires but I am not allowing the sale to go through. I am blocking it." The sheiks were furious, Derrick was furious, but I knew it was the right thing to do. That was the first time I had ever stopped Derrick doing anything. Derrick and I had a shouting match and during it I said, "Either I run this business, or I am off. You are still a 50/50 partner, but I have to be the one to make these decisions."

When we converted Cloudfm into a group business I got thirty-three per cent of the shares, Derrick got thirty per cent, James got twenty-eight per cent but I had a 'nuclear button' in the contract, which meant I always had the final say. For all my criticisms of him during this process, it is always worth remembering, the business would never have got off the ground without Derrick. He knocked on doors until his knuckles were bleeding. He was tenacious, reliable and had great skills with clients, our initial success was down to him, and he worked tirelessly for us for years. He made countless decisions and the vast majority of them were spot on. As for everyone else? Andrew Frith and Chris Gallop have also added huge benefit to the business. They both worked for 18 months for nothing, and Cloudfm's success is partly based on their commitment, talent and endeavour.

The lesson is: **when seeking investors or business partners, you need to find people who will put skin in the game.** Not everyone has money to invest, but people should be able to dedicate their time and effort and commitment. If they are willing to give that, then they should get your attention. If money is their sole motivating factor, leave them be. They don't truly care for the company or the purpose, they only care about cash.

In the early days, we had also appointed former *Vogue* model Nicky Page to the board, who had hit the headlines when she had an affair with former Tory minister John Redwood. She was put in touch with us by another bloke Derrick met who supposedly had the contacts to transform our world. She had her own design business and apparently had the political connections which might help us to break into some large government FM projects. To be fair to her, within a few weeks she introduced us to a number of politicians – which included John Redwood, funnily enough – but that was as far as it went. She was a lovely lady, but in my opinion, she wasn't really adding anything, and we let her go which made her quite upset. As for Frank Hodgson? Eventually, he left his flat in Mayfair, moved to Gibraltar where we spent months tracking him down to try and buy him out of the business. He was a silent partner who had been brought in to introduce us to people who would change our business. In the end in my mind, he didn't even introduce us to a McDonalds' breakfast. We finally got rid of him in December 2019. It was a seven-year nightmare. Frank wanted £4m. Eventually it went to mediation and it cost us a million pounds.

But companies are not built in the boardroom. Crucial to Cloudfm's success was the team I created to actually do the work and to grow the company. At the start I cherry-picked some of the exceptional people I had met in the past. David Harris and James White had both originally been ISS engineers but had moved into the ISS office when I was there. David had broken his leg playing football and after being at home for three days said the boredom was killing him and there must be something he could do in the ISS office. He came in and started to learn the help desk process. It was the best thing that could have happened to him. It opened up a whole new career path rather than just being out on the road fixing things.

James White saw the progress David was making and had the foresight to want to make the change too. He came into the ISS office and started doing planned maintenance organisation. Both these fellas took big salary cuts to do this as they were no longer getting engineer pay and overtime bonuses, but they saw the long-term picture. Being an engineer was great but it was a limited role in the great scheme of things. They wanted more. Both of them were incredibly useful because as former engineers they could put jobs in context, knew what it would take to solve them and distribute the work accordingly. The rest of the industry would just employ admin people in those roles but I knew expertise paid off in the long run and so I snapped them up. I also knew when they joined us at Cloudfm in April 2012 that both were incredibly hard-working, saw the positives rather than the negatives, and would be great contributors to the team. We couldn't pay them what they were getting at ISS, but we gave them some share options which would have value when the company reached a certain size and a Volkswagen Fox company car each. The cars were almost identical, and we said, "Choose which one you want." James picked the one in slightly worse nick and said to Dave, "You have the better one, it's on me, you have that one." James had noticed the number plate on the other car started PED 0. Both are now in senior positions and their shares are theoretically worth something like a quarter of a million quid each. It pays to look long-term.

Tim Hickman also came in from ISS in January 2013 where he was working as an estimator. When jobs are required which are not part of the standard contracts, estimators tell the clients what they will cost. He came in to head up our estimation department and his work ethic remains an example to everyone in the company. I also took on Barbara Mardell who I knew from back in my days at Auxilia. Barbara is a lovely Yorkshire lass in her seventies and back at Auxilia she took me under her wing when she realised that I was working to midnight every night and living on take-aways. She soon started bringing in sandwiches, lasagne and other food for me. The problem with my technology at that time was it had no capability to log and create an invoice. She knew everything about this process, and so we worked together to build it into my system and before long she was working until midnight too. As soon as I set up Cloudfm, she was always calling me looking for a job, but the problem was she lived one hundred and seventy miles away in Cannock. However, when we needed to upgrade our invoice processing system, I knew she was perfect for the job and so she became our first full-time home worker, popping down to see us every couple of months.

Ian Fieldwick was my management accountant at ISS and was young, dynamic and desperate to move into commercial and financial accountancy rather than just auditing. When we needed a head of finance, he was the perfect choice. He was another person who took a salary cut to join us and we gave him some shares on top. He left us in 2018 and we bought the shares off him, meaning he walked away with a very healthy lump sum. My daughter's best mate from primary school, Stacy Barnard, joined us as a trainee management accountant. Because she had joined us from the start, two years ago she was also rewarded share options and left late in 2019 with our blessing and she will always be part of the Cloudfm, and my personal, family.

Lewis McLennan joined us early to help James Blackman as a

programmer straight from university and is now a senior developer in a thirty-five-strong team and was also given share options. Chris Gooch was one of my peers at Middleton and another lovely, funny guy who was great at leading teams of engineers. I had always vowed never to have our own engineering team at Cloudfm. The problem with engineers is unless you have enough work to keep them busy one hundred per cent of the time, sometimes you can be paying for them to sit at home. When Aurora paid us to take on their engineers it made financial sense to do it, but I agreed solely on the understanding they would just do maintenance and compliance work. This meant we could diary them to be busy every single day. It then made sense to divide Cloudfm into two – integrated services (the main business) and shared services which employed the engineers. The engineering company was treated the same as all our other contractors, in that when they do work for a client, they bill us, and we then bill the client. Chris was the ideal bloke to run it, and he developed it from twelve engineers to one hundred. He stayed with us for five years before retiring with the help of the shares we had given him.

Sally Frost joined us as a payroll and purchase ledger clerk in March 2012 and now runs the payroll for the entire group on her own.

Then another daughter of mine joined the business, Hayley. Hayley had trained as a hairdresser and loved her job. She would often get frustrated around the dinner table when me, Michelle, Kelly and Natalie were talking about the business. Then after a year or so, she got the bug and I offered her a position as a trainee. She would later set the world alight.

Helen Tidswell, who also joined us early to manage our brand, also made it onto the board. It is one of the unfortunate aspects of the FM industry that there are not enough women in the top jobs. At Cloudfm over the last four years we have employed four hundred people, about eighty of them in senior positions. For each of those positions there has roughly been twenty men applying for every one woman, which means the odds are already heavily stacked against a woman getting the job. We would love to have more women in senior roles but the problem is one with society as a whole and not always with the employers.

Anyway, issues about gender aside, most of these people had one thing in common. They were willing to take a step back, either in career or salary terms, and join Cloudfm because they had the foresight and vision to see they would benefit in the long run. Those who were already working in FM were great people in a rotten industry and they knew what my ambition for Cloudfm was. When they saw our technology, and the culture we were creating, they bought into my dream as well.

Cloudfm's HQ. One of seven offices across the UK and Europe.

One of the keys of starting and running your own business is realising you can't do every job yourself. Instead, you have to bring in people who will maximise their value and help grow the business, but most importantly, they have to believe what you believe. Success is impossible without them, you cannot do everything yourself. As my earliest experiences showed, finding them is not easy, but it is vital that you do. You need to have the confidence and foresight to employ people who are on the same page in terms of what you need from them to help the company grow. Businesses talk about getting everyone pulling in the same direction, how a team is always stronger than the sum of its parts, but many are just paying lip service to the principle. I always like to think about businesses like orchestras. It has brass, wind, string and other sections and they all do their bit at exactly the right time to try and produce perfection. Dance groups are the same. If one person is off, the effect is ruined. The goal with a business is to get it operating like an orchestra where everyone is acting in unison, knowing when to blow a note, when to hit a drum, play that chord. That should always be the goal. A big part of being an entrepreneur is employing the right people around you.

In 2020 we were changing people, and also looking at bricks and mortar.

COVID June 2020:

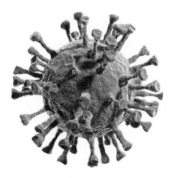

Building for the future

From the start of the furlough process, we had warned our staff we had no intention of returning to our buildings before January, 2021, at the earliest. We did not want to give people an understanding they might return in August for example, and then if we didn't they would be demoralised. We were managing expectations. By telling people January we had made it clear and everyone knew they would have to learn how to work at home. Like everyone else in industry, we had some suspicions about home-working but after a couple of months we saw productivity had gone through the roof. Working from home proved incredibly efficient for us. Once people had got used to it, they realised it gave them immense freedom. People were not spending time and money commuting through traffic for two hours each day, young Dads and Mums weren't missing out seeing their children grow up. People stopped being measured on presenteeism and what time they got to the office, but rather on their output, which is what most people prefer. People have varying abilities and if you are being paid the same as colleague A, but get the job done better and quicker, why should you have to sit in an office for eight hours just because colleague A needs to?

We did a survey at the start of lockdown on working from home and seventy per cent of people hated it. They were having to home-school their kids as well as work, they were being interrupted, they were finding it difficult to switch off. Two months later, when people were used to it, another survey and eighty per cent said they loved it. Working from home gives individuals a much greater degree of freedom over how they structure their days. It improves their quality of life. They can take their kids to school, they weren't having to commute and their quality of life went up three hundred per cent. There were other benefits. In an office environment if you want something from someone you wander into their office, ask them a question and the person has two choices, to interrupt what they are doing or say, "Come back in an hour". Either way, you have distracted them from their work.

Instead, we instigated a system using TEAMS technology where video conferences could be held when need be, otherwise calls which were not vital and time-critical could be scheduled. For routine matters we were sending simple messages asking, "Are you available for a call?" If the person doesn't respond immediately that has to be tolerated. If they say they are available in two hours that's fine. If they say, "I am available now, make the call," the individual can control, and plan their own workload efficiently, rather than being constantly interrupted. Of course, there has to be a degree of trust and understanding, but those are the core values of our culture and business. And people also know they cannot abuse such trust without consequences.

We then asked ourselves, do we need all our seven buildings across the UK? We knew we were losing staff and the business was going to shrink as the casual dining industry suffered. So, we began negotiating with landlords to get out of leases and managed to extract ourselves from five of them we deemed surplus to requirements. The savings amounted to £1m a year. Again, we had created margin without sacrificing services to our clients. We maintained our HQ at Charter House in Colchester and the Innovation Centre, where our digital team is based.

Of course, working from home is not without issues. People can become isolated and sometimes face-to-face meetings are more appropriate. For that reason, Charter House was converted into a company meeting space where people can meet to chat, hold meetings, engage with colleagues and work on joint projects. However, it will never be a typical 9am – 5pm office again. Only time will tell how these new working practices will evolve but we remain confident they will improve our company for clients and staff.

But the changes were not finished yet, and these would be personally painful. Back in 2015 though, we were all about expansion.

Chapter 14

Spreading our wings

"Winner winner, chicken dinner" as gamblers like to say! One of the first clients we had ever approached was KFC but it was obvious we were too small back then to look after their business. We had kept in touch, Derrick would periodically woo them, and by 2015 we were in advanced talks with them for the third time. A chap called Adam Clayfield had recently joined us as commercial director with a great pedigree, having been partly responsible for the design, implementation and deployment of BT Sport. He was also a former property director for Lidl across Europe, and Wicks, the DIY company. He was the first person we took on through a recruitment process rather than being someone we knew and he walked in, showed his teeth and within five months had secured KFC. We needed the deal badly. Gondola had got rid of our financial problems but KFC was the deal which was going to turn us into profit. When we won it, we held the biggest party we had ever had. We weren't looking after KFC's franchise restaurants as they were individually owned, but we looked after the two hundred and forty head office "owned" restaurants. The contract covered all their hard FM, from the catering equipment to the fire alarms, and it was worth £13m a year. KFC enjoyed the same immediate benefits Gondola had enjoyed and we saved them £2m in the first year. They also started increasing their spend with us annually as well, until 2017, when they started selling off the branches to franchisees, leaving us about fifty to manage.

Getting KFC was another massive feather in our cap. It is the second most recognised brand in the world. Our head had gone above the parapet with Gondola, so to win KFC put us firmly on the map in terms of credibility, brand awareness and reputation. It was also important as we won it from our biggest perceived competitor, Bellrock (formerly SGP), which was Derrick's old employer. They had the contract for a number of years, but their contract was only worth £300,000 to

£400,000 a year. When they saw our press release saying we had won a £60m contract - £12m a year for five years – they nearly fainted. The reason for the difference was Bellrock had simply offered a managed service and the contractors would invoice KFC directly, much as we had done for Poundland, but we had managed to secure the whole shebang. When I met the Bellrock owners a few months later and explained the deal to them they said, "Geez, how stupid were we?" I could only reply, "Yeah, that's what we thought too."

KFC was a turning point. When we had started the business, we had never envisaged it would take us five years to really get into profitability but the experience had taught us two things. Problems like Republic going bust owing us £250,000 could take years to recover from, and it also showed us that perseverance was the key.

After winning Gondola and KFC, we threw a huge Christmas party in London for the two hundred staff and their partners.

By now we were also keen to move out of doing FM in just the casual dining sector. Derrick had been doing consultancy work on a daily fee basis for the American-owned BPP university, which has twenty universities specialising in law, business and technology, accountancy, nursing and health. It wanted an accurate insight into its FM assets and future liabilities and its FM provider – one of the big four – couldn't even supply them with that information. They were thrilled with the level of detail that we supplied them with and asked why we weren't trying to sell our services to them. Derrick said, "You have employed us as consultants and we never try to sell things to people they don't want." They asked to come and look at our operation and soon signed up. It was only a £1.5m contract but it helped diversify our work and was a first step into moving into the education sector.

Just as important as diversifying was making sure we remained at the technological forefront of the industry. For example, we created an app for our engineers. Previously, people had been creating standard web browser sites which looked good on a mobile phone, but there was no fancy app technology. Then HTML 5 came out which allowed you to create specialised apps you could download through the Apple Store or Google store, or wherever. We created an app for our contractors and engineers so when they went to our client sites, they could log all the data of their work onto the app and it would send it to us in real time. Even when they didn't have a signal on site, it would automatically upload it when they got back online. It was ground-breaking. Derrick then got Wolseley for us as well in the same consultancy way. They were the biggest trade counter company in the UK with around one thousand sites, supplying builders, plumbers and decorators and the like. He was doing consultancy projects for them and won us a contract to replace all their standard lighting with LED lights in their Leamington Spa distribution centre, which was massive. That project was £1m alone. They immediately showed great savings in energy costs, became interested in what else we could do for them and eventually signed up. That was a £12m annual contract. It was fair to say things were going well.

In six years, our turnover had gone from £1.7m in 2014 to £65m just four years later. We were growing faster and faster and faster. The days of sleepless nights over £300,000 debts were a thing of the past, far bigger issues were keeping me awake. The next company to come on board was Tui, the largest travel company in the world. When I was at ISS, a guy called Simon Walker had been head of FM at Harrods, left the role and was looking for a new challenge. Mutual acquaintances put us in touch, and he came to me at ISS for a job. We sat down, he was a great guy, but we did not have a vacant role I thought he was suitable for. He went on to get a job at the phone company 'Three', and then moved to Selfridges. We had kept in touch and would periodically go out and have a few drinks – during which he would always call me a bastard for not giving him a job – and he learnt more about our technology and my aspirations for the industry.

He then became head of property at TUI, said he wanted to make a difference to its operations and asked if he could come in and see us. He presented us with his challenges, I told him what we could do, and he was impressed. But at Cloudfm, new companies are not just our clients, we seek real partnerships. Part of this process is being sure we want to work with that company and it is also crucial we get their whole organisation onboard. We need to know they are prepared to think differently, to realise our relationship will be totally different to the ones they have had in past, that our FM principles and practice are totally different to anything they have experienced before.

The first part of this process is to get the client to visit us so we can have a three to four hour-long meeting. We gauge what their needs are and, most importantly, what their mindset is. We explain all our processes, show them the technology, the Engineers Academy and gauge their reactions. Some people say, "We already do that, we already have that," and we know they are not the clients for us. We know they are deluded and talking rubbish, so we politely show them the door. If we think we can work together, we then tell the FM manager they need to get more people onboard. It isn't fair on that individual to try and implement the change the company will experience if it is all on their shoulders. The stress will kill them. We tell them you need to bring your whole senior team here and create an environment where they want this as much as, if not more than, you do. That means, rather than the FM manager carrying the burden of whether it will work, there are thirty people in his company carrying it. If they are managing a team of twenty, at the next meeting, we want to take at least half of them through that same process, so they are excited by the opportunities too. Once we have enough people onboard, we will go through the due diligence process. We will then present our findings and finally insist we meet the people at the very top of the business, the chief exec, the MD, the chief financial officer. The reaction is we will never convince them to come to Colchester, their diaries will be too busy, and they have delegated this stuff to the FM manager already. However, for the process to work, they have to know the value we are adding, how different our relationship is going to be and we won't proceed unless they do. It's a deal-breaker for us. We won't work with clients unless they truly embrace and share our methods, beliefs and the way we work together. It must always be a partnership.

In the history of Cloudfm, we have walked away from perhaps a dozen major deals because we weren't sure the customer was the right fit for us, or they were merely paying lip service to embracing the changes which would be needed. Those dozen deals were worth maybe £80m, but we were better off without them. Thankfully, Tui got it, they understood our philosophies and were willing to embrace them and so we took over FM management of their six hundred UK shops. We brought the benefits we always promise and they extended their contract with us less than two years after it had started. The one time we bypassed that process? We had our only major failure with a client. As I have said before, we avoid working with small companies. Economies of scale mean we can't positively impact them in the same way we can for larger firms and, just as importantly, they also have a different mindset. With larger companies if you have four hundred stores, a £10m contract and 400,000 assets, you appreciate one slowly dripping tap in the toilets is not a crisis. You have bigger things to worry about. You know our engineer will fix it on his next monthly visit, or even pop in if he is passing because we take pride in the job we do. Of course, if it's something bigger we will be there in four hours, but if it's a slightly dripping tap you put it into perspective. However, if you have five stores you will obsess over the tap and be on the phone three times a day shouting for it to be fixed. It's just a headache we don't need.

Sometimes, even when companies experience rapid growth, they maintain this mindset. Their business has got much bigger but their mentality hasn't. They want everything done yesterday and everything for nothing. We won a contract with such a company. We went through the normal diligence, got to know them, but I had reservations as to whether they were the right match for us. You know the voice you get in the back of your head, the one that reminds you to look left and right before you step into a road which stops you going under a bus? That voice was telling me to walk away. **Always listen to the voice in your head before you listen to anyone else. Whatever anyone else is saying to you, that inner voice is speaking with years of experience, knowledge and instinct.**

With some reservations, we took them on. It was a nightmare from the start. We knew millions of pounds were being wasted in their business through faulty equipment and poor FM practice, but they were constantly questioning every single aspect of our operation. If one of their store managers authorised an engineer getting a new £50 cage for their dishwasher because the old one had holes in it, and items were dropping through it and breaking the machine, head office was on the phone to us demanding why it was necessary. This questioning, micro-managing and attitude was constant, it was drawing away all our energy. We held countless meetings with them, where we would say, "Look, this is our process, these are the benefits we are going to bring you, these are our structures, this is our agreement, work with us as partners and reap the benefits." They would agree and then two weeks later would be shouting at our help desk, "Why have you ordered four replacement bulbs for that site when it only needed two? We would reply, "Well, because then you have two spare the next time one goes and we can replace it immediately." They would fire back, "But the bulbs cost us £3 each and we didn't need two of them right now." Even though it was a £10m account, we eventually said, "We can't do this anymore, we have to walk away." Of course, we did so properly, agreed to professionally disengage with them, carried out all the work required so they could comfortably, sensibly and safely transition into working with someone else. At no point did we give them a deadline or stop doing any of the work. We came up with a plan and worked through it together. We could not wait to get rid of them but we did so professionally.

That mistake aside, things were going well. Turnover was shooting up, new clients were coming onboard and everything was rosy.

Communication is key at Cloudfm and we regularly hold events with staff to discuss the business and inspire them to even greater heights.

Then I did something which astounded everyone at Cloudfm and the entire industry. I slammed the brakes on and told my team to stop selling. No new contracts, no more consultancy projects, we didn't want any more work. I told the team we were like a block of flats. We had experienced fantastic rapid growth over a short period of time and it would have been easy to let it run away with us. Get another client, get another client, keep growing. We had built the foundations and then added floor after floor as the company grew. However, a couple of things were occurring which made me think, *Hang on a minute, on the upper stories of these flats I can feel the occasional wobble.* The warning signs were subtle, but they were there. **Never ignore early warning signs, it will inevitably smack you in the face.**

For example, clients were starting to take more and more credit and we were not alert enough to the dangers. Our business model meant we were always cash rich. Because our clients were paying us within five days, but we had forty-five days to pay our contractors, we always had lots of money in the bank. Because of this, we had stopped getting worried about people who weren't paying us on time. People were saying, "What's the problem? We have got loads of money, why are you worrying about it?" What was I worrying about? Cloudfm had almost collapsed when Republic went bust and, long before that, I had faced ruin with Essex Air Conditioning when ENI Coward had folded. People were getting complacent and, like a disease, it was spreading.

Our technology was so robust it also meant every job we did for clients should have been fool-proof but we had missed a couple of compliance issues. With our ethos of transparency, honesty and trust, we had highlighted these errors with the clients, rather than hide them, but they should never have happened. We had taken on a large number of staff, some of the existing staff were increasingly comfortable in their roles and we needed to instil in everyone a new sense of focus. **Complacency is a normal human trait. You can't change human behaviour and human spirit, so you need to put checks in place to make sure you don't fall victim to it.** We needed to tighten things up and shore up the foundations before we went up another five floors. We had to re-educate people about what was important and what risks were being run. The culture of the business and its four principles of integrity, humility, empathy and freedom were as vital as they had been on day one. Following these was the number one priority every single day above all else but, as we grew, it was more difficult to ensure they were truly embraced right throughout the company.

It was a major decision, and a year-long process, but the majority of people reacted positively to it. They knew our turnover would continue to grow with existing clients and, unlike most FM companies, we were not a high-pressure business which was all about *sell, sell, sell*. We were there to change the industry. Of course, there were some concerned voices. For some people, getting new clients is inbred into their DNA, it's what they thrive on. They understood our philosophy, but it came second to the chase and the thrill of getting new clients. Getting bigger and getting richer was the goal for them and if the foundations were shaking a little their view was, "Don't worry, it will be all right." I knew it wouldn't be, so I had to keep them on a tight leash. But that didn't mean the business stood still. It was time to grow in other areas.

My daughter Natalie, who had risen to one of the highest levels in the business, was becoming frustrated at the growth slowing down. She decided to become a bigger fish in a smaller pond and took on a director role in one of our supplier's businesses. She left with my blessing, although I wasn't convinced it was the right move for her.

After Natalie had left, there was a large hole in management of the helpdesk and operations and, what seemed like overnight, my daughter Kelly appeared to grow these huge wings, and in no time had taken ownership of Natalie's role with a totally different style of management. It was obvious that she had lived in Natalie's shadow for the last few years and suddenly blossomed. Our operations became even slicker under her stewardship.

Kelly and I in 2012 as Cloudfm began to grow.

For years, we had kept our head below the parapet in terms of publicity, but it was time to grow the brand. In 2017 we sponsored the ground-naming rights at Essex County Cricket Club's ground, which was renamed the Cloudfm County ground. Essex Cricket is an international cricket brand, its players frequently play for England and other international teams and, because of its traditions and reputation, it is known worldwide. Sponsoring the county's ground fitted in with our ethos of supporting the local community and it gave real credibility to us. Lots of people sponsor a shirt for a year but sponsoring a ground is a ten-year process, it's a longstanding commitment and says, "We are here to stay, we are a serious business."

When the deal was announced we were getting contacted by American magazines, the coverage was off the scale. Essex cricket gets three hundred hours of live coverage from Sky TV every season and our name was constantly being broadcast into people's living rooms. We were getting massive exposure for £75,000 a year. If we had tried to match that exposure in Premiere League football, we could have kissed goodbye to £40m.

Sir Alistair Cook and I, after we signed the ground-naming rights deal.

I believe because of this one deal, and all the PR we were enjoying, everyone in the £200 billion UK FM industry now knows who Cloudfm are. We might be small compared to the FM giants, but everyone knows our name. A massive amount of that is down to sponsoring the cricket club. Another reason we did it was because of the culture of the club and the sport. Football's reputation is that, at the top level, the game has been tarnished by too much wealth. We can all picture millionaire players acting like prima donnas, walking round with their headphones on and misbehaving. Cricket is nothing like that. Despite recent international scandals, it is still seen as a refined sport. As for the players, they act with humility, integrity and genuinely appreciate what the sponsors bring to their club. They will come into our corporate box and engage with us and our guests, not because they are contractually obliged to, because they genuinely value the fact that we are helping their club. Sir Alistair Cook is a worldwide giant of the game, one of the sport's best ever batsmen, but every time we are at the ground he will wander into our box at some stage and start shaking hands, saying hello and thanking people for their support.

Culturally, our two organisations work well together, and it has been money well spent. When they were doing well in the County Championship in 2019, to further motivate and inspire the players, I said if they won it, I would take them away on a golfing trip to Portugal. I approached the other major sponsors, we each chipped in a few grand and after they won, we all went away for a long weekend. The brilliant thing about the trip was the players themselves, they were all so humble, well-behaved. People such as the former England captain Graham Gooch, who has been at Essex Cricket Club man and boy, and Ronnie Irani, another Essex and England legend, have instilled a culture where players are responsible for their own actions. They have been so well educated in their environment over the right ways to behave. In four days not one player did anything stupid, said anything stupid, they never stopped saying thank-you, were polite to everyone. Their behaviour was humbling. Can you imagine taking top footballers on such a trip? Once again, you are the product of your environment.

Essex Cricket went on to win the T20 and the Championship double in 2019, which had never been achieved before. Being associated with such success helps, and I hope we perhaps contributed in a small way towards it.

Myself and Graham Gooch, one of the world's leading batsmen. He is now a Club Ambassador at Essex Cricket Club.

Cloudfm also began to spread our wings internationally. With the Brexit furore escalating, we opened an office in Dublin, not merely to serve a number of sites our clients had over there, but also to have a stronger foothold in post-Brexit Europe. Then one day I got a LinkedIn message from a guy called Ignasi from a company in Spain called Optima Facility. They are a family business, have existed for forty-five years, know everyone in Spain, are roughly the same size as Cloudfm, but they concentrate on soft services - cleaning, security and the like. Ignasi said FM in Spain was as broken as it was everywhere else, they wanted to offer something different and could they come to meet us? Ignasi flew over and when we met him it was obvious that he was a Spanish version of me. My colleagues started referring to him as 'Spanish Jeff'. His frustrations, principles, aspirations and approach to business were exactly the same as mine. Before we met, they had initially thought the big difference we brought to the industry was our technology, which is what a lot of people think. So, Ignasi had initially scoured the world looking at technology. He had been to Dubai, India, Italy and America. When he was in America, he met Cushman and Wakefield, one of the largest asset management companies in the world, and they had told him you need to go and see Cloudfm in the UK. That made my day for a start!

When we sat down, I said, "Before I tell you about Cloudfm, tell me what the challenges are in Spain." They were identical in terms of culture, behaviour and attitude. It was like an epiphany. Our problems were the same. Within a few weeks more people came over from Optima, we met the family owners, and we started talking about forming a partnership in Spain, supplying hard services. The talks took a year until we agreed to set up a Spanish division of Cloudfm. We agreed it would be a joint venture and would financially be split 50/50, but we would have the final say on everything to protect our brand, reputation and the model we are delivering.

Myself (left) with Ignasi and Alejandro Casamada (both standing) and their father Ignacio (seated), the owners of Optima Facility. Sadly, Ignacio became a tragic victim of the COVID epidemic and will be sadly missed.

Optima continues to trade entirely independently and we are trying to build Cloudfm Spain together. It is a partnership based on having the same mentality and absolute trust. We launched in October 2018 and by January 2019 we got our first client, Serunion. It is a catering and restaurant business which has three thousand kitchens throughout Spain in places like factories, schools and other establishments. One of their kitchens is even in football superstar Messi's personal box in Camp Nou. Having a European footprint is important because a lot of major companies are pan-European, so if you don't have a foothold there it's a massive disadvantage. The new company also proves we can work in different cultures, in different languages and is another sign we are a growing business.

Another marketing boost came in 2018 when we were given one of the *Financial Times* 'UK's Top 1,000 Businesses to Inspire Britain' awards. These independent awards look at rapidly-growing businesses, the quality of their clients and the strength of their balance sheets. It is a real accolade because it is not based on buying adverts or sponsorship - the evidence of worthiness has to be there in black and white. It is difficult to quantify the financial benefits of such awards, but they all added to our awareness, brand equity and reputation as a growing force in the industry. Awards like these are great as self-affirmation, but our philosophy is always to remain humble. Despite our growing international reputation, when anyone else in the industry wins an award or does anything else of note, Cloudfm is the first to contact them to say congratulations. We never want to be a threat, we don't engage in seeing who can piss up a wall higher than anyone else, we want to be humble. Even when we are consulted to audit the work of other FM companies, and our research shows they are failing, we are always respectful and say, "We have been asked by this company to look into this matter, and we are simply doing the audit the same as you would in those circumstances." We are always careful, cautious and focussed on behaving respectfully.

The break in sales drive also allowed us to focus on what comes next. Brains a lot bigger than mine, like the UN Committee for Climate

Change, say if industry is to stop wasting money, time and energy by 2050, more than fifty per cent of this change will be reliant on technology which does not yet exist. Our technology has always been at the core of our business, but we realise it is going to change beyond comprehension in the next few years. That is why our Mindsett programme was born.

Simply put, we want Cloudfm to be at the spearhead of technological evolution. This aim sounds simple, but in an ever-changing digital environment, it is a massive challenge. Its first major achievement? Creating a system to monitor our clients' assets and save them a fortune. In the last few years, it has become relatively commonplace for expensive ovens and other equipment to come complete with sensors. These transmit data to people's phones and laptops about its energy usage, when the door has been opened and if maintenance is needed. These are fine in isolation but for companies running hundreds of sites, with dozens of assets in each, all supplying their own data, the system is unwieldy and of limited value. The restaurant owner might know what his oven is doing, but he isn't getting data from any other equipment. If he is, he then has to open seven apps for the seven different pieces of kit in his kitchen and try to make sense of it all.

At Cloudfm, we have done away with all that. We have designed and manufactured our own range of sensors and gateways, which monitor the performance of every sort of asset from ovens, hot water systems, air con, refrigerators. You name it, we have the technology to fit sensors to it. These then feed the data to a transmitter, which passes it along to a cloud from where it is accessed by our Artificial Intelligence system. The AI then creates user-friendly insights, which appears on an app giving an unheralded insight into how your assets can be better run. It tells you when your equipment needs urgent maintenance and when it is cost effective to replace it. It alerts you to problems, highlights examples of best practice across your hundreds of sites. It tells you what actions to take which will benefit your business immediately. Users do not get raw data to try and make sense of, they get simple reports a child can understand. We typically put about fifty sensors in each building and the benefits are immediate. The technology is still developing but our philosophy is always to get it out there, and then build on it. We want our customers to reap the benefits of it before every T has been crossed and I dotted.

Initially, when we were building the prototypes, the cost was high. You are paying top dollar because you are buying one component rather than a million of them. On January 15, 2020, the cost of installing these sensors was £10,000 a site. By May 2020 it had dropped to £1,000 a site because we have started mass-manufacturing them. We usually start by looking at clients' energy use as it is the fastest to get the best return. With one of our clients, we analysed what times they turned their ovens on every day at different sites. The data showed that some turned them on far too early, others left them on far too long. Simply by looking at the data and standardising their oven times we worked out we could reduce their energy bill by fifty-five per cent.

After energy, we then examine the data to assist with compliance and risk, predictive maintenance and then environmental control. As ever, we are able to tell clients, "If you pay to install this technology it will save you X over the next few years, or we will write you a cheque." For a couple of years, we had looked for software partners to get such a system operational and four times we came very close to getting into bed with them. They all either went bust or got bought out by another company. That would have left us with buildings full of sensors which the company was no longer making or supporting. Eventually, it just made sense for us to control the whole process. We build and run every single aspect of it, from the sensors to the transmitters to the AI learning system and app.

At the core of this system is the Artificial Intelligence system, which is so complicated we simply refer to as 'the brain'. Its capacity to interpret data and self-learn almost defies description and understanding for us common folk, but thankfully we have some very big brains of our own working on it. In 2019 we began a relationship with Essex University and the government's Innovate scheme, which gives PhD students a start in the commercial world. For two years the government pays half their salary, and we pay the other half. They get the opportunity to learn, work in the real world and initially earn around £20,000 in a commercial environment. The beauty of these PhD students is their attitude.

We have had supposed experts walk in who want £70,000 a year and they never succeed in building anything. These students are talented, ambitious and extremely clever but they have not been tainted by greed or opinions of self-worth. Their purpose is not to chase money, but to build things and broaden their experience. Of course, because they are creating such cutting-edge technology, more money is the result of that. For example, our chief developer joined us on £18,000 a year in 2014. Four years later his salary had almost quadrupled.

One of the major issues in the FM industry is the goals set by clients – for example, the four-hour response times we mentioned earlier. These are often simply not realistic. No-one can employ enough engineers, or have enough third-party contractors, to ensure every demand can be met anywhere in the UK within four hours. However, clients will insist on four-hour response times because it gives them a measurable response time and, crucially for their balance sheet, allows them to financially penalise companies if they fail to meet them. The fact is, because of supply and demand, these windows simply can't always be met.

Such issues are common in other businesses. Take Uber. It was set up because there were never enough taxis to meet demand. Uber realised there were millions of people with cars who want to earn some extra money. It came up with the idea of matching the demand for taxis with this supply of cars and it used technology to set up direct links between the two. Airbnb did the same. The hotel industry has always said, however many new hotels get built, it can only meet around fifty per cent of demand. Airbnb realised there were millions of people with spare rooms they might be willing to rent out. So, again, they matched supply with demand. At Cloudfm we have done the same with Augmented Reality. We are never going to be able to employ enough people, take months fully training them as engineers capable of fixing every bit of kit they come across, and then pay them full engineer salaries just to meet the fluctuations of demand. It is also true that an awful lot of maintenance and repair work does not need highly skilled engineers to do it. Why pay expensive engineers to change lightbulbs?

We realised to match supply and demand, we needed to find engineering-minded people who could perform basic tasks and AR allows us to do this. For example, when an individual walks onto a restaurant site they turn on their iPad, which can immediately see all of the assets on the site. When he points the iPad at a cold room, he sees a 3-D image which tells him how the cold room has been operating, a history of its temperature readings, its service and repair history and, most importantly, if something is not working properly. Having identified the problem, the iPad then tells you how to fix it using short videos. The reason for using videos is simple. If you buy a wardrobe from IKEA and there is wood and screws and fastenings everywhere, and it comes with an instructional manual in seventeen languages, you lose the will to live. Instead, if you can watch a step-by-step video on YouTube or somewhere on how to do it, it is so much easier, and you do it ten times faster. With the help of such videos, anyone with enough common sense to use a spanner can safely fix a huge amount of problems. People are getting real-time training in right there on site. If the problem is more complicated, they can either have a real-time video chat with someone more qualified who can talk them through it. Of course, if the situation demands it, we will have full engineers on site as soon as possible. Through AR, we have matched the resource with the demand.

The cost of the whole Mindsett programme has been about £1.5m over two years - £250,000 of which came from a government grant – and the majority of that has gone on twenty people's salaries. The benefits it will bring us, and our clients, will dwarf that figure. And the benefits of this technology are not just related to traditional FM. For example, we were asked to go and see a doctors' surgery on January 30, 2020, about a common problem in the NHS. It keeps losing expensive and temperature-sensitive drugs to theft and fridge faults. If the fridges break down and the temperature rises, the drugs are ruined. Within twelve days we had created a sensor, transmitter and app, which allows them to see when the fridge door has been opened, which drugs are being moved in and out, what the temperature is in the fridge and it alerts them if there is unusual behaviour such as the temperature rising. That is the sort of speedy response our technical team are capable of.

The technology should also be of massive interest to the asset-manufacturer's themselves. Fridge-makers, for example, are really good at making fridges, putting them in a test chamber and proving they meet quality standards. But it is a controlled environment. As soon as you put the fridge in a commercial kitchen it is operating outside the environmental parameters it was designed for. This is also a common trick they use to void any warranties should it break down – they say you have been running it in an environment which is too hot. People spend a fortune on these warranties, and they are void the second they switch the fridge on. However, our technology will give the manufacturers real-life data about how their machines operate in the real world and how to improve them going forward. By summer of 2020, moving forward was at the forefront of all our minds.

COVID July 2020:

Hard decisions

Redundancies are terrible. They bring anger, fear, disappointment and stress. No company likes to make them but sometimes the demands of the business mean they are inevitable.

In total, from our three hundred and thirty staff, we put two hundred people at risk of redundancy. Of these, one hundred and thirty were engineers but we TUPED across more than eighty to the new independent engineering companies that we had helped to set up. Others got a job on the newly restructured helpdesk that we renamed – 'Technical Support Centre'. Because we had worked hard at communicating to all affected staff as early as possible, we had enabled them to immediately begin seeking alternative employment with our full support. We tried to be as honest as we could with everyone affected by such cuts. We did not just hand people an envelope and a cheque. From July, for two months, the HR team's sole major role was to help find new jobs for as many of those affected as possible. This was another example of our culture in action – albeit in difficult circumstances. We are more than just slogans and words. We are passionate about trying to help as many people as we can.

I could never promise to find every one of the hundred or so people affected new jobs, but I did my best. I even personally emailed our clients and everyone in our supply chain saying, "These are quality people who have been highly trained. If you have vacancies, I have every confidence you will be grateful you took them on." For example, one employee who had been with us for a number of years said she was looking for work on LinkedIn. I shared the post and added a message including, "Anyone who is lucky enough to secure her for their organisation will be acquiring an incredible asset. She is a talented and tenacious individual who is purpose-driven." The post had more than two thousand views and even included a response from a senior person at Amazon encouraging her to keep an eye on their vacancies site.

The end result of efforts like these? We helped to find new jobs for the majority of people affected. In fact, the final number of people that had not secured a new role by the time the process had ended was in single figures. This alone was a major achievement. These were catastrophic times for commerce, and we saw our total head count reduced from three hundred and thirty people to around a hundred. And the changes did not stop there. They also affected the very top of the business. How times change. Just a couple of years before, things were going incredibly well.

Chapter 15

A right royal result

In the FM industry there are lots of different awards. The governing body is the Institute for Workplace Facilities Management and they have a massive annual black-tie event at the Grosvenor Hotel with about fifteen hundred people getting drunk. We were always being asked to enter the awards, but my view was we are here to tear down and change the industry, not be congratulated by it. Instead of entering the awards, we would sponsor them. We did this for about four years then stopped because we perceived - admittedly with no real scientific evidence - that other companies which sponsored the awards tended to win quite a lot of them. Strange that!

One day, I went to meet a Southend landscaping company called Ground Control, which was interested in doing some work with us. They had grown the business from nothing to £100m in a short space of time, and I was fascinated to see what they were about. As I walked up their stairs, they had this big plaque on the wall saying they had a won a Queen's Award for Enterprise. Even though these are among the most prestigious awards in the country, I didn't have a clue what they were. I was shocked when they told me winning it had transformed their business and had played a major part in growing them from £60m to £100m. I fancied some of that and so, when I got back to work, I asked my marketing team to look into it. They reported one of the reasons it is such a prestigious award is because it is so difficult to win. There were countless hoops to jump through, the submission document needed reams of detail, but I said, "If it is the award worth having, then let's have a go." I left them to it. They spent six months preparing a document of evidence which eventually ran to one hundred and sixty pages. It was brilliant. Detailed but easy to understand, exceptionally well-written. We submitted it for the Innovation category and then I forgot all about it.

One day in March 2019 I got a call from the head of marketing saying, "We have only gone and won it." I thought she meant a contract and I replied saying, "Great, which client?" and she replied, "No, the Queen's Award."

It hadn't been at the forefront of my mind because I knew it was incredibly difficult to win one, never mind at the first time of asking. She forwarded me the email from HM The Queen's office with the details, and it stated you are not allowed to tell anyone until April 23 when the results are officially announced in the *Guardian* newspaper. I was over the moon, it was brilliant. This is one accolade you cannot win by buying advertising space or sponsorship - it is the UK's premium award and a totally independent recognition of excellence. It is the best a business can win, simple as that. It was a massive affirmation of everything we were doing. In June, we went to Buckingham Palace to receive it and mix with the other award-winners. Two people were allowed to attend, and Derrick magnanimously said James Blackman and I should go because the award was for innovation and technology, which is mine and James' field. He also said he had met the Queen before. She was old news for Derrick!

We went down with a film crew to record the day before the presentation so all the staff could see what went into it and feel part of it. At 6.30pm, James and I rocked up to Buckingham Palace. It was amazing. The event was in five or six massive rooms which were unbelievably ornate, luxurious and regal, with famous paintings on the wall I had only ever seen in history books. The frames alone would buy my house three times over. It was overwhelming. We could see into the gardens which were also spectacular, all the staff were in pristine footmen's uniforms, complete with gold buttons which were polished to the hilt. It was an incredible experience. One of the other people there approached us, said she was one of the judges for Innovation and asked what we thought of the process. We sheepishly admitted our marketing team had put the submission together and we were still a little in the dark about what the exact process was. She explained it is a seven-stage process. First, there is the written application which goes before a committee to see if it warrants consideration. If approved, your company then goes

James and I receiving the Queen's Award at the Palace.

through financial due diligence where a team of accountants study your published accounts over the last three to four years. A lot of companies fail at this stage. Then, HMRC investigates the company's tax behaviour and the personal tax behaviour of the people who own and run it and ninety per cent of the remaining firms fall at that hurdle. They then start studying the technological innovation aspects of the company and bring in experts to comment on it. Knowing people get the crest for five years, they then look into the business's longevity before it is presented back to the full committee for consideration. About five hundred companies get put forward to Her Majesty the Queen and she alone picks the winning companies, which usually ranges in number from about one hundred and fifty to two hundred and fifty across all the different categories.

The big shock was we didn't know any of that when we entered! We are a squeaky-clean business - as winning the award proves — but we might have shied away from it, having known teams of accountants were going through everything with a fine-tooth comb, including our own personal accounts. Prince Charles made a speech, and I was getting stuck into the free champagne, when up walked Princess Beatrice. James Blackman started charming her and I thought I had better contribute and blurted out, "I hear your Mum and Dad are getting back together?"

James immediately turned and walked away, and she looked me in the eye and said, "I don't think that's an appropriate question, do you?"

To be fair, she was right, but she hadn't drunk a bottle of champers. She seemed like a nice girl, but it is fair to say I won't be on her Christmas card list.

It is too early to tell if having such a prestigious award will have a dramatic impact on the business, but we got so much national and international PR from it, it was amazing. We had the crest put on all our vans, all the staff got special Queen's Award pins to wear and yet again, it sets us apart from the competition. It is a massive confidence-builder and a massive seal of approval for everything we stand for. My one regret was that my father was not alive to see it. He passed away on August 14, 2017. It knocked me for six. It made me rethink my life and how quickly it can end. I idolised him. He had instilled in me values which I still cling to today and his death made me re-evaluate a lot, but mostly how valuable time is. I realised I had spent an awful lot of my life working every hour I possibly could. I vowed to spend more of it doing things I liked with the people I love. It also made me re-evaluate the business in terms of at what point I would be willing to sell it.

COVID July 2020:

Helping out

With the country still in crisis, our thoughts naturally turned to what we could do to help combat COVID.

The government launched an INNOVATE grants scheme to help find quick solutions to some of the problems the NHS was facing. Because of our long relationship with Essex University, and because we were already working with the NHS on some IT projects, we got together and said, "What can we do to help?"

The result was a project looking at UV light to help combat the virus. The university did the research, we made the equipment for UV solutions which will nullify the virus. We are close to a safe solution.

Chapter 16

Who wants to be a millionaire?

There are very few people on the planet I actively dislike. One of them is 1966 World Cup-winning hat-trick "hero" Sir Geoff Hurst. I can't stand the bloke. But in a weird way he was partly responsible for a seismic change at our company. For years, we had gone through a process of trying to secure one or two clients a year and enjoyed almost a one hundred per cent success rate. We thought we had the process sewn up. Aim for a target, hit it. Having put the brakes on the business for a while to allow us to refocus, by 2018 we were talking to three major clients and were very confident. They were making all the right noises and we anticipated landing about £35m of new contracts. We thought in the worst-case scenario we might lose one. We lost all three. One was a £20m contract and the business concerned decided to buy a massive national restaurant chain to add to its portfolio, so it wanted to concentrate on integrating that instead. Another one disappeared because the guy who was in negotiation with us got caught with a brown envelope in his back pocket from a supplier. It had nothing at all to do with us, but the company decided to get rid of him, and cancel any deals he was negotiating. The third collapsed because they did not like our negotiator. It was a catalogue of bad news. At every previous stage of my career before now my reaction would have been, "Oh shit, we are in trouble now." That was not the case at Cloudfm. In my previous jobs, we needed new contracts because we were constantly trying to fill a leaking bucket. At Cloudfm, we didn't need to win a single new client to survive. We had purposely set up the business not to be under that kind of pressure. However, it is only natural and helpful to set targets and goals you want to reach.

Back when the company was still a pipe dream, Derrick and I had settled on a magic figure to reach - for the company to have a turnover of £100m. Bearing in mind we were two men working from a shed, it was a tall order, but we thought it was possible. When we got to 2017, we were nearing that £100m benchmark. We had £30m of contracts we were confident of signing and we were five years into an original seven-year plan. It was time to take stock. I took all the senior managers to Portugal and spoke candidly to them. I said, "We have all invested into this company, either financially or with blood, sweat and tears and we are reaching a major benchmark, so I need to know who is in and who is out? Who is exhausted and who wants to go again? It's time to be candid. If we are going to make another massive push and grow the business to the next stage, we need to know who has had enough, who wants more?" Everyone said they wanted to carry on. But before too long most of them had left the company.

So, Sir Geoff Hurst. Back when I owned Clacton FC, we had end-of-season events and I wanted them to be the best in the league. I always paid for a star guest and one year it was Sir Geoff. I paid him £5,000 to come along and present all the awards, two hours a night for three nights. The events did not just cover the senior team, but the thirteen kids' teams as well. The under-sevens wouldn't have a clue who Geoff Hurst was, but at least their parents would be excited. On the junior evening, a shy little seven-year-old approached Sir Geoff and said, "Can you sign my football please, sir?" He said, "Of course, who should I sign it for?" and the kid said, "I don't know yet, my Dad and my Grandad both love you but I don't know who I will give it to yet." Sir Geoff looked at the kid and said something along the lines of, "Sorry son, due to copyright and people abusing my signature on memorabilia, I have to write who it is for, so whose name is it going to be, your Dads or your Grandads?"

The kid started crying. I wanted to lump Sir Geoff - he would have been crying too. Instead, I pulled him to one side and said, "I am paying you five grand, if you want your money sign the ball." By contrast, the next year I brought in Peter Shilton on the same deal, two hours a night from 6.30pm to 8.30pm for three nights. He turned up at 3pm, spent three hours with the youth teams and their parents before the event started, and then stayed till 10pm, moving from table to table, talking to everyone. At the end of the night, he was helping the old ladies do the dishes. He was brilliant. Comparing him to Sir Geoff Hurst made me dislike Sir Geoff even more. Of course, inevitably, every football fundraiser or award night I went to, Sir Geoff was there. For years I barely restrained myself from walking up to him and saying, "You have been trading off your hat-trick for fifty years, why don't you give it a rest?"

In 2019, it began to dawn on me that in the upper levels of Cloudfm we had some great people who had done great things, but most of it had also been years ago. Examining this realisation took me to a decision which almost killed me emotionally. Having rebuilt the business from the foundations, I now started looking at the very top of the company. We had got bigger and bigger, we had more senior people, more shareholders, but I was no longer sure the right people were on the bus, never mind in the right seats. The last couple of years had seen us fail to win contracts and growth had slowed. This alone wasn't keeping me awake at night, but the reasons for it puzzled me and I suspected that, although the top team had stayed the same, they had changed as people. It was challenging to undertake this process because we had always been a happy, positive organisation. At senior management level we were just like a family, we cared for each other, had each other's backs, and turned a blind eye when people sometimes dropped the ball. The whole basis of our management culture was always to remove obstacles from the top down. My job as CEO was to ensure the rest of the senior management team had everything in place to allow them to perform brilliantly. My role was to say, "What problem is preventing you from doing your job better?" and then ensure it was solved. This could be anything from a piece of technology the business relied on not being up to scratch, to issues with their personal life – for example if they had marital problems or wanted to spend more time with their families. My job was to give them all the support they needed to do brilliantly. That was their main role as well, to ensure middle management had everything in place to manage properly. This principle goes right through the organisation from the very top, to the people dealing with clients on a day-to-day basis. Everyone should be able to perform superbly because the obstacles to doing this have been removed. The team on the coal face should never have to tell a client, "We can't fix that problem because we don't have the right equipment," or, "Management will not let me dedicate the time to it." All the problems which might prevent them being one hundred per cent customer-focussed should have been removed. However, if senior management was failing in the process, the trouble cascaded all the way down. Coldly sitting back and asking if these top people were performing, and if we still needed them, was upsetting. I was upfront with the team and spoke about my fears. I said that we have grown at speed, had a lot of fun, largely stress-free growth, but maybe it is time to move from being a teenager to an adult.

I said, "If we want to turn this into a £250m business, we are going to have to be a lot more focussed." I spent two months doing a lot of soul-searching, holding one-to-one meetings with the senior team and, to take the emotion out of the process, we also did a lot of real analysis into the benefits these people had given us. The analysis showed some were living on past glories. Not to Sir Geoff's extent, but it was still an issue. We had people who had secured major contracts for us a couple of years before and thought they were superstars but had won little since. We started asking, "Why are we failing to get these contracts? What's different to before?" and we suspected as the process was exactly the same, it must be the people who had changed. For whatever reason, they were not achieving the same results, we suspected some had a touch of arrogance and clients were sensing it. In one case a prospective client rang me and said, "Don't ever send that bloke to see me again."

That was an alarm bell going off I could not avoid hearing. Suddenly, it seemed people who used to be largely responsible for our wins were contributing to our losses.

At the end of this process, in September 2019, I made my decision and moved at lightning speed to implement it. I called eight people in who had been with us from almost the very beginning and told them their services were longer required. All were gone within three days. These were good people and it hurt to do it. However, I felt when they had joined us, they had eye of the tiger like in the Rocky films - they were hungry, nothing would stop them. But the board now felt they won some fights, got a little complacent and the tiger was gone. They still looked good in the ring, were good people, but they were unknowingly going through the motions.

When removing people, the HR rules are laid down in stone. You begin a consultation process, hold meetings, give people a chance to say why they should be retained etc. In the real world such consultations are a paper exercise. The course of action has already been decided and everyone knows what the end result will be. I had no time for that. These people were my friends and I was going to have adult conversations with them. I sat them down, one by one and said, "You know we have been going through this process. I am trying to analyse what is right for the business. I have some big plans going forward and unfortunately you do not feature in them."

It was one of the most difficult things I have ever had to do. I didn't sleep for days leading up to these meetings. I had spent years with these people and cared for them. Some were in their late forties and early fifties and their company shares were their nest egg, the job was going to see them through just a few more years until they took early retirement, and I was taking that away. It was awful. At some of the meetings what made it even worse was the individuals concerned were worried about how I was coping with the process and said I looked terrible. I was getting rid of them and they were worried about me. That's testament to the individuals concerned. At the meetings, I said, "I realise you have shares, notice periods and redundancy payments due. We want you to leave the business right now, but let's meet up again in three weeks when the shock has passed. Our values mean we are going to do the right thing by you, and we will talk about how we can best structure your package for you."

The reason for the delay was two-fold. Firstly, it would allow us more time to go through the complexity of freeing up their shares. Secondly, as these people had helped grow the business, I also thought it was right they should have a chance to have their say in how we shaped the severance packages. It wouldn't have been fair to have handed them an envelope and say, "This is what you are getting, the door is that way." The trouble with the three-week gap was it allowed people time to get over the shock, and a lot of anger and denial to build up. While we were trying to be fair and generous, the fact is when you go through a divorce, either personally or in a business sense, there is little happiness. Worries about how I was faring emotionally during the process had understandably gone out of the window at the second round of meetings. By then some of them would have preferred to throw me through it. A couple of them were misguided about what the business was worth compared to a genuinely independent valuation we had done. When they got their own legal advice, they knew our estimate was beyond dispute. It was an awful time for all concerned, but you have to ensure these types of negotiations are done right.

Ironically, during this period I was helping a former colleague who had been kicked out of his own company by the board of directors after he was absent due to ill health. Eventually, legal action was the only way forward for him to get his share of the business, which was around £1.5m. However, his legal fees were going to cost up to £200,000 and he did not have the cash. I knew him, respected him and cannot stand to see people being abused, and so I pesonally financed his legal fight. My attitudes towards fairness have never changed over the years. The deal was, if he won, I would get three times back whatever I gave him to finance the case and, in the end, this totalled £50,000. After three years of legal battles, he won £800,000. However, by the time I had taken the £150,000 I was entitled to, and the lawyers had taken their massive fees, the poor bloke would have been left with next to nothing. The lawyers asked me if I was prepared to take a drop in fees, to which I replied, "Are you prepared to take a cut in yours?" In the end I settled for my £50,000 back with £25,000 on top, and the lawyers also accepted a reduced fee.

Thankfully there were no such legal issues at Cloudfm. We went through the process properly. **Causing pain is not what anyone goes into business to do, but sometimes the toughest decisions are the right ones, even though it hurts to make them.** I also have personal experience of doing the wrong thing.

Earlier in my working life an episode occurred which was so shameful that, if I think about it now, it can still keep me awake at night. In one of my previous roles, I had employed a brilliant woman who was smart, engaging, meticulous and a superbly fast learner. From starting in an office role, she soon became indispensable and was my PA. There was nothing she couldn't do. She could think two steps ahead of me, she knew what I was going to ask next. She solved every problem. If I had asked her to get me a place on the next space shuttle she would have asked if I wanted a window seat. I had paid massive salaries looking for people like her and I happened upon her by chance. She was also stunningly attractive.

However, one of my senior managers who was deeply involved in deals which the business's very survival depended on, had a flirtatious, playful nature and, despite the fact he had an attractive, jealous wife, would flirt with anything in a skirt. One day he pulled me to one side and said, "Jeff, I have a problem. You know my missus is the jealous type… well, I pinched your PA's arse and she slapped me round the face and got the raving hump. If my missus finds out she will leave me and I can't work near your PA anymore. We are going to have to let her go."

She slapped him in the face… I wanted to punch him. What a prick! Forget changing attitudes to sexism in the workplace over the decades, pinching women's backsides wasn't acceptable then, nor will it ever be. If that happened in my company now, I would run to the phone to ring the police and say there had been a sexual assault. She should have reported him and sued the arse off our company. What particularly hurt me is I pride myself on my working relationships being based on trust. Firms should be like families, you can fight, disagree, grow closer and apart, but you should always have each other's back. Because of his actions the business, and his family, were in danger of being ripped apart. Either she went, or he was going to. I should have torn up his contract in front of him and told him he was gone, whatever the massive implications for the company. Instead, to my lasting shame, I sat her down and presented the problem to her. To her lasting credit, she said she understood and she decided to leave the company. She warned me he was a "wrong un" and to watch my step around him. Then, to save the business, she left.

I didn't sleep properly for weeks and the whole episode still shames me today. She left her job because she was attractive and this bloke acted like a dick. Very soon afterwards I realised that I wished she had sued us. It could have cost us tens of thousands, but nothing would have made me happier than writing that cheque. My justifications – I was saving the business and his marriage - ring hollow in my ears even today. Sometimes business life can be cutthroat and we do things we regret. We can upset people, threaten their lifestyles, make competitors go bust. But that episode taught me **when you have to make morally uncomfortable decisions, you should always take time to consider if they will bring you long-lasting personal regret, whatever the benefits to the business might be. If they will, then don't make them.** She left her job to help me when she had been the victim. Thank God, she went on to bigger and better things. I have made many business mistakes in my life. That episode ranks among the worst.

Years later, at Cloudfm the senior management redundancies were painful but justified, and we started to reap the benefits quickly. We went from a board of twelve people down to five and it re-energised the business beyond measure. I also spent a long time reflecting on my own performance. As the owner, there is no-one to give me marks but I knew one area I had succeeded was in purposefully surrounding myself with people who would not hesitate to question me, give me negative feedback or criticise me if I was underperforming. If I ever suspected they were not telling me the truth, then there would be a problem and I would immediately question why they were being reticent.

With the Queen's Award under our belt, it was time to get the show back on the road – or even on the railway. Doing FM for rail companies should be an attractive proposition, it is a repetitive revenue-generating sector which is always going to needed by the consumer and we had been trying to get into the sector for a while. In FM terms, we do not touch the trains or the track, but the barriers, air con, CCTV, waiting rooms, emergency lighting and fire regulations etc.

For nearly a year, we had been in negotiation with ScotRail and were at the final hurdle of getting a £20m contract but it was proving troublesome. The railways are more heavily unionised than almost any other industry, and ScotRail was also in the middle of a massive scrap with the Scottish government because the company was failing to meet its obligations. It got to a stage where they were tearing chunks out of each other and it was a painful process. We didn't want to get caught in the middle of this dogfight, it could have been bad for the business and the brand, and so we took a step back. We opted to wait and see what would happen rather than trying to drive change and, in the end, ScotRail decided it was too difficult for them to bring in the changes we needed, and we were probably lucky not to win a client embroiled in a political dog fight. There would have been no winners.

But, as part of this process, we came to the attention of the rest of the rail industry and Chiltern Rail - a smaller franchise running between London's Marylebone and Birmingham - came to us to see what we could do. They had massive cost pressures, wanted to half their FM bill from £6m to £3m, and we started negotiating. Normally it takes seven months to tie everything up but, again, because of the politics and union issues, the process was slower than a train with leaves on the line. Eventually, after around twelve months, we signed the deal in January 2020. Northern Rail was also interested but it too was under massive political pressure because of its lack of performance, and I had that feeling at the back of my neck that this was going to go pear-shaped, so I insisted we step away. Not long afterwards they lost their franchise. But soon we had other major problems as a result of the restructure.

Despite Derrick being my co-founder, his influence was slowly disappearing. He had played a major role in establishing the company and Cloudfm would not have been a success without him. However, as the company had grown bigger, the board judged his contributions had waned. Part of growing a company means you have to take on people with ever-increasing expertise and acumen. Eventually, you should be employing people who are far better at their jobs than you are. Circumstances change and you must embrace it. **Clinging on to past performance, roles and responsibilities will simply mire your company in the past. In personnel terms, businesses are sometimes like sports teams - you have to keep improving who is in the team if you want to keep raising your standards.** I had adapted to these changes, which wasn't always personally easy, and had left some areas of the business to be run by others who were more qualified to do it than I was. I simply supervised them and put my energy into other areas where I could still have an impact.

However, I and the board believed Derrick and James had struggled more with this process. Derrick's consultancy division had performed well in 2016 and 2017 but, despite carrying major costs, had brought in little business since. Similarly, James had helped create the IT the business was built on, but when the IT department had expanded from six people to thirty, managing these people was not James' passion. We had brought someone in to run the department who was more technically and digitally experienced than James, and James was fully supportive of this. However, as he was used to calling the shots, we felt he slowly started to lose interest in the development side. He also didn't always agree with decisions that were being made which was frustrating for him.

As a result, James became more and more absent from the business, despite taking a full salary. I tried to re-invigorate him several times, but the feeling among the board was he had lost his mojo, and being absent on a full salary was enabling the development team to question our judgement. It was beginning to cause much bigger problems internally.

While Derrick's unhappiness at losing his seat on the board was entirely understandable, it was also draining having to deal with it. We felt his unhappiness was a like a constant shadow. It needed to be resolved. None of us had ever set up Cloudfm with the intention of retiring aged sixty-five while still running it - the plan had always been to change the industry and then sell the business. So, as pressure continued to build, the time had come to bring everything to the surface and ask the difficult questions.

I asked them, "What is it you want? What is going to make you happy? Stop talking about company valuations, what Cloudfm is worth now and could be in the future, forget all that. What is the number that makes you both feel you have achieved what you wanted to when we started out eight years ago?"

Their answer? £X million each. They wanted enough cash to live comfortably for the rest of their lives. Fair enough. I said, "Great, I will go and see if I can find a solution which will allow you to exit with £X million in your pockets. You will be very rich men and you can ride off into the sunset knowing you have been well paid for all the value you have added."

Under such a deal, I could also have been a very rich man as well as my shares would have been worth more. However, I had no interest in disappearing. I knew there was still massive potential at Cloudfm to grow and continue to revolutionise the industry. I knew I could still play a major part in this process and the work still invigorated me. As I have said before, my motivation was never about making money – **money is a natural by-product of success.** But it was time to sit back and ask if we were selling part of the company, what sum did I want in my own bank account so I never had to worry about cash again? My figure was much, much smaller. The challenge was now to find an investment firm willing to put sufficient cash in the company to pay off James and Derrick, give me a much smaller lump sum, but still be happy for Cloudfm to continue under mine and the board's leadership. Finding such an investor would be difficult enough. Finding one who agreed with our principles, ethos and vision should have made it even harder.

We needed companies which understood who we were, and could be honest enough about themselves to share their own vulnerabilities and concerns about buying in. From that, you get a great foundation of trust you can build on. However, in the end the search was not too difficult because there were an awful lot of interested people who we scratched off the list straightaway. The old saying goes, "Never get into bed with someone you are not ready to marry," and from initial meetings with some potential partners it was obviously never going to work, and so we did not waste time with them. We eventually found two contenders. The first was a major international investment company. The market value of Cloudfm was about £35m. They came to see us a number of times, liked what they saw and made us an offer of £20m. James and Derrick would get their cash but I would leave the majority of my money in the company. The plan was as Cloudfm continued to grow, I could then sell my remaining shares at any time in the future. Our business projections saw Cloudfm eventually being a £200m company and, if that happened, my existing share would be worth nearly £50m. But, again, it wasn't about the cash. If in five years I walked away with £50m what on earth would I do with it? Leaving that amount of money to my kids would probably ruin their lives, and my grand-children's lives as well. I just wanted to continue doing what I loved.

I could have sold up and started again but it made no sense. Why would I walk away from a company which had momentum, credibility and authenticity? We had got the company three quarters of the way up the mountain and I wanted to finish the job. As we went through the process, the company said all the right things but when they put together the final proposal it was so complicated, I just did not trust them. For example, one of the clauses said if the deal didn't go ahead for any reason - including them deciding to pull out of it - we would have to pay them £500,000 in fees. I said, "Why on earth would we agree to that? You might pull the rug from underneath us, stop the deal and we would still get billed half a million pounds? You are having a laugh." They said this was normal practice but I wasn't going to deal with a company who thought that was normal.

At the same time, another investment company was also showing strong interest, so I told them we had received an offer, we hadn't moved into any sort of exclusivity deal, but if they wanted to get involved, they would have to move quick. I was clear about what the other company was proposing in financial terms and said, "I am not trying to screw you down here, but if you want to be in the prime spot you are going to have to improve the offer." They came back with a bid of £25m, which was a magic figure because it allowed all the other smaller share option holders to get paid full value on their shares. Remember, many senior people had joined the company and not been paid for a couple of years because they believed in the business. This would be their reward. Just as importantly, the new investment company understood our way of thinking.

It was a win/win for everyone. James and Derrick would have got more than the £X million they wanted. I was going to take a much smaller sum and roll the rest into the new company, leaving me with a twenty-five per cent shareholding. The minor shareholders were going to get their windfall. Everyone was happy. After months of stress and unhappiness at the upper echelons of the business, there was light at the end of the tunnel, and the light was shining on big cheques for those who wanted them. For the first time in months, I could see an end to the unhappiness and stress everyone was feeling. Money aside, I just wanted to move forward without being weighed down by the unhappiness of other people's emotions.

Of course, none of us was naïve, we understood the investment company wasn't nearly as interested in changing the FM industry as we were. They wanted to make cash. Recognising this, the deal was structured to give the management team massive financial rewards to hit certain targets. For example, if we reached a turnover of £200m in four years the management team would share a £50m windful. We entered the process on February 20, 2020, with a view for the deal to be done before March 30 at the end of the financial year. Normally this process takes months, but we were doing it in six weeks.

On March 10, I spoke to the company, everything was great, the cheque was being written and it was happy days. Then those people in China started coughing.

The deal was off. No millions were coming our way.

COVID November 2020:

Lessons learned

After a summer of declining numbers of COVID cases, the Autumn months saw number begin to rise across the world. In the UK, businesses were again being closed, the economic future was uncertain and Cloudfm's fortunes were once again, along with almost every other company. Thankfully, because of the changes we had made, we were prepared.

One of the lessons I learnt some time ago was to **"begin with the end in mind"**.

This means when you decide what you want to achieve, try and build your business accordingly from the start. When we started Cloudfm, and were only turning over £1m per annum, I wanted us to strive to become a £100m company. For that reason, I got people on board like Christopher Gallop and Andrew Frith who were £100m company people. As you know, we couldn't afford to pay them a bean but I sought out people who believed what I believed, could help us grow, and they also knew when we got going they would receive their just rewards. The value of getting such people onboard early to help your business grow is incredible.

As we approached Christmas 2020, we had an incredibly energised business with just a third of the staff pre-COVID, our costs were massively down and our profit ratios up. Our new technology platform was gaining a lot of traction and will be the next huge step in transforming the industry.

But we are still thinking with the end in mind. My next target is to make Cloudfm a £200m company by 2024 and our latest appointments follow this philosophy.

Graeme Smith, who I knew back at ISS, is a major player and has been responsible for generating and overseeing £350m of business every year for years. He has been appointed head of business development.

Haydn Mursell has an incredible pedigree operating as CFO, and latterly CEO, of the huge Kier Group. He has become our new CFO advisor. These are £200m people and we are delighted to have them onboard.

Another change COVID has brought us will also save us almost £1m a year and help the planet. About three years ago I started banging on about how we had staff driving hundreds of miles for twenty-minute meetings and I thought it was nonsense. We had video conference technology and people could do it from the office, but my philosophy is always to listen to what people tell you. Everyone said the same, "No Jeff, people expect face-to-face meetings, the company will suffer if we don't do them, clients will not like it etc., etc., etc." So I listened and said, "OK, we will do it your way."

And, while I am hardly a green eco-warrior, I also knew this business model was environmentally-damaging. While you won't find me preaching from Speakers Corner about global warming, as I have grandchildren I would actually like to do my bit to ensure they have a planet to grow old on.

For this reason, I had made sure the Cloudfm offices were environmentally managed and I swapped my love for big V8 engines and got a Tesla electric car, encouraging the rest of the board to do the same.

Suddenly, COVID showed us these journeys were not needed and video conferencing has become the norm. Previously, we were paying £90,000-a-month on expenses and now this figure has fallen to £3,000-a-month. And all our company cars have gone back too, with people recompensed who previously had them. Just as important as the cash is the fact that we are saving £87,000-worth of pollutants being pumped into the air every month.

The third major lesson COVID taught us was focus. I previously said no-one tries to totally redesign and rebuild a ship when it is successfully powering its way across the Atlantic. COVID stopped our ship and, albeit it in terrible circumstances, gave us an opportunity we would never previously have had to re-imagine our business and make it better.

As the virus continues to play havoc across the globe, my advice to all businesses would be to make sure you are stronger when this awful episode ends than you were when it began. Only that way, in the business sense, can we ever triumph over COVID.

Chapter 17

The hardest goodbyes

The two biggest redundancies which were brought about partly by COVID were also the most personally painful for me. The board of directors decided that if we were shaking up the company and taking a fearless approach to ensure we prospered long into the future, everyone's role had to be examined. After long and difficult discussions, it was decided it was time for Derrick and James to depart the business completely.

It was a gut-wrenching decision. Emotions aside, their work and contribution to the company between 2011 - 2017 was off the scale, it was massive.

Derick had set up Cloudfm with me and James had joined very soon after. Without them, it is possible the business would never have succeeded. Derrick had stood by my side from day one and brought energy, enthusiasm and the self-motivation to keep banging on customers' doors no matter how often he was turned away. He had strengths I didn't have and the company's success was down to him as much as anyone else. In the early days, his keenness to make a deal had driven me potty, but, as the cliché says, what doesn't kill you makes you stronger. The Pret and Poundland deals, to name two, had earned us a few quid and helped grow our reputation. Just as importantly, they had reinforced the direction we wanted the company to move in. I had spoken to Derrick numerous times every single day for years and the conversation we had about him leaving was an awful one for us both.

James had put a lot of trust in Derrick and me, joining our new company with no salary and just the promise of shares if it didn't go belly-up. He had taken the basic technology I had built and commercialised it. Cloudfm remains at the forefront of technological innovation in the industry and James had built the foundations of this. Getting in touch with him that first time long ago with the calendar software problem was one of the best decisions I ever made. However, times change and as outlined in the previous chapter, their influence had waned.

The truth is, though, as with all such decisions, it also comes down to pounds and pence. Derrick's consultancy division carried a lot of costs. It had made a major contribution to profits in 2016 and 2017 but had never reached the same dizzy heights again. The division was all about chasing the next big project and if we didn't secure that contract, the cost figures in the accountancy ledger soon started to add up. In James's case he was a brilliant guy, but he was on a major salary and even he had admitted he had lost his mojo, his enjoyment and enthusiasm in being part of this new, bigger company. As a result, he had been absent from the business on a day-to-day basis for more than a year.

Breaking the news to them was awful. We had stood side by side for years and I knew the decision was going to cause incredible anger and distress. There was only going to be one bastard in this script, and it was going to be me. I knew they would not see the decision as being based on performance in their roles, but more on me wanting more control on the direction of the business. The unfortunate thing was they didn't realise my view was shared by almost everyone senior in the business. Making people redundant is always terrible, but when it is two people you have been so close to, personally as well as professionally, it is devastating for everyone. In the end, Derrick decided he didn't want to be made redundant, so he decided to resign instead.

The one saving grace, which allowed me to sleep at night, was we had the financial ability to make sure neither of their lifestyles would suffer. The company had recently been valued, admittedly pre-COVID, at more than £30m. Since then, we had reduced our costs so much, that even with a reduced income, it was actually worth a similar amount.

They had shares worth millions and to simplify the financial details, they could borrow money from the company against those shares. Say they wanted to borrow £150,000 a year, if the company was sold down the line at its pre-COVID price, they would each get £X million each, minus the £150,000 a year they had borrowed. Nothing in life comes without risk, so the only downside was if the company went belly up and the liquidators were called in, they would be chased for the money they owed. However, that would mean the business had collapsed and we were all down millions of pounds anyway. I was never going to let that happen.

Of course, when money is involved emotions are high. However, I will not stop until I have ensured they receive the financial reward they deserve for what they added to the journey, and that is my number one priority. They will be multi-millionaires before the end of 2021.

I hope one day we will be able to sit down without anger and resentment and look back fondly on those early days when we didn't have a pot to piss in, but that time may be a little way off.

I know the decisions I took, and even parts of this book, will infuriate them. The truth is, Cloudfm would never have existed in its current form, or succeeded, without them and its success is testament to all of us.

Chapter 18

Marks out of ten

In 2018, something occurred which changed my life.

A few months previously, Cloudfm's managing director at the time, Christopher Gallop, told me he had recently met someone called Kevin Johnson at a networking event. This Kevin bloke was the chair of a peer group for CEOs called Vistage.

I have always tried to be open-minded, but the thought of a "peer group" where we would all sit down and presumably discuss how great we were all doing, using the latest buzzword bullshit, was not that attractive. I politely declined but Christopher Gallop said he had researched it, it might be useful and because I trusted Christopher's judgement, I reluctantly agreed to meet Kevin.

We met in October 2017 and over two hours he interviewed me extensively about my history, Cloudfm and my personal life. It's fair to say we did not immediately hit it off - he was attentive but very commanding.

He explained Vistage was a global organisation bringing more than twenty thousand CEOs in twenty countries together from across the world. It is structured in groups of twelve to fifteen across the UK and membership is by invitation only from the chair of the relevant group.

He said one was being established in East Anglia in January 2018 and urged me to sign up as I was the sort of humble but ambitious person he was looking for. I asked a lot of questions about the group, its purpose and values, but most importantly, who else was going to be in the group?

He said there would be CEOs and company-owners from across the East of England, with businesses ranging from £5m turnover to £100m turnover, making Cloudfm the second largest company in the group.

Kevin explained the group (called V375) would meet monthly at different locations for a whole day, and that the commitment was at such a level that missing a meeting was simply not an option. Then, once per year, the group would go on a 'retreat' for two days and an overnight stay in a hotel. In addition, I would receive 'one-to-one' coaching every month.

Somewhat reluctantly, I went to my first couple of meetings in January and February of 2018 and met the other members. We would talk about various issues that members had (business or personal) and begin to peel the onion layers back on the various people in the group. It's fair to say that, even after these couple of meetings, I was still full of scepticism and wasn't feeling I was getting too much out of it.

Nevertheless, as I was taught back in my childhood with the karate and then lagging pipes in my first job, sometimes if you stick with things it pays dividends. The realisation was not a thunderclap but came to me slowly. I found I enjoyed sharing my knowledge and experience with the group, and realised I was also learning from the experiences they were sharing.

One of the most powerful lessons I learned was how to see through all the mist, false perceptions and second-guessing when it came to people.

In Vistage, we have a process at the very start of every group meeting called the 'Sign in'. You have to write your name on a flipchart and then score three sections out of ten – how you are doing at work, in your personal life and your own wellbeing. You then add a statement of the most important thing you need to address within the next thirty days. When you have scored yourself, you then explain why. When it comes to your personal score, if you aren't comfortable explaining the reasons for your score, you don't have to. However, to illustrate just how open and honest the group is, in the three years I have been in Vistage, not one person has ever declined to explain.

The beauty of this process is that if someone gives themselves a score of three on their personal or business life, you know they need help and support. This scoring process simply solves one of the challenges we all face, establishing how people are actually feeling and if they need support.

I use the following analogy to explain it - if two people were standing talking and an old lady walked past and fell over, what would they do?

We all know the answer - they would rush to help her to her feet. That's because we could physically see her fall over and the human spirit in all of us wants to help anyone in distress.

The scoring technique enables us to know people have fallen over in the mental sense, as opposed to the physical sense, and guess what, our natural reaction to help and support them is the same.

In the meetings that is what we do. Our challenges become the focus of the meeting and we get under the skin of the problem, ask detailed, probing questions to get to the nub and then offer our observations on what we have seen and heard to try and help them with it. It is like an out-of-body experience.

The people on the receiving end of this process suddenly become alive, focussed and strong, and when asked to score themselves again, the three inevitably becomes a six, or an eight (sevens are not allowed!).

The process is obviously confidential but nationally it has helped people with issues such as a CEO who was trapped in a toxic relationship with his company's owners. His group gave him the confidence to stay true to his values and beliefs and he left the firm, began a new, now very successful business, and is a man reborn.

Another was an MD having marriage problems that he felt he could not discuss with anyone else. After caring, but challenging questioning, some damaging behaviour patterns emerged he had not realised were taking place and he committed to change them, with the group holding him to account to do so.

There were many such issues which arose in our own group over the years and were successfully tackled with overwhelming results. Basically, the group's power comes from the strength of its values in "doing the right thing," and from the many different business leaders, each from different sectors and with their own outlook, being united in a desire to learn, grow and help their peers do likewise.

I am pleased to say I have learnt more than I could ever have imagined from it.

I learnt that to be vulnerable creates an inner strength that cannot be challenged. To be vulnerable attracts help and support you could never dream of, yet most people in society believe vulnerability is a reflection of weakness. It's absolutely not, it's a reflection of unrivalled strength.

This whole process changed the entire way I operate and the way I think about everything. As an experienced businessman, I believed direction and strength created success. I believed having the answers to problems that your colleagues were struggling with showed leadership. Vistage taught me I was deluded.

If I am in a meeting room full of ten people discussing a subject, how do I spot the leader?

He/she is the person asking the great questions and never giving the answers. This is because a true leader's job is to help your teams find the answers together, then they own the solution and they are engaged in solving the problem, rather than simply following instructions from above.

I learnt the most powerful traits of any leader (or human being) are:-
Empathy
Humility
Integrity
Freedom

These happen to be our company values, and thanks to Vistage, I now truly know why.

I learnt the most dangerous traits of any leader (or human being) are ego and pride. They are the biggest barriers to happiness and fulfilment.

So how did I learn so much in such a short space of time? Well, the other great thing about Vistage is that it operates an inner circle of 'world-class' speakers. We hear from people who have been there, done it and got the T-shirt. Their happiness now comes from giving back to people their knowledge, experience and wisdom.

Being a Vistage member, we enjoy receiving key notes from some of the world's most accredited speakers every month on almost every subject you can imagine, and there are common threads which link them all - people, culture, empathy and vulnerability. Above all, it is about values and always doing the right thing. It also shows the value **of surrounding yourself with experienced people, with great** values and wisdom, and being prepared to learn from them. Often the only way you can improve is to seek negative feedback. If you only ever accept praise you will become complacent. And whatever you do that affects people, you must always create a win/win outcome.

At Cloudfm we also use motivational speakers to try and educate and inspire our staff. These have included the amazing Mandy Hickson, the former Royal Air Force pilot who flew forty-five missions over Iraq.

Throughout the pages of this book I have highlighted a number of life lessons which only now, looking back, I realise if I had followed them could have saved me a lot of trouble on my journey. It would be easy to say that by following them, people will become successful. But the real question is, *what is success?* Many people perceive it to be having millions in the bank, a gorgeous house, a fancy car.

Working in pursuit of such goals *might* (and it's a very big *might*) bring some people happiness. But life has shown us countless times that achieving such targets does not always make people happy.

I believe the one thing every human actually strives for is fulfilment, which can, of course, be widely different things to different people. It goes beyond bank balances, job titles and personal life goals. You could be living in a mansion and be less fulfilled than someone living in a shack.

So, how do you establish what fulfilment looks like for you? A brilliant tool is Ikigai – the translation from Japanese loosely means '*A reason for being*'.

At first glance it's an easy process but is actually difficult to do properly.

How does it work? In simplistic terms it's a formula for working out fulfilment. It asks four simple questions:

What are you good at? This might be engineering, sports, managing people or simply listening.

What do you love? What would get you out of bed every day for years, punching the air with excitement?

What can you get paid for? You and your family need to eat, right? Therefore, you have to ensure you can get paid for what you do, to live the life that makes you truly happy.

What the world needs? This doesn't mean solving global warming or curing cancer, though everyone would like to do both. In Ikigai, it means what can you do to improve the world in some way which will bring personal fulfilment? If you are a car park attendant and you realise the traffic flow is wrong and delaying motorists, what the world needs could mean getting this changed, giving you a sense of achievement through knowing you have helped others.

To simplify it, if you do something you are good at and love doing every day, if you can make a real difference and get paid enough to live to the standard you desire, you have reached fulfilment. People always get hung-up about the financial aspect of this, but as I have said before, money comes to those who make a positive difference, rather than those who chase it as a goal in itself.

Answering these questions is not as easy as it sounds because firstly, most people have never asked themselves these questions, and secondly, we are all quick to jump on what we think the answers are without

Ikigai

A JAPANESE CONCEPT MEANING "A REASON FOR BEING"

really, deeply thinking them through. It will take most people a few months, or even a year to truly establish their Ikigai.

The key to establishing your Ikigai is to 'begin with the end in mind'. This means to project yourself forward and think deeply about how you believe you would feel. An example might be, "I really want that Mercedes E class. If I had that car, my world would be great. I could drive in comfort, feel like I have progressed etc. The cost of the car will push me to my limits, but that's OK, I will manage."

Now, in most cases, this is what people believe in the moment. But when you can project yourself forward, you ask different questions, such as:

After driving for a month, how will I feel? After driving for a year, how will I feel? How will I feel after six months when the car has become just a car, it needs cleaning every week, I am stressing about every scratch on it and the £600 per month it is costing me could be spent on better things? In most cases like this, we regret the fact that we bought the car.

This is because we thought in the moment, short-term happiness rather than 'begin with the end in mind'.

But once you have worked out your real Ikigai, you will accelerate your journey to fulfilment at lightning pace.

You read earlier in this book about my love, passion and enjoyment when I was at Clacton Town football club. But I realise now that it was not sustainable because I couldn't get paid for it. Similarly, at ISS I was being well paid and doing something I was good at, but I couldn't influence the ISS business model and, because of that, I did not love the work. Cloudfm was the perfect living vision of my Ikigai.

What was I good at? Engineering, technology, IT, managing people and getting them to believe what I believed. My biggest asset was being able to link technology to engineering due to my programme-coding experience.

What did I love? I loved the idea of improving an industry that I was passionate about and knowing I had the capability, skills, knowledge and tenacity to implement such a change. I knew that starting my own business meant that I - and not other people - would control the barriers to success.

What did the world need? The FM industry needed a new way of operating and Cloudfm was proving there was a better way through focussing on culture, behaviour and simply doing the right thing.

What could I be paid for? The success of Cloudfm meant I was financially secure.

The irony is I only discovered Ikigai after I had achieved it. I wonder how different my life could have been if I had known of it at the start of my journey. As for Vistage, it also helped me during one period of my life which could have emotionally destroyed me far worse than the bankruptcy had. It was about family.

Chapter 19

Do the right thing

For the rest of time, 2020 will be forever remembered as the tragic year of COVID, but for me, it will always be about new life and not death.

Throughout the hundreds of pages of this book, my family life has rarely been mentioned even though it's importance to me is beyond measure.

Family is at the heart of my fulfilment, but this book is not the place to talk about people I love deeply and throw our shared experiences open to the world. But one family event affected me so deeply I have to share it.

Anyone who is a parent knows it is the most complex task in the world. However much love, help and support you give your children, you are always wracked with guilt that you did not give more. To be a perfect parent is an impossible task and, if perfection is the benchmark, God knows I have failed, despite always doing my best.

I was blessed with loving parents who gave me all the love and guidance I needed in raising me, my brother Paul, and sisters, Wendy and Sally. Anyone with brothers and sisters will know, as the decades come and go, your relationships strengthen and then ebb, but whatever differences we may have had, or are still to come, the love I have for them will not change.

It is the same being a father. As your children grow and become adults, they make decisions you might not agree with, do things that worry you, frustrate you and anger you, but, whatever happens, your love for them cannot even be dented, never mind destroyed.

As we read earlier in the book, I had two children, Sarah and Michael, with my first wife Heather. The guilt I carry about not being there for them in the early years will never go away. When I used to tell my Mum how not being part of their lives was tearing me apart, she would say, "Son, I know it's tough, but trust me, one day they will come and find you," and I clung onto her advice.

My Mum and Dad in the late 1990s.

When Sarah was sixteen, and Michael fourteen, they made contact with me via their Mum and I met them in the Toby Carvery in Clacton. They asked me the most challenging question I have ever faced, "Dad, why did you leave us?"

Sarah and Michael when they were young.

Thankfully, from that moment on, I started seeing them regularly and over a long time our relationship grew. I am so grateful to have been given the chance to have them in my life again. I was blessed to be able to help Michael become an engineer and he eventually found his niche at Cloudfm in training people in our technology.

Sarah is my one child who has never become involved in my businesses. She progressed to become a senior manager of a high street opticians and then was then bitten by the bodybuilding bug, has won numerous events around the UK and Europe, and now runs a physical training company.

Michelle and I have been blessed with three daughters who were brought up in an atmosphere of love and financial comfort. They all initially carved out their own careers. Kelly went onto run a major Yates pub which was taking in more cash on a nightly basis than Clouldfm was at the start of the business. Natalie had always loved children and so went onto work at Montessori, while Hayley fulfilled her dream of becoming a hairdresser.

However, they all had my genes and as Cloudfm grew and we needed well-educated, streetwise people with good values, they all joined the company. A lot of people will be shouting, "Nepotism!" and think I was showing some sort of favouritism by employing my daughters, but there are some easy answers to that.

Firstly, if you own a company, if you can't give opportunities to your family who are suitable for the roles that need filling, who can you give such opportunities to? Was I meant to not consider them for roles because they were my kids? They shared my values, they knew what the company stood for and they all went on to contribute to the business and help make it a success.

The second point is the chat I gave them all before taking them on, and it was a stark one. I said, "At work I have no family, I have employees. I stop being your Dad as soon as I walk through the office door. I will give you the opportunity to work for the company but I will never, ever carry you, show you favouritism of any kind or treat you differently.

"I will never allow myself to be in a position where I could be criticised by anyone in my business for treating you differently. If you constantly mess up, I will fire you like anyone else. Of course, as your Dad, outside of work I will support you, put a roof over your head and feed you, but, believe me, in work you are on your own, your surname carries no weight. Mess up, or if the business changes and your roles are no longer required, you are gone."

As proof of this, without going into the details, two of my children are no longer with the company. Hayley, on the other hand, has flourished and is now a major cog in our operation. But some things are far more important than business.

In 2010 I became a Grandad when Sarah had Lana, followed by Michael's son Ethan. Hayley, our youngest, then became pregnant and had Quinn in 2015. Becoming a grandparent is a special moment in anyone's life and Michelle and I were obviously over the moon.

Also, in 2010 Natalie became pregnant but lost the baby through an ectopic pregnancy. This meant she also had one of her fallopian tubes removed as a result, and she was told it was unlikely she would be able to have children. As you can imagine, this was devastating for her and for us, especially knowing how much she loved kids and how much she enjoyed working with them and educating them through Montessori.

Thankfully, in 2017 she announced, against all odds, she was pregnant again and had a son, Tommi, a miracle for us all.

Michelle and I in 2017.

But, as well as these joyous births, there was another tragedy. Kelly, our oldest, who had always been desperate for a child, became pregnant. We were thrilled beyond belief, her prayers had been answered. Her life, and ours, would be complete.

Then our world seemed to end. In October 2018, after some complications, Kelly gave birth to a still-born girl they named Maggie. I have never experienced anything like it. Michelle and I felt a double blow. Not only did our grandchild not make it, the worry we had for Kelly and her partner James intensified our grief. Kelly was so looking forward to her child, it was all-consuming.

As you can imagine, Kelly and her partner James's, world was turned upside down. For the next couple of years, Michelle spent hours and hours with Kelly on a rollercoaster of emotions that seemed to never end.

I was really worried about Kelly who had slipped into a shell, was suddenly lacking in confidence and carrying a huge amount of guilt when she had nothing at all to be guilty for. It was the first time I had experienced a problem or a challenge that I couldn't fix. I felt totally helpless. My beliefs, strengths, money, experience, they were all useless in the face of this tragedy.

We have lots of memorabilia for Maggie. She will never be forgotten and she is in our daily thoughts.

The devastation we felt as a family was beyond words. All her life, Kelly had given to others, never ever said, "What about me?" Now, the one thing she desired more than anything in life had been taken away from her.

Our family's incredible joy at having four grandchildren was always tinged with the pain of Kelly and James' loss.

And then, in February 2020, she became pregnant again. And the truth is, I struggled to cope with it. Forget going bankrupt, forget saving the business during COVID or the fact that the collapse of the deal to sell Cloudfm cost me millions of pounds, as 2020 dawned the one thing that kept me awake at night was worrying about Kelly's pregnancy.

I knew, if something went wrong, it would destroy her and it would also destroy me at a level I barely dared contemplate.

We have all dealt with losses in our lives, seen loved ones pass, but somehow, I knew the indescribable pain she would feel on losing another child would pierce my soul in a way that could never fixed.

Now, I am proud of my vulnerability and honesty, but I couldn't even talk things through properly with Michelle. She had enough worry on her plate about her daughter without me revealing I was consumed with fear as well. Sometimes, I felt my inner happiness was so dependent on Kelly's dream finally coming true.

For months, I felt like I was holding my breath every day, and in the end, I had to share my fears with someone and so I opened up to the Vistage group. I sat with them and told them how I was feeling, like I was standing on the edge of a precipice, and what made it far worse was there was nothing I could personally do to affect the outcome. Without their support I would have been in a dark place.

On October 9, while Michelle and I were in Portugal, we received a call at 7pm. Kelly had been suffering back pain and was on her way to hospital. *Oh God no, please no.* At 7.20pm we got another call: her waters had broken two months early.

You can imagine the panic, forget COVID quarantines and laws, and the fact there were very few flights between Portugal and the UK, we would hire a private plane and break the law if need be to be with our daughter.

At 10:20am on October 10, 2020, Kelly gave birth to a premature but very healthy baby boy, weighing 3lb 7oz. Stanley (as he was named) was proving to be a proper little fighter. He was breathing on his own and the hospital was impressed with how well he was doing. On October 26, he was allowed to go home.

I am fifty-seven. God willing, I have a few years left. COVID prevented the sale of the business and I lost millions of pounds. I don't care. There are business dreams I still want to achieve, industries to further change, technologies to invent and lives to be altered. I also know there will be failures and missteps on whatever road the future takes us down but I know, right now, whatever happens, with our grandchild, my world is complete. And there is one last valuable business lesson there. It is crucial to creating success whatever you do.

Business is not about products and balance sheets and job rates and tenders - it is about people. It is about caring for people, always trying to do the right thing, creating win/wins, not losses. It is about empathy, not exploitation. If you succeed as a person in always trying to do the right thing, more often than not your business will succeed as well.

Epilogue

I am writing this on New Year's Eve of 2020.

In terms of COVID, despite a year of worldwide lockdowns and scientific breakthroughs, the virus is again out of control. A new, more contagious version of the virus has swept through the UK like a tsunami.

Hospitals are again filling up, the number of deaths are rising and businesses across the country have been forced to shut their doors, yet again.

Two different vaccines are just starting to be distributed and we are told the worst will be over by Easter, when millions of people will have received their injections. We can only hope and pray that is true.

At Cloudfm, thanks to the massive structural changes we have made to the business, we are in a far better position to ride out this latest storm.

Having seen our revenues fall by 95 per cent during the first lockdown, this time we are also being helped by the fact many of our clients have only reduced their spending by around 25 per cent. They have become pragmatically resigned to seeing out the crisis as best they can and realise doing essential maintenance will mean they are better prepared for when their doors can re-open.

After working with us throughout the year, they also recognise we are here to help them as their partners, and our principles of integrity, humility, empathy and freedom have not become weakened by COVID, but their importance has been strengthened.

At Cloudfm we are prepared for the future, we are on the cusp of even more astonishing technological breakthroughs and in terms of revolutionising our industry, there is still much more to come.

As the poet Alfred Lord Tennyson said "Hope smiles from the threshold of the year to come, whispering "it will be happier".

We all hope that will be the case in 2021.